To Ethan

In appreciation
and friendship.
                    Cynthia

With Your Own Two Hands

Self-Discovery Through Music

With Your Own Two Hands

by Seymour Bernstein

SCHIRMER BOOKS
A Division of Macmillan Publishing Co., Inc.
NEW YORK

Collier Macmillan Publishers
LONDON

Schirmer Books
A Division of Macmillan Publishing Co., Inc.
866 Third Avenue, New York, N.Y. 10022

Collier Macmillan Canada, Ltd.

Library of Congress Catalog Card Number: 81-51014

Printed in the United States of America

printing number
    3   4   5   6   7   8   9   10

Library of Congress Cataloging in Publication Data

Bernstein, Seymour.
    With your own two hands.

    Includes index.
    1. Piano—Instruction and study. I. Title.
MT220.B52   786.3'041   81-51014
ISBN 0-02-870310-3   AACR2

To
Ronald Herder

I never dreamt
that with my own two hands
I could touch the sky.

Sappho

Contents

Preface   *xiii*

Acknowledgments   *xv*

PART I
A Reason for Practicing

1   Why Do You Practice?   3

    Who Am I?   4
    Practicing—A Key to Integration   6
    The Ultimate Goal   9

2   Why Don't You Practice?   11

    Aloneness   11
    Your Own Best Self   13
    You and Your Teacher   14
    The Class Experience   16
    Case Histories   19
      Pupil No. I (The Lifeline)   19
      Pupil No. II (The Commitment)   22
      Pupil No. III (The Sacrifice)   24
      Pupil No. IV (The Cookie Jar Is Empty)   26
      Pupil No. V (The Pianist from Wall Street)   30
    Conclusions   35

3   Concentration   39

    Natural and Deliberate Concentration   39
    Sight-Reading   40
    Inducing Concentration   45
    The Automatic Pilot   47

A Close Look at Mistakes   49
A Close Look at the Whole and Its Parts   51
A Close Look at Fingering   54
Anticipation—The Archenemy of Concentration   58

4 FEELING   62

Notation   63
Breathing   65
Physical Adaptability to Sound   67
Conclusions   73

PART II
The Disciplines

5 TEMPO–RHYTHM–PULSE   79

Some Definitions   79
The Effect of Rhythm on Your Behavior   80
How Fast Is Fast? How Slow Is Slow?   81
Physical Response to Slow and Fast   84
Adaptation for Fast Playing—The Joints of Stabilization   84
Long Notes   86
Don't Rush Weak Beats   92
Rhythmic Control in Crescendos and Diminuendos   93
Balance and Control   94
Eurhythmics   95
The Child in Us   96
Slow or Fast Practicing?   98
Coping with Difficulties   102
Summary   107

6 LISTENING   110

Listening Naturally   110
Supervision   114
Tuning In and Out   115
A Musician Listens   117
Activating Your Vocal Cords   120
Listening to Others   120
The Audience Listens   121
Absolute Pitch   123
Relative Pitch   125

7 You and the Piano   127

Introduction   127
Arm Weight   128
The Relaxation Myth   129
Natural and Controlled Tension   130
Experiencing Natural Tension   133
How Much Tension   134
My Arm Is Falling Off!   136
Taut Fingers   137
The Three Key Positions   138
How to Voice Chords   139
Pedaling   143
Fingers, Fingers, Fingers!   152
Endurance   155
Grounded   156
Scales and Arpeggios, Yes or No   159
Preparation for Scales   162
Stabilize Your Arms   171

8 Choreography   173

Introduction   173
The Movements of Your Upper Arm   175
Curves of Energy   180
Revelation Number One: Adapting
Physical Movements to Accents   187
Revelation Number Two: The Three Spheres   192
Conclusions   196

PART III
Fulfillment through Performing

9 Performing   201

Who Performs and Why   201
Performing: An Incentive to Practice   205
Contests   206
Reviews   210
A Measure of Your Own Worth   212
The Four Stages of Learning   214

10 MEMORY   219

Historical Survey   219
Why Memorize?   220
The Keyboard Memory   222
Repetition and the Conditioned Reflex
(The Automatic Pilot)   226
Conscious Memory   228
Deadlines   229
Consciously Freeing the Automatic Pilot   231
Aural Memorization   233
Memorizing Away from Your Instrument   234
Memorizing Backwards   234
Memory Slips   235
Outline for Memorizing Music   238
Implementation of the Outline for Memorization   240
Some Afterthoughts and Conclusions   258

11 NERVOUSNESS   260

Being Responsible   260
Being Irresponsible   262
Self-Destructiveness   263
  Self-loathing   263
  Delusions of Grandeur   264
  Self-Sacrifice   264
  Victimization by Others   266
  Priorities   267
Try-outs   268
  *Importance of Try-outs in Insuring
  a Successful Performance*   268
  Transcendental Preparation   269
  Making Your Try-outs Productive   270
  Overpreparation   271
The Day of a Performance   272
  What to Eat   276
  Drugs   277
  The Artists' Room   280
The Day after a Performance   281

12 FINALE   283

NOTES   287

INDEX   289

Preface

If you play an instrument or sing, you will no doubt agree that life's experiences influence the way you practice. But has it ever occurred to you that the opposite may also be true: that the skills gained from practicing—namely, the refinement and control of your emotions, your thoughts, and your physical responses—can influence your life?

Your acceptance of this idea would depend upon how you view your talent and the place it occupies in your life. If, for example, you believe that you and your talent are one, if you can say with full conviction, "I am what my talent is," it should follow that the synthesis of feeling, thought, and physical co-ordination experienced through practicing can quite naturally affect all that you do apart from music. Since virtually every activity in life engages feelings, thoughts, and physical movements in various combinations, it is reasonable to assume that the intense coalition of these three functions achieved musically can be directed into other channels as well, thereby fortifying you for all of life's demands. In other words, through an organized and consistent process of practicing, it ought to be possible to harmonize everything you think, feel, and do.

This book addresses itself to the kind of practicing that achieves this end. It begins by recognizing your individual talent—regardless of your age or degree of accomplishment—and it encourages a dedication to practicing that can lead to self-mastery. Motivated by a love of music and possessed of a clear understanding of the reasons for practicing, you can establish so deep an accord between your musical self and your personal self that eventually music and life will interact in a never-ending cycle of fulfillment. Since all of this is accomplished with your own two hands, I invite you to practice.

Acknowledgments

Throughout the writing of this book, I was spurred on by a collective interest on the part of my family, friends, colleagues, and pupils. Supporting my belief that practicing music can influence one's life, they encouraged my every effort to bring this book to completion. As though to uphold what I believe to be the underlying principle of teaching, they also cared whether or not I succeeded, and they expressed their caring by giving me of their time and talents.

I am especially grateful to Sir Clifford Curzon, my master, whose artistry remains to this day a model toward which I direct my practicing and teaching; to David M. Clay, who kept me on the road to "Minsk," when I was about to veer off to "Omsk"; to Christopher Lewis, who not only typed two versions of the manuscript but also made constructive comments along the way—all done with the same exquisite taste that informs his artistry; to Dr. Thomas Darson, brilliant pianist, teacher, and musicologist for his expert advice on technical and historical questions; to Robert Levin, musician extraordinaire, who "harmonized" the *Outline for Memorizing Music*; and to Sheila Aldendorff, one of the finest teachers I know, whose enthusiasm and helpful suggestions inspired my best efforts.

The following were also of inestimable help to me: Marin Alsop, Simone Belsky, Dr. Helen Boigon, Professor George Bozzini, Oliver Brittain, Carolyn Bross, Dr. André Dupuis, Professor Lillian Feder, Claude Frank, Felix Galimir, Maxine Giannini, Richard Goode, Lynn Grasberg, Irene Rosenberg Grau, Liora Hendel, Margaret Howard, Dr. Michael Jacobs, Natalie Jaffe, Yi Yin Huang, Denise Kahn, Michael Kimmelman, Seth Kimmelman, Ernest Levenstein, Professor Samuel Levin, Rabbi Z. David Levy, Dr. Owen Lewis, Stephen Mayer, Mark Preston, Robert Resnikoff, David Rissenberg, Professor William E. Rutherford, Richard Shirk, Joseph Smith, Rosalie Sutherland Stump, Alexander Tcherepnin,

Dr. Baylis Thomas, Eleanor Thornblade, Harriet Wingreen, Eve Wolf, Elizabeth Wolff, and Mitchell Zeidwig.

This book could not have reached its present state without the help of my friend, mentor, and pupil, Flora Levin. A classical scholar and a dedicated student of music, she patiently led me through the discipline of writing with a sensitivity born of her regard for language. Inasmuch as I teach her music, we have become both pupil and teacher of one another. The interaction of giving and receiving, our mutual strivings toward a common goal, and, finally, the gratification we earn from even the slightest advancement of our efforts all relate in a very real sense to the thesis of this book. Certainly, her devotion to practicing and her keen awareness of its harmonizing effects upon the personality have lent support to my theories on this subject. Beyond editing my manuscript, she often interjected her own wise observations, many of which have found their way into the final copy. Always sensitive to my thoughts and uncompromising in her standards, she approached this project exactly as she practices—with artistry, thoroughness, and enthusiasm. It would not be an exaggeration to say, therefore, that Flora Levin's mind permeates the pages of this book.

Part I
A Reason for Practicing

1 Why Do You Practice?

I once had a gifted teen-aged pupil who would argue no matter what I suggested. Sensing that her defiance stemmed from guilt at not fulfilling her assignments, I patiently tolerated her insolence while trying my best to motivate her to practice. But at one point during a particularly quarrelsome lesson, I decided that matters had gone too far and that she needed a firm appraisal of her behavior. When I pointed out that her hostility really reflected a lack of discipline at the piano, she glowered at me with her customary obstinacy and exclaimed, "I didn't come here to be psycho-analyzed. You're just supposed to give me piano lessons!" "And what makes you think," I replied, "that I'm interested only in giving you piano lessons? Do you think for one moment that I would separate you, the person, from your musical talent? A teacher, as I see it, ought to influence qualities of humanity in his pupils, and as far as you are concerned, I intend to achieve this by developing your pianistic skills." To think that I could be interested in her as a person apart from her talent stunned her into silence. It was a turning point not only in her life, but in mine as well. It was the first time that I articulated to a pupil what I had previously only sensed—that practicing can influence the person as well as the musician. When my pupil recognized that I cared as much about her as I did about her musical progress, her attitude changed noticeably. Her lessons became models of preparation during which we both enjoyed a constant exchange of ideas and feelings. Gradually we built a relationship based on mutual trust and affection.

Nothing can be more gratifying, of course, than reaching someone's best nature through teaching. But my successful experience with this particular pupil had a much greater meaning for me—one that affected my approach to teaching from that time on. It is our talent, I realized, that gives us our special individuality and identity.

3

It reveals, in fact, who we really are. I reasoned, therefore, that the more fully one develops one's talent, the greater one's powers ought to become in all the other aspects of his life. This seemed to me to be the real purpose of studying music—to unite ourselves with our special gifts in such a way that one would add strength to the other. It was this thought that led me to a very important discovery: the practice and performance of music can promote self-integration. In the following pages I have attempted to explain why this is so and how it can be brought about.

WHO AM I?

When I was a young student, I occasionally sensed that practicing had some sort of bearing on my whole life. But since I did not understand that there was a connection between my feelings at the piano and my feelings away from it, I was not able to use this intuition consciously. Around the age of fifteen, however, I knew for certain that when my practicing went well, I left the piano with a sense of well-being that stayed with me the entire day. The result was that I was a better son, a better friend, and a better student in school. On the other hand, when I was confused and unproductive at the piano, everything else I did was adversely affected. I pondered what there was about practicing that could exercise such a strong influence on my behavior.

I remember finding in the piano a refuge from ambivalent feelings arising from social encounters. Basically, I viewed myself as playing two different roles: the person who sat at the piano and the person who related to his family and friends. For example, I had the false notion that others liked me solely because I played the piano and I thus felt awkward in social situations. It would have comforted me had I known then that even a figure such as Beethoven was disturbed by the same conflict. "It troubled him that his acceptance by others appeared to derive from his talents rather than from his qualities as a person."[1] Actually, this conflict is quite common among individuals who reveal artistic gifts at an early age. But since no one had ever explained this to me, I viewed this role-playing as a serious hindrance to my growth. I was not only puzzled by having to play two different roles, but I was also uncertain in my own mind about which role reflected my real self. I am sure that many people grow to maturity accepting and fashioning their lives around this sort of conflict without taking steps to re-solve it. Of course, it never occurred to me at the time that the answer lay in all that I was experiencing at the piano.

This duality in my personality caused such distress that when war broke out in Korea, I secretly looked forward to being drafted. I thought that if I were detached from my musical life, I would then have the opportunity to discover if I could be liked as a person. I would put my personality to the test once and for all. The two years I spent in the army proved to be extremely valuable. I discovered that my buddies liked me just for myself. With the piano no longer used as a prop, I sensed for the first time that perhaps my musical self and social self were in fact one and the same. But more than that, I suspected even then that my years of discipline at the piano made it possible for me to endure the rigors of forced marches while others who seemed more athletically inclined either fell out or fainted.

As luck would have it, though, the piano was not to remain a silent relic of my civilian life. On one of those rare occasions during basic training when I found a piano to play, a special services of-ficer happened to hear me. Through his efforts I was put into a special service unit and later sent to Korea with Kenneth Gordon, the violinist. There, we performed as many as three concerts a day on the front lines for the United Nations troops. I had come full cir-cle. Armed with a new regard for my strength, I rejoined my former self, as it were—that musician of whom I had unreasonably made a social misfit.

It wasn't until I was in my thirties, however, that I had my first indication of what it felt like to be an integrated person. I did no-thing to bring this about. Perhaps I unconsciously began to see a relation between my growth as a musician and the patterns of my everyday life. This enabled me to experience such a state of well-being away from the piano that the role-playing was no longer necessary. Although the process which brought this about per-plexed me, the results were gratifying; I became more communica-tive as a person as well as a pianist.

I was aware that this feeling had come upon me spontaneously and thought no more about it. Then one Sunday in August 1970, I came across an interview in the *New York Times* commemorating the sixty-fifth birthday of Arthur Koestler. The editors of *L'Express* in Paris "drew him out," the article said, "on a life spent seeking 'a universal explanation, a key to everything.'" The headline was an eye-catcher: "A Fighter for Men's Minds Now Studies Their Brains." The famous polemicist, novelist, and political thinker had now turned to psychology. At the time of this interview, he was engaged in research on the brain with Dr. Paul H. MacLean. The following excerpt is taken from that interview:

Q: How did you get back into psychology? Did you write to MacLean and tell him you wanted to work with him?

KOESTLER: Yes. I got in touch and went to see him, a humble assistant. MacLean has established that there is a lack of coordination between the old and new regions of the brain. A duplication of functions. No real integration, no harmony. The old parts of the brain [i.e., "old" in terms of evolution] are dominated by the emotions. As for the neocortex [the new brain], it is concerned with what we call reason, symbolic thought, abstraction. A strong emotion distorts our logic, leads to unreason. . . .

Q: Is all emotion in the old brain?

KOESTLER: It's a little more complicated than that. There is an interaction. In other words, there are moments when our thoughts are dominated by emotions. We know this. To a certain extent the new brain can control the emotions of the old brain.

Q: Are simple gymnastics enough, or is chemical intervention necessary?

KOESTLER: Nobody likes to say it, but are tranquilizers anything other than a chemical intervention? But current chemotherapy is still in the Middle Ages. In ten years, tranquilizers will be replaced by harmonizers.

The import of this final statement overwhelmed me. For it suddenly dawned on me that one could synthesize emotion and reason through practicing and thus arrive at the integration to which Koestler referred. Chemical intervention indeed! Why not consider practicing as the ultimate "harmonizer"?

PRACTICING—A KEY TO INTEGRATION

Although I felt indignant at Koestler's proposed method for synthesizing emotion and reason, I was encouraged, nonetheless, to know that such a distinguished figure was also studying the problem of self-integration. In this respect, Koestler's remarks reinforced the idea that practicing can actually influence behavior. Since music constantly integrates thought and feeling, it demands of the practicer a continuous coordination of reason and emotion. And it is this very kind of coordination of our innermost faculties that makes self-integration possible.

I had already experienced a correlation between myself as a pianist and myself as a person. The interview with Koestler, however, led me to look for its cause. Was it practicing, something in my personal life, or a combination of both? If it was practicing, as I suspected, I had to discover how it had brought about this integration. Moreover, I had to see if it also influenced the lives of my pupils. I thus began to observe my pupils and myself at the piano and away from it with greater objectivity. I discovered that those who were well-integrated and happy had achieved a balance between their systematic practicing and the way they related to others. This led me to conclude that those who had not established this balance were not likely to do so by concentrating only on the *social* aspects of their lives. For even though one may be extremely close to a person, one cannot always predict the other's behavior. Paradoxically, this unpredictability contributes an element of novelty to a relationship, very much like those unexpected harmonic progressions in a Schubert work. Nevertheless, in striving for integration, it is necessary to engage in a process that is as predictable as possible. And no process is more predictable than practicing.

The organizational aspects of music epitomize the order and harmony you seek in yourself and in your relationships with others. By applying yourself to music through the kind of practicing discussed in this book, you can establish within yourself that same order and harmony you find in music. As this process of practicing unfolds, you grasp it, absorb it, and relate it to your every activity.

It is possible, of course, for a musician to excel in his field and yet be a misfit socially, although such incongruous behavior does not belong to the arts exclusively. One would assume that a person dedicated to the noble art of music would himself become ennobled, but the many instances in which musicians behave as though their personalities were untouched by their art contradict this assumption. In an attempt to understand this contradiction, I questioned some musicians on this subject and got some surprising answers. One told me that he goes out of his way to protect his art from the "contamination" of his social world. In other words, he tries to bring about the very separation which I have suggested should be avoided. Furthermore, he thought that great art and irrationality went hand in hand and he thus concluded that irrational behavior was, in fact, desirable. Another musician told me that his art and his neuroses were synonymous, that he was afraid to tamper with the latter for fear of disturbing the former. Because they accept this theory, many musicians perpetuate their own neurotic behavior, seemingly unaware of the well-integrated figures who grace the field of the performing and creative arts. But the fact is that there are many gifted musicians who vastly increase their artistic output only after they have succeeded in establishing a balance between their art and their relationships with people.

A musician who separates his art form his personal life does so at a price both to himself and to others. For in his desire to focus exclusively on his art, he forfeits much of what he might contribute as a human being. When this is carried to the extreme, he becomes unsatisfactory in all his other activities. He harbors the distorted notion that by virtue of being an artist he may behave in any fashion he chooses. Successful artistic accomplishments coupled with unhappy relationships become habitual for such a person. And since destructive habits are hard to change, he may even go so far as to justify them. That is, he may convince himself that art flourishes when it is fed by irrational behavior. Curiously, though, an artist may continue to develop his talent in spite of his own destructive tendencies. Certainly, there is nothing in music itself that would cause a musician to behave in this fashion. Rather, the cause lies in two specific areas:

The Wrong Reasons For Studying Music

The professional world is filled with musicians who were often forced by ambitious parents and teachers to practice four or five hours a day from early childhood on. Instead of viewing practicing as a means of discovery, they were taught that it was sinful not to practice. Adults who were victims of such tyrannical upbringings continue to suffer guilt every moment spent away from practicing. Some manage to bridge the gap between their unhappy childhood and adulthood, but others are often left with scars of resentment caused by abnormal stress at too early an age. Still others actually leave music when they are mature enough to rebel against their parents and teachers. It is a rare stroke of good fortune when a gifted person is born into a healthy, constructive household and finds, at the same time, a competent, sensitive teacher.

Some musicians feel an exaggerated need for praise and adulation which they seek to gratify through applause and publicity. This indulgence gives them a false sense of accomplishment which itself becomes a prime incentive for a career in music. Others have an abnormal competitive streak which often makes them hostile to their colleagues. Perhaps the gravest consequence of studying music for the wrong reasons befalls the musician who fails at a performing career and is thus obliged to earn his living as a teacher. Instead of viewing teaching as a privilege, he resents his pupils and thus wreaks havoc upon them and upon himself.

An Inability to Relate Practicing to the Social World

In this area we see a musician creating a world of beauty and order through practicing. As long as he is engaged in his art he feels happy and productive. But in social situations he tends to ignore that hard-earned comprehension that enables him to define and express his talent. The conflict, as we have seen, arises when he experiences the contrast between the fulfillment of his talent and his inability to relate to people. As this book progresses, we will examine the various ways in which practicing can resolve this conflict.

THE ULTIMATE GOAL

During the last few years, when I came to understand the real reasons for practicing, I began to hold seminars for teachers and pupils. At the opportune moment, I invariably asked, "Why do you practice?" The most common responses were: "I practice to perfect my technique so that I will be able to play more beautifully" or "I want to make my New York debut and eventually go on tours." More disturbing was the comment, "I've never thought about it." The most encouraging answer was simply: "I practice because I love music."

Naturally, you want to perfect your technique; perhaps you will even make a successful debut one day and eventually go on concert tours. Certainly, it is hard to imagine your doing all this without loving your art. Yet, there is an ultimate goal that transcends all these possible accomplishments: *Productive practicing is a process that promotes self-integration.* It is the kind of practicing that puts you in touch with an all-pervasive order—an order that creates a total synthesis of your emotions, reason, sensory perceptions, and physical coordination. The result is an integration that builds your self-confidence and affirms the unification of you and your talent. You can begin by believing that such an integration is possible, and that through it you can achieve a wholeness that affects your behavior in everything you do. The benefits you can thus bring to the lives of others justify the process of practicing.

2 Why Don't You Practice?

ALONENESS

You enter the office and are greeted by familiar sounds—voices of executives, secretaries, typewriters; the coffee vendor is pouring you one with cream, no sugar; you exchange "good mornings" and some conversation with your friends; you look forward to more of it as the day wears on.

As you settle down at your desk to begin the morning's work, you suddenly recall the *Fantasia in D minor* by Mozart that you were practicing the night before. The themes fill you with an indescribable longing, but some of the technical passages continue to defeat you. You wonder if it will be ready for your lesson four days from now. Obviously, music is a powerful force in your life. Still, you can enjoy being in the office. Even though some aspects of the job are difficult or troublesome, there is, nonetheless, something secure about the predictable routine from day to day. Besides, you like to be with people and they seem to like being with you. The environment of the office, your desk, the work that awaits you, all afford you a measure of comfort. In contrast to this, practicing is a very solitary activity indeed. Yet, your communion with Mozart fills a need within you that no other experience can offer—that is, when you finally bring yourself to practice.

After eight hours, you say good-bye to your fellow workers and leave the office to meet a friend for dinner. You arrive home at 8:30 P.M. rather weary and close the door to your apartment. For the first time in twelve hours you are alone. In just a few moments, you are at the piano, eager to resume your work on the *Fantasia*. But as soon as you attempt to unravel the difficulties of the first technical passage, your mind begins to wander. You think of a friend you would like to see. You love music, you love Mozart, but loneliness crowds out your concentration. You won't have it; you force

11

yourself to practice; you try the passage over and over again. Alas, it is no use. By now, you know very well where you would prefer to be. Guilt overcomes you. Yet your need to be with your friend overrides your need to practice. In a moment you are on the phone. "I know I ought to be practicing," you explain to your friend, "but the musical world will have to survive without me this evening. I'll get to it tomorrow. Let's meet for a drink."

Such ambivalence is very common among amateurs; even professionals experience it at times. Knowing what you must do, but being incapable of doing it, can cause guilt, frustration, and, in some cases, unmitigated torment. Even though you may sense that practicing harmonizes your musical self with your personal self, the question remains, "How can I get myself to practice?"

Loneliness is perhaps the major deterrent to practicing. It may stem, on the one hand, from a compulsive need to be with others; it can, on the other hand, come from an incapacity for self-discipline. If the kind of organization necessary for practicing seems to extend too far beyond your present abilities, you may feel utterly defeated even before you begin. Your sense of futility in the face of an overwhelming challenge can indeed make practicing a very lonely activity. Yet, these are problems that can be overcome. One way is to peer into the minds of confirmed practicers and try to discover what makes them keep working. For some, the answer, paradoxically enough, is that practicing, through its harmonizing effects, dispels loneliness. One of my pupils, a secretary by profession, has constructed her entire life around her need to practice, even taking a job that has enabled her to devote more hours to her music. Once, at the end of a lesson, I asked her if she ever felt lonely when she practiced. "Not at all;" she replied, "loneliness has never been a problem for me. On the contrary. It is only while I practice that I feel in touch with myself and with others. It is as though the great composers are speaking for me—through me. Their music awakens feelings within me that seem to reflect my true self. You can see, then, why I feel a deep rapport with the minds that have fashioned music; I believe that composers speak for the entire human race; I not only feel a spiritual bond with them, but also with others who love music as I do."

My pupil's inspired response did not surprise me in the least, for I had already deduced from her playing and even from her demeanor that she was a well-integrated person. Practicing, we both agreed, was the factor that had unified her personality. The harmonizing influence of music had enabled her to preserve her need to practice within the framework of her busy life. Moreover, it had established within her a spiritual bond with the human race. But not all people view practicing in this way. Some musicians experience anxiety at the very thought of practicing alone. They may even avoid the piano and look upon practicing as a sacrifice instead of a necessity. Their desire to fulfill an artistic calling, however vital this may be, means to forfeit an even stronger need—human contact. They believe that each hour spent at the piano separates them from those they love and any attempt to concentrate is shattered by the specter of aloneness. You can see, then, why such individuals may come to resent music as well as their teachers.

Both extremes—that is, total isolation or a constant need to be with others—are counterproductive. Rather, it is important to achieve a balance, as was exemplified by my pupil, between practicing (being alone) and communicating with others (being social), and to relate one experience to the other.

YOUR OWN BEST SELF

In order to help my pupils achieve this balance, I had to search back to my earliest recollections to see if I, too, had ever felt lonely during my long hours at the piano. What I recall is that I practiced for certain individuals whom I looked upon as models of excellence. The mere awareness of them enabled me to feel a connection with someone I admired. They inspired me to emulate the high standards that they themselves demonstrated by their achievements. Interestingly, the Greek author of *On the Sublime* (long thought to have been Longinus) advocates this principle of emulation when he advises the poet to imagine that Homer is standing over his shoulder.[2] Robert Schumann in his *Rules for Young Musicians* offers similar advice: "Always play as if a master were present."[3] Both Longinus and Schumann understood that the idealized image of a master motivates a student and leads him toward the realization of his own best self.

My own best self was inspired by my teachers. Like Homer, they stood over my shoulder and spurred me on toward greater achievements. With each hour of practicing I would imagine their voices either approving or disapproving. When something went well, I would think how delighted they would have been with my accomplishments. My love of music, coupled with this image of approbation from those I held in such high esteem, became the primary source of inspiration during my practicing. Later, friends and colleagues whose opinions I respected joined with my teachers in a fantasy audience.

YOU AND YOUR TEACHER

I believe that I created this fantasy audience as a means of warding off loneliness. It was my way of establishing that spiritual bond expressed by my pupil. My teachers and friends, of course, had no notion how often I sought their guidance and encouragement by merely summoning them to my imagination. It is, however, one thing to imagine Homer standing over your shoulder, but quite another to have a teacher to guide you from lesson to lesson. Similarly, a fantasy audience, symbolizing your highest ideals, may serve as models during your practicing; but such an audience cannot always provide you with a realistic evaluation of your efforts. For unless you have already achieved self-realization through practicing, you may use your fantasy audience to tell you only that which you desire to hear. But there was a real aspect to my fantasy audience that had nothing whatsoever to do with my imagination. That is, the people I called to mind really cared whether or not I practiced. In fact, it was their caring that enabled me to make progress. Usually, it is your teacher who is chiefly concerned with and involved in your practicing (although family, friends, and colleagues often share this concern). Yet ultimately, it is your teacher who must care not only about your practicing, but also about your individual response to music. This caring will, moreover, draw you into a closer bond with him, one that will transcend mere music instruction. For his caring about your practicing means that he cares about you personally. Further, he must earn your abiding respect by being himself an example of excellence, both musically and personally. He can care about you only in proportion to his capacity to care about himself. He expresses this concern by practicing so that he remains the eternal student throughout his teaching career. If he is a performer, he encourages engagements for himself as an incentive to practice. If he is not a performer, he still seeks the advice of other musicians who challenge him to greater achievements, all for the sake of his own development and his pupils' enlightenment.

Just as your teacher encourages your best self, you in turn strive to do the same for him. This notion of a pupil encouraging a teacher has not received the attention it deserves. Yet all relationships flourish in reciprocity, and the relationship you have with your teacher is no exception. The most effective way in which you can encourage your teacher is by practicing. You thus show him that you can take yourself seriously and are ready to achieve the standards of excellence agreed upon between you. Since your capacities differ from those of others, you should discuss this with your teacher as well as all other issues pertaining to your musical goals. You should, of course, guard against the tendency to minimize or exaggerate what you perceive to be your own capacities. But don't be overly concerned about this, for your teacher will always be there to guide you and, at the same time, encourage you to view your capacities realistically. Once you commit yourself to an assignment, you will discover that your motivation will increase proportionately. Your progress will then be assured and your accomplishments will indicate both to you and to your teacher that you are a serious and responsible student. Moreover, he will view your seriousness as a sign of respect for him. Inspired by your devotion and progress, he calls forth his best efforts on your behalf. The circle of giving and receiving is then complete.

Such a relationship between a teacher and his pupil is rewarding in itself. However, I have always thought that our artistic achievements extend beyond ourselves and our teachers to become part of a larger circle that includes all gifted individuals. In this respect, the degree to which you take your practicing seriously affects the others in this circle. That is why I have often told my pupils, "If you don't practice, I don't have to, either." Talent, after all, is a sacred trust to which we must be responsible. When we practice, we fulfill our share of responsibility in the circle of giving and receiving. When we neglect our practicing, however, the shadow of our failure falls upon the others. Finally, the choice is yours: you choose your teacher as you choose a friend; you either inspire each other through a shared devotion to high principles or you ignore your responsibility to those principles and allow your teacher, your friend, to do all the practicing, all the giving. Your love for music will lead you into making the right decision. A good way to begin is to find a teacher who embodies the highest ideals and helps you to attain them for yourself. Such a relationship can become a model for all your other relationships, for it epitomizes the essence of giving and receiving.

THE CLASS EXPERIENCE

Your lessons with your teacher and your relationship with him or her are vital links in your quest for self-realization. As this relationship grows and you come to know each other's strengths and weaknesses, you are heartened to learn that someone not only accepts you even with your faults but also cares enough about you to help you overcome them. As you have seen, your teacher is interested in your personal development as well as in your musical growth. Nonetheless, it would be unrealistic for you to assume that such a relationship alone can prepare you to cope with "that world out there," as one pupil described it. I decided, therefore, that in conjunction with private lessons my pupils needed frequent performing experiences that would serve two purposes: first, an audience would evaluate their progress without necessarily replacing their teacher or their fantasy audience; second, performing situations would provide them with a vigorous training ground for the development of performing techniques. This would enable them to achieve their secret ambition to perform for others. I used to invite outsiders to serve as an audience for my pupils. Whereas this atmosphere proved ideal for the professional students, it created difficulties for the nonprofessionals who were unaccustomed to performing before a large number of people. At present I restrict the audience to my own pupils, although I occasionally invite others to listen provided that they are sympathetic to the efforts of all the students—whether they be of artist caliber or not.

The classes were more successful than I could have imagined. It was primarily the experience of performing that convinced my pupils of the necessity for conscientious practicing. The criticism that followed a performance proved to each pupil that his achievements were regarded seriously by the group of which he was a part. The class thus became in a sense his musical family, strengthening the existing bond between his love for music and his relationship to his teacher. As a member of this musical family, each pupil felt motivated to perform his best, not only to preserve his own integrity, but also to benefit the others. This led the class as a whole to draw inspiration from the progress of its individual members. Thus, trying one's best became the only criterion for such progress. If, for example, a student who usually had many memory slips succeeded in having only a few, his performance was greeted with great enthusiasm. On the other hand, the class might respond negatively to a seasoned performer whose note-perfect performance did not measure up to the high standards expected of him.

A successful musical performance is in itself a heroic feat. Because my pupils recognize this, they learn to formulate their responses to the efforts of others with clarity and discrimination. This in turn furthers their own progress, often with spectacular results: novices succeed in outdoing themselves, gifted pupils reach high standards of artistry, and teachers begin to take on the attributes of true masters. In addition, the personal interaction that develops between the pupils becomes useful to them even in nonmusical situations. Being a member of a society challenges your ability to balance your individual needs (the soloist) with the needs of the group (the class experience). In a musical sense, this is best exemplified by a chamber music performance in which the principle of interaction depends on the conscientiousness of its individual members and a collective dedication to a musical ideal. It is to foster such interaction that I urge my pupils to play chamber music whenever possible. The same kind of interaction is of course required of families, institutions, and even governments, for the goal in each case is not only to uphold certain tenets but also to maintain a harmonious interplay between the individual members.

As a participant in these classes, I have been privileged to witness one victory after another. I have heard exclamations of joy from one pupil who overcame a fear of performing before others. On another occasion, I received a warm, tearful embrace from a pupil who finally succeeded in performing from memory. But the most touching tribute to the members of the class came from a young man who told me that the enthusiastic response to his playing enabled him to view himself for the first time as a person worthy of love and respect. In light of all these successes, I consider the classes to be an essential part of instrumental training and unhesitatingly recommend them to other teachers, especially those who have difficulty in motivating their pupils to practice.

When my pupils had begun to feel more secure as members of

our musical family, they would initiate stimulating discussions after the playing ended. This was perhaps the most valuable aspect of the class experience. The range of subjects was wide, often extending beyond musical matters and touching upon problems I could never have anticipated. It was during such discussions that I learned, for example, about loneliness and the adverse effect it has on practicing. I also learned about other obstacles to musical progress such as self-loathing, destructive parental and pedagogical influences, and a general lack of motivation for practicing. I began to observe that some of my pupils actually revealed the effects of these problems in the way they performed in class: they were either insufficiently prepared, unable, or reluctant to involve themselves emotionally in the music they played or at times were hostile to me and to my other pupils. I felt that these were symptoms of a deep inner struggle and that these pupils were in fact crying out for help. To stand idly by in the face of these human dramas, knowing that these pupils were being deprived of the benefits of practicing that I had myself enjoyed, was unthinkable for me. I had already told one pupil several years earlier that my sole intent in teaching her was to influence her growth as a human being. Now, I thought, was the time to put this intention into practice. For if I were to maintain my effectiveness as a teacher, I would have to involve myself in the hearts and minds of my pupils and, in short, deal with their total personalities.

Although I was trained to be a musician and not a psychologist, I am nevertheless fully aware of the role that psychology plays in a teacher–pupil relationship. Inasmuch as it is the science of the human mind and deals specifically with human behavior, psychology has a particular relevance to the relationship between teacher and pupil. Although volumes have been written on what constitutes emotional health, psychologists agree in principle that it requires a balance between emotion and reason within the framework of a healthy, functioning body (although psychologists tend to neglect the body). This is, in fact, the primary aim of practicing. When a musician succeeds in capturing the musical intent of a composer, isn't it because he has achieved this kind of balance? But again, we must be clear about our goals with respect to this balance and not confuse musical realization with self-realization. As we have seen, a musician may successfully balance thought, feeling, and dexterity in his playing without necessarily correlating this balance to his relationships with people. My task, then, was to show my pupils how the process of practicing could be applied beneficially to nonmusical areas, or, to put it another way, how their artistic strivings might be brought to interact with "that world out there."

Firmly convinced that I could teach my pupils to harmonize themselves through the techniques of practicing, I tackled their emotional problems in the way I knew best—through music. I began by convincing them that it really mattered to me whether or not they practiced. I knew that once I got them to practice consistently and productively, the process itself would restore their faith in themselves. Alas, I was not successful with all of my pupils. It would, of course, be unreasonable to expect such an approach to be effective with everyone. Yet, the results of my efforts with many pupils went beyond anything I could have predicted.

The following case histories demonstrate how a teacher–pupil relationship based on an involvement with music through practicing can lead to self-integration. My love and concern for my pupils elicited from them in return touching testimonials, some of which are included as part of their histories. They are undeniably flattering to me, but more important, they provide valuable insights into the relationship of music to life. Certainly, I cannot help but be gladdened to know that I, like Homer, have been called upon to stand over the shoulder of a pupil and inspire him to great heights. This image reaffirms my own connection to others.

CASE HISTORIES

Pupil No. I (The Lifeline)

When Pupil No. I came to his third lesson unprepared, I looked at him sternly and asked why he hadn't practiced. "Practice?," he repeated in disbelief. "What do you mean, practice? When I wake up in the morning, it is a major decision whether or not to brush my teeth, let alone practice!" Hearing this and considering his abject misery, I could hardly suggest that he conjure up an image of his piano teacher peering over his shoulder and inspiring him to work. The situation steadily deteriorated as my pupil became more and more depressed over his inability to motivate himself. Whatever progress he would manage to make was always followed by a decline. The problem stemmed, as he put it, from his sense of utter loneliness and his lack of a reason to practice. Finally, when the situation had reached a desperate stage, I confronted him with an ultimatum: "I've been thinking about your problem for a long time. You know how eager I am to help you to do your best. With a talent such as yours, it seems to me that you have no choice in the matter. Your talent must win out! As I see it, you can't motivate yourself to practice because you obviously don't have the capacity to love and respect your talent. This is another way of saying that you don't love and respect yourself. If you won't practice for yourself, then your only hope is to do it for someone else. Therefore, as your teacher, I am taking matters into my own hands. Either you agree to my conditions, or our relationship has got to come to an end."

I gave him a few days to think about this before proceeding further. After all, it would take a leap of faith for a young man so racked with difficulties suddenly to place himself in someone else's hands. After agonizing over the decision, he finally telephoned me to say that he had reached the end of his rope and was ready to do whatever I suggested.

The solution I reached for him subsequently helped other students who found themselves in a similar predicament. It consisted in the following: I not only asked him to practice four hours a day, but I instructed him also to telephone me each morning and report exactly what he intended to accomplish. On the following morning, he was either to reaffirm his commitment or explain why he was not able to fulfill it. This would be followed by a new commitment for that day. After continuing this routine day after day for about six months, the most promising incident occurred. One morning, when I hadn't received his call, I began to feel concerned that he had perhaps slipped back into his old habits. But during the afternoon, Pupil No. I did 'phone me, embarrassed to say that he had forgotten to call because he found himself too deeply involved in his *practicing*. Interpreting this as the first sign of victory, I suggested that he call every other day. After a few weeks, we both agreed that it was no longer necessary for him to report to me.

On that morning when he forgot to call, Pupil No. I had succeeded in transferring his sense of responsibility to *himself*. He had taken his first step toward conquering his loneliness and finding a reason to practice. Above all, by having to account for his actions, he felt a connection with someone. It gave me great satisfaction to hear his expressions of joy and gratitude at being able to trust himself, perhaps for the first time in his life. But more than that, he told me that the sense of continuity he experienced in his practicing encouraged him to reapply it in his relationships with people. Although this success could not by any means solve all of his personal problems, it did indicate his potential for future achievements, both musically and personally. In the years that followed he experienced successes as well as setbacks. Despite the latter, his progress has been, on the whole, steady and consistent. At this writing, he enjoys an excellent reputation both as a pianist and as a teacher.

The real significance of an experience is sometimes understood only after its actual occurrence. A sense of distance made it possible for Pupil No. I to put his experience into proper perspective. He reveals in the following statement the inner torment of a deeply sensitive person, not only describing the feeling of loneliness but also explaining the process that helped to alleviate it:

I remember feeling that no one cared, that I had been abandoned intentionally. I therefore felt free to do whatever I wanted. This invariably took the form of self-destruction since no one was there to observe my behavior or even to care what I did with my life. By not practicing, I avoided loneliness. This developed into a need to defend myself by thwarting the attempts of others to involve themselves with me. Holding them off only increased my loneliness. When you delivered your ultimatum, I was tortured by ambivalent feelings. On the one hand, I experienced rage and hatred toward you for trespassing on my sacred ground of aloneness. On the other hand, I didn't want to risk losing you. This rage was heightened by my sense of guilt at the ways I was neglecting myself. The worst guilt of all was the realization that I had failed myself. I chose isolation so as to numb this terrible realization. I was able to suppress it so long as no one forced me to bring it to consciousness. The daily phone calls established a kind of umbilical connection to a source outside me. Because of those calls, I found the courage to be myself and explore my talent. It was as if someone were leading me by the hand and staying with me while I ventured into my own inner realm, an area into which I had been terrified to enter. Had it not been for the constant assurance of another's presence, I could not have endured the loneliness of my work. Slowly I recognized that I could be left alone for increasingly longer periods of time without disastrous results. In fact, being alone kindled my first feelings of self-sufficiency and self-respect. After succeeding in carrying out your ultimatum, I discovered two fundamental truths about my personality: one is that I must be accountable for my actions; the other is an instinctual need to overcome loneliness by feeling a connection to others.

Thwarting either of these causes me shame and guilt. Finally, when you forced me to make a choice, I was willing to abandon my defenses and suffer the truth of my failings. You see, I couldn't bear to lose my teacher—the one person who really cared about me. That would have been a greater hell.

Pupil No. II (The Commitment)

Neither of my parents was emotionally communicative. In my house, feelings were either not important or were tacitly disapproved of. It wasn't considered desirable to express oneself on an instrument, or in any other way, for that matter. Father told me that he thought playing the piano was a form of self-indulgence. He even told people that he thought I was prepared to hide behind my talent for the rest of my life. Even my mother and sister have only a passive interest in my desire for a career in music. But as far as my father is concerned, everything I have done to advance myself musically has invariably incurred his disapproval. Even today, I'm afraid to tell him about any successes I've won because I know it will only upset him. Now I understand that what kept me from practicing was an unconscious desire to fulfill my father's unspoken conviction of my worthlessness as a human being. As long as I failed by not practicing, I was living up to his expectations. No sooner would I present him with tangible evidence of my attainments—such as a successful performance—than he would begin to get very upset. Since the expression of feelings is looked down upon or else totally ignored by my family, I always seem to shake up their whole constellation whenever I succeed at making my feelings known—through music. To me, succeeding in general means playing well or just plain practicing.

After reading this account of a son's feelings for his family—and for his father, in particular—you should not find it hard to imagine what a male piano teacher represented to Pupil No. II. When he came to study with me several years ago, he had no motivation to practice and his relationships with people brought him great unhappiness. He was not only unable to prepare for his lessons, but he would even enter competitions having attempted to learn the repertory only a few days before—tendencies that invariably led to his defeat. It is not unreasonable, I think, to resent a pupil who behaves in this way. Although I believed in his exceptional talent, understandably enough I soon began to dread my encounters with him. Apart from the unhappiness he caused me, everything he did seemed to increase his own depression and misery. What is more, he appeared to be completely oblivious of his own destructive behavior and my distress in dealing with him. When all attempts to reason with him failed, I took a new approach and devoted his next lesson to a serious discussion. When we were face to face, I told him the following: "How long do you think I will sit back and watch the annihilation of your talent? Your attitude toward music is sacrilegious and your behavior toward me is insulting. You have turned your back on yourself and on everything else that is important in your life. I, for one, will no longer tolerate your actions. Therefore, here is my ultimatum: if you don't write out and adhere to a contract of specific goals and a program of practice for a minimum of six months, I will be forced to discontinue your lessons. You have one week to come to a decision."

The week that followed was as tense for me as it was for him. He suffered unspeakable anguish over his decision. At first he telephoned to say that he couldn't go through with it and was leaving music. A few days later he told me that a letter of commitment was in the mail. But before the day was over, he 'phoned again and instructed me to tear it up without reading it.

Finally, a letter did arrive. Pupil No. II had succeeded in outlining carefully a project to which he vowed strict adherence. I in turn promised my full support in helping him fulfill his commitment. It was a triumphant day for both of us and a turning point in his life. When I asked him what enabled him to take this positive step, he replied, "I didn't want to lose my connection with you. Also, I interpreted your ultimatum as proof that you really cared about me and wanted me to practice, that it mattered to you whether or not I realized my potential. It was the first time in my life that I felt like this. I am certain that my parents, my other teachers, and even my friends never really cared whether or not I fulfilled myself. Otherwise they would have encouraged me to practice."

Pupil No. II lived up to his commitment. He began to practice diligently and succeeded in giving his first successful recital. He shows every indication of developing into a pianist of major proportions, and his goals are projected as far as a year in advance. His success at the piano has also had a startling effect on his personal life. When he finally learned not to compromise his talent, he could no longer tolerate superficial relationships with people. Practicing, he told me, made him feel productive and gave him a sense of self-worth. Having experienced this, he felt he would always be able to practice. Moreover, learning to use his natural resources filled him with confidence and gave him the courage to communicate with others more easily. He was free at last to satisfy his urge for artistic expression both as a pianist and as a person.

Pupil No. III (The Sacrifice)

When Pupil No. III sits at the piano, he gives the impression of being totally in contact with the music—even before he sounds the first note. His playing represents the kind of synthesis—emotional, intellectual, physical—that was discussed in the first chapter of this book. But it wasn't always that way. Perhaps he plays more beautifully today because of the suffering he endured most of his life.

He began taking lessons at the age of five from his mother. Curiously, he remembers no communication with his mother or father except through music. Since his mother supervised his practicing every day, he recalls vividly how each session filled him with security and love. But suddenly, when he was eight, his mother announced that from that time on, he had to practice by himself. Imagine the trauma he suffered when the only means of communication he had with his mother came abruptly to an end. Being only eight, he imagined that his mother had stopped talking to him entirely and that a lifeline had suddenly been broken. Silent as he had been, he became even more withdrawn. Practicing the piano now generated feelings of anger and spite directed against his mother who, he thought, had abandoned him. He built up such hatred for her that, as he told me, "I remember making a lot of mistakes when I practiced. It even occurred to me that if I made enough of them, it would kill her."

At sixteen, when he came to study with me, he was sullen, morose, and lacking in motivation. He was very pale and his eyes were lusterless. His playing, which reflected his emotional state, was withdrawn, unfocused, and lacking in detail. To make matters worse, he fell victim to drugs and his physical health deteriorated. He transferred from one school to another, unable to concentrate on any of his subjects. Finally, at the age of seventeen, he applied for admission to a clinic which had a special program for teen-aged students who have problems with motivation. After he was tested, he was accepted under one condition: he had to sacrifice his personal freedom and cut himself off from all contacts with the outside world—no visitors, no mail, no phone calls. The stipulations were severe and the decision was a difficult one to make. Nevertheless, his dream was to become a concert pianist and he was prepared, therefore, to do anything to achieve this goal.

During our last meeting together, we both expressed optimism about the future. I pointed out that his own determination to help himself would be the strongest factor in bringing about his cure. Moreover, we were encouraged to know that the program was highly regarded and that he would be in competent hands. Still, it was a sad farewell.

After being discharged a year later, his first telephone call was to me. I was overjoyed to hear from him and in our excitement we both began to speak at the same time. Finally, after we regained our composure, he asked me if he could have a piano lesson as soon as possible. I was deeply moved by this, for I felt that such a request—his first after a year in the clinic—indicated his recovery of an incentive. When the doorbell rang several days later, it is hard to say which of us was more joyous at our reunion. His outward appearance was somewhat the same, but with this difference—he looked healthy and there was a light in his eyes. His personality had undergone such a transformation, however, that in this sense he was unrecognizable. Fortunately, there was a piano in the clinic so that he was able to practice and learn repertory on his own. The intensity and passion with which he played the *Concerto in A minor* by Grieg and *Fireworks* by Debussy brought tears to my eyes and left me dumbfounded.

Now, at the age of twenty-one, Pupil No. III is developing into an artist, even though his emotional problems are not completely resolved. His practicing, which he still does sporadically, continues to be marred by feelings of anger and spite, cruel reminders of his childhood. No matter how hard he tries to circumvent these feelings, they loom up again and again, appearing sometimes as impenetrable obstacles to his progress. When, as a child, he was left alone to practice, he felt that he could never satisfy his mother's wishes. Even now, as an adult, he continues to feel inadequate in the face of the most simple demands, although he knows rationally that what is asked of him is easily within his grasp. Blessed with all the natural talent necessary for a career in music, he discovered how easy it was for him to win adulation with the least amount of effort. When he plays well, he thus tends to greet praise with contempt, knowing that a minimum of time went into his preparation. I pointed out to him that by not doing his best for me and his friends, he is in effect withholding his love and respect, thereby transferring unconsciously to us his long-held resentment toward his mother. This observation has helped him to gain a clearer perspective into his problem, for it enabled him to understand how his present conflict has its roots in his painful past. Although explaining this to him did not eliminate the conflict, it helped him to view it more objectively. While his work is still not as consistent as he would like, no pupil I have ever taught approaches the art of practicing with his special kind of imagination. His desire to make progress, coupled with my expectations of him, give him the courage to strive for the highest goals. Each time he conquers a musical or technical problem and communicates his feelings to others in performance, he reaffirms his ability to surmount the difficulties of the past. He is spurred on by the knowledge that his fellow students and I want him to succeed. We are confident that some day he will overcome his problems and share his artistry with the world.

Pupil No. IV (The Cookie Jar is Empty)

This pupil is a married woman whose need to practice and develop her talent has presented her with various difficulties, the major one being how to reconcile her artistic inclinations with her responsibility to her family. Her inability to achieve a balance between her personal ambition and her devotion to her family caused her to suffer from feelings of guilt during most of her adult life. She assumed that each hour spent at the piano was time she should have given to her husband and children. She battled with conflicting thoughts such as: "Should I be working on an *Etude* of Chopin when the cookie jar is empty?" or "How will my husband feel when he realizes that he can't satisfy all of my needs, that a part of me can be satisfied only at the piano?" At one point, she even considered living alone in order to pursue her studies freely, but this idea was quickly rejected as selfish. Instead, she tried to find a less drastic solution. "I wanted desperately to be a concert artist," she told me, "but not at the expense of my husband and children."

After years of struggling with this problem, she finally decided to give up practicing altogether and accepted a post as director of a music school where she also taught various musical subjects. "I reasoned," she explained, "that the only way I could really demonstrate my responsibility to my family was to contribute to their economic security. By devoting myself full-time to teaching and abandoning the piano, I thought I could at least gain their acceptance as a breadwinner if not as an artist." Her decision lasted for fourteen years. By denying herself the right to practice, she attempted to act out the image she had of herself as a devoted wife and mother.

It was a grave miscalculation as the catastrophic results proved. Her health deteriorated and she developed ulcers. In a desperate attempt to stabilize a precarious situation, she decided (with the encouragement of her husband) to resign her post at the school and return once again to practicing. She did, however, continue to teach a few private students. In 1974, at the age of forty, she invited me to a piano recital, her first in seventeen years. Although this period of inner conflict had been extremely trying, she gave a creditable performance of a most demanding program. Her fingers were expertly accurate, but her playing sounded emotionally constrained.

I didn't realize at the time that the invitation to her recital was her way of approaching me for lessons. Hearing her made me eager to teach her. I felt confident that once she put the piano into its proper perspective, she could more easily resolve her other problems. When she came for her first lesson, I began by explaining how all emotion must be synthesized with corresponding physical gestures. I then showed her how sound is achieved through various appropriate movements of the entire body. Heretofore, she had concentrated on her fingers only, not knowing how to make use of the adapting motions of the wrists, forearms and especially the upper arms and torso. The events of her progress were impressive. Her sound became more pliable and resonant, and her musicality found a channel through which to express itself. When her efforts produced such positive results, her entire personality changed for the better. Physical freedom brought with it emotional freedom as well.

Many months later, Pupil No. IV told me that what had helped her more than anything else was her new appraisal of perfection and error. She had grown up assuming that mistakes are simply forbidden and that love and approbation are earned by accuracy alone, even at the expense of emotional content. Like so many gifted people, she was intimidated in early childhood by tyrannical teachers. At seven, she attended a professional school for exceptionally gifted children where each day her practicing was scrupulously supervised. Her encounters with the director, before whom she frequently had to play, were moments of sheer terror. But the glamorous student recitals at the end of the year were occasions of joy. She loved to play for people, especially in the formal environment of an auditorium. At one such recital, she performed the *Sonata, Op. 49, No. 2* by Beethoven and suffered a minor mishap. As it happened, this lapse neither affected her poise nor the audience's appreciation of her playing. The director, however, took a completely different view of the situation. Approaching her menacingly, he bellowed, "Don't you dare to make a mistake like that again!" Small wonder that when I met her thirty-two years later, she wouldn't allow herself the right to play Chopin *Etudes* anywhere near up to tempo until she had practiced them slowly for a year. To risk even one mistake at the indicated tempo was unthinkable for her.

My approach in teaching her stressed her *right* to express her feelings, to disagree with me if she wished, and, above all, to make mistakes. This brought her the first freedom she had ever known and the courage to follow her own convictions. She was now armed with a confidence gained from her newly acquired artistic freedom—a confidence which she then transferred to her personal life. Soon she became more responsive to her family in ways she had never thought possible. The piano, which had formerly estranged her from her family, now became the catalyst that produced the harmonious union she had always wanted to achieve. I once suggested to her that practicing seemed to make her healthier both physically and emotionally and that in this state she was far better equipped to be a loving wife and mother. She now understands that her right to express herself at the piano actually benefits her family. The joy she experiences from her musical accomplishments radiates out to her husband and children, bringing them comfort and serenity. They in turn sense a world which, though detached from them, brings balance and reconciliation to their lives. "I finally realized," she told me, "that denying myself does not necessarily make my family contented and happy. Going back to the piano and accepting the disciplines of practicing helped me to make that discovery."

You should not assume that practicing is in itself a panacea for all difficulties in a relationship. However, there are certain aspects of practicing that have a direct bearing upon human relationships. In Chapter 11, for example, you will discover that it is possible to be deeply involved in the music during a performance while still listening to yourself as though you were, in a sense, a member of your own audience. It is exactly this kind of musical objectivity that is applicable to life. For one of the requirements in maintaining a mutually satisfying relationship is the ability to be objective about the person you feel close to, without disturbing in any way that strong thread of feeling that binds you together. Just as you become enraptured by a musical phrase—or a person—a part of you must stand aside and witness objectively the whole miracle—the whole personality. By sensitively balancing your initial feeling with your knowlege of what it is you feel, your love for the source of your feeling doubles upon itself. Pupil No. IV was in the process of achieving this objectivity, not only musically, but also in the way she brought her need to be an artist into balance with her responsibilities as a wife and mother.

After practicing on a new program, Pupil No. IV decided to give another recital in the same studio where she had played the year before. She assembled the same audience of family and friends, augmented now by my pupils, all of whom had become her ardent fans. How did she play? Ordinarily, I would never disturb a performer during intermission even to praise him. For intermission is more important for the artist than for the audience, giving him the chance to catch his breath and harness his forces for the second half of the program. This time, however, I could not restrain myself. I felt compelled to tell Pupil No. IV that love came pouring out of every note she played, a gift from her to her audience. But it was she who best summed up the significance of the occasion. In a voice charged with emotion, she told me the following morning, "I gave the recital I have wanted to give all my life." She wept tears of joy and sadness. When victory comes after a lifetime of struggle, attainment is often bittersweet. But mixed with her tears was the triumph of the human spirit—a triumph that has encouraged her to continue accepting one challenge after another both at the piano and in her personal life. "A relationship," she told me,"is very much like practicing in that you can't miss a day of nurturing it—like watering a plant. It always needs your attention. I have a need to serve both my husband and my music. The truth is that I can no sooner live without him than I can without the piano. By assuring him of this, I bring harmony into our life."

You don't have to be a professional musician to understand the significance of this inspiring story. Pupil No. IV began to function as an integrated person only when she confronted herself through her talent. The two compelling drives in her life—her need to be a pianist and her love for her family—vied for supremacy. When she chose to neglect her musical talent, she denied the artistic truth in herself and thus suffered the grim consequences of her decision. Even when you reason out your priorities in life and consciously place them in what you think is the proper order, your body recognizes a higher truth and responds accordingly. We saw this manifest itself in Pupil No. IV. For when she relegated her musical talent to second place in her hierarchy of needs, ulcers developed as a painful, symbolic admonition, as though her talent was crying out for recognition. It was only when she acted upon her right to be a pianist that she was able to balance the priorities in her life.

Pupil No. V (The Pianist from Wall Street)

At forty-one, Pupil No. V plays like an artist. Although he is an investment analyst by profession, the piano is a sacred and vital part of his life. But this was not always the case. His story is an account of a man's struggle against circumstances that kept him from developing his musical talent.

From the age of five until the time that Pupil No. V came to study with me, no one had ever shown him how to conquer his technical limitations. He therefore assumed that unless you are born with technical ability you can never hope to achieve it. He wanted desperately to perform for people, but his preoccupation with his technical deficiencies distracted him from the emotional content of the music he played. He thus created a false image of the piano literature as being merely a vehicle for technical display. And since he considered his technique to be inadequate, the area of performing seemed closed to him forever. "I never looked upon piano playing as an experience that could be personally fulfilling," he told me, "and so I followed my family's suggestion and pursued a career in business."

While studying at the University of Chicago, he had his first experience playing chamber music. Caught up in the sheer beauty of the literature and inspired by the dedication of the musicians with whom he played, he temporarily forgot about his technical limitations and sensed for the first time the true communicative power of music. His proficiency in this literature grew to such an extent that one summer he was accepted at a well-known music festival. There he studied with an eminent pianist and participated in chamber music performances. But even this experience did not enable him fully to view himself as a pianist, for his technique was still unpredictable. Not yet understanding the significance of music in his life, he continued his university studies and earned a degree in accounting.

At twenty-six, Pupil No. V moved to New York City with an excellent job, but no piano. I met him one day at a social gathering and played some four-hand music with him. He was not only an expert sight-reader, but one of the most musical pianists I had ever heard. My admiration for his playing inspired me to help him in any way I could. He agreed that he could not continue to live happily without an instrument and at my insistence we went together to choose a fine upright piano which afforded him endless hours of delight. But it had taken him twelve years to realize that music was an integral part of his life. Finally he decided to study seriously. Years of searching had led him to understand that even if he could not be the best pianist in the world, he could still fulfill himself through music.

As he gradually learned how to control sound for specific musical intentions, his imagination caught fire. For the first time in his life he understood what intelligent practicing could produce. When my students heard him play, they thought he was a professional pianist masquerading as an investment analyst. He in turn enjoyed the security of a musical family that could appreciate him for his true worth. He eventually replaced his upright piano with a beautiful Steinway grand that inspired him to new heights.

In the years that followed, he developed a degree of confidence far exceeding his expectations. As he told me, "No one had ever before proposed to me that practicing could be a way toward happiness. I never would have believed that practicing could have so positive an effect on me. Practicing, to me, had always been a destructive experience—something to be avoided. When you're told as a little boy, 'Don't get dirty!', you try to avoid getting dirty by keeping uninvolved. The trouble is, you can end up on the sidelines always looking in. What I eventually learned from practicing is that if you don't recognize problems and solve them, well, you just can't learn to play the piano. However simple or obvious this may seem, its application has not only affected my musical progress, but my personal life as well. Still, I don't think I could have motivated myself to practice if you had not cared whether or not I did it."

My discussions with Pupil No. V prompted me to hold a special meeting of the class in order to learn how my other pupils viewed practicing. To my surprise, I discovered that many of them looked upon practicing as nothing more than a dutiful preparation for their lessons. Some even expressed a secret fear, as had Pupil No. V long before, that they could never hope to solve their technical problems no matter how long they practiced. Discouraged from devoting sufficient time to their practicing, they could not hope to achieve tangible results. Least of all could they be expected to focus on the ultimate objectives beyond practicing. I was determined to clarify these issues for them and redirect their views so that they could accept practicing as a process leading toward self-realization. Unfortunately, I could not use the story of Pupil No. V as an example of someone who had benefited in this way. Although they observed how his musical and technical expertise was matched by his personal growth, they were not about to accept practicing as the factor that brought it about. I decided instead to direct the discussion toward the men and women of genius, those born with a "freakish physical set-up" that enables them to play anything. As I pointed out, geniuses have to practice just as anyone else. We learn from them that practicing first entails finding an explanation for purely instinctive attitudes. Thus, the most gifted among them will ask, "How did I do that?" "What made that passage work?" While he practices, he looks over his own shoulder, so to speak, and examines and reexamines each and every note, drawing conclusions that strengthen his confidence: "I play that F sharp softer, not louder; I raise my wrist when I make a diminuendo on that trill; I increase the pressure in my lower arm for that passage . . ." The whole process is one in which he synthesizes his natural, intuitive faculties with a controlling intellect. Although he may revel in the naturalness of his talent, his integrity tells him that an unexamined note is in fact not worth playing.[4] "Well," one of my pupils protested, "all that is fine for a genius, but where do I fit into this picture?" "You fit into whatever place you make for yourself," I said. "If you value your gifts—and I mean really value them—you will *act* like a genius even if you cannot be one. And that means paying serious attention to *what* you are. Instead of complaining about what you are not or succumbing to the view that you need not practice conscientiously or study with a master teacher unless you are headed for a major career, look upon your talent as something uniquely yours and *develop it*." After all, measuring your gifts against another's is really as futile as comparing the various manifestations of beauty in the myriad forms of nature. Thus, since our fundamental goal is to synthesize emotion, intellect, and physical coordination, it is from this that the benefits of practicing accumulate, no matter what one's individual gifts may be.

At this point in the discussion I was moved to read a letter I had just received from a pupil who, at age thirty-nine, recently gave her first recital. Like many of those present, she used to think herself incapable of ever achieving technical proficiency. To perform from memory before others was always unimaginable to her. Although her letter generously acknowledges my teaching, its greater message, from which I have excerpted the following, concerns practicing and what it can do for the nonprofessional musician:

> You have to be told in writing how my recital has changed my life. The musical development it represents has unquestionably brought me more emotional stability, confidence, and poise than I have ever known before. But more than anything else, it was your belief in me that led me to trust myself enough to rise to the occasion. Whatever the flaws in my playing, I have learned from this one step forward (small for mankind, giant for me), how much a positive attitude can accomplish. My gratitude goes to you for giving as much care and attention to a student who will never win prizes or become a concert pianist as you offer the professionals in your class.

Because talent is a composite of strengths and weaknesses, it remains for each of us to strengthen our weaker traits. For example, one person may be technically adept but musically wanting. The process of practicing for that individual entails a strong focus on the emotional content of music. Everyone who practices, gifted or otherwise, must engage in this sensitive balancing of all his faculties. It doesn't matter whether you arrive at it through one piece or ten, in one week or a year, in Carnegie Hall or in your own room. Your chief concern should be to experience this balance through practicing, no matter how long it takes and no matter where you perform. Once you synthesize all the factors that make up your talent, you will in time learn to apply this synthesis to nonmusical situations. With this as an ultimate goal, everyone—professionals as well as nonprofessionals—cannot help but grow from practicing. One thing is certain: your progress will be proportionate to the quality and quantity of the effort expended. Far from being defeated by the capabilities of a genius, draw instead inspiration from the creative way in which he practices and the extraordinary standards he upholds when he performs. Find within yourself that passionate dedication which you see in the artist. Be assured that even though your playing may not reach his level, the benefits of practicing are nonetheless the same for you as they are for him. Can it be anything but heartening then to know that you are engaged in a process shared by the immortals?

Pupil No. V learned to apply these principles to his own practicing. In the last few years he has given three recitals, the last one in particular surpassing all the others. "It is curious," he told me recently, "and I didn't realize it until I started studying seriously, that when I used to sit at the piano, I never really listened to what I was playing. I only heard what I wanted it to sound like. I was therefore disconnected from what I was actually doing. Now I am confident that if I continue to listen to my own practicing, I will eventually fulfill the image I have of my playing."

Soon, he began to see a correlation between his musical growth and his personal life. When he discovered that a lifetime of pianistic difficulties could actually be solved, he was encouraged to approach problems in other areas with the same degree of patience and insight. As a result, he feels more optimistic and hopeful about everything he does in life. In fact, to him music and life are inseparable. As Theodor Leschetizky, the great Viennese pedagogue, used to say, "No life without music; no music without life."

Mastering an instrument is a constant challenge. Confronting this challenge means *confronting yourself.* Because musical and technical difficulties will always exist to some degree, the battle is a perpetual one. But confidence comes from knowing how to succeed—how to grapple with problems and eventually solve them through a *process.* As Pupil No. V told me, "It is a battle between the self I used to be and the self I always wanted to be. You helped me realize this. Of all the people I know, you are the one most interested in me as a person and as a musician. I know this just by the way you open the door and greet me when I come for a lesson. You appreciate me for what I can do. The various degrees of talent among your students are not the important issue for you. It is what we can do *individually* that matters to you. This removes all competitive feelings among us. It is not that you don't criticize our playing. Yet you never behave negatively toward your students.

You are constantly optimistic about our development and we in turn respond to your belief in us."

Pupil No. V is planning a New York debut. His playing certainly warrants the decision. And provided that no unforeseen emergency in the stock market distracts him from the piano, he will do it, too.

CONCLUSIONS

Some of my friends and colleagues reprimand me for spending too much time and energy helping my pupils solve their problems. They feel that I should use that time for myself. However, I think that three minutes a day on the phone is not too great a sacrifice to make if I can thereby establish a lifeline with someone whose emotional health may be at stake. Furthermore, if I am to uphold the principles discussed in this book, my chief responsibility as a teacher is to show concern for the personal development of my pupils.

In all my experience as a teacher, I have never had a pupil who did not show marked improvement in his personal life once he understood the far-reaching implications of practicing. Yet, there are times when even this knowledge cannot remove certain barriers to practicing. If your teacher, family, and friends all fail to motivate you, it is possible that your problem is psychological. For example, you may feel that someone close to you resents your practicing (see Chapter 11). As in the case of Pupil No. III (The Sacrifice), your inability to practice may stem from an internal rebellion against a loved one toward whom you dare not vent your rage. But a teacher who cares about you, a friend, or a psychologist can help you resolve these problems, thus enabling you to organize your energies for even a minimal approach to practicing. Such a humble beginning is all that is necessary, for once you embark on the process of practicing and experience the satisfaction that comes from honest effort, you will feel, like Pupil No. II (The Commitment), that you "will always want to practice."

We live in an age of technology in which practically everything is reduced to a formula. Words like "caring," "loving," and "feeling" are often dismissed as being embarrassingly sentimental. I deplore this tendency and consider it a primary obstacle to practicing and, for that matter, to all human growth. Even doctors have admitted that beyond a certain point of scientific knowledge, the deep concern of one individual often becomes the determining factor in a patient's recovery. These case histories show the beneficial effects of such concern. For the one factor that determined the progress of my pupils was the knowledge that someone really cared for them and demonstrated this care by a genuine interest in their practice habits.

Pupil No. III (The Sacrifice) expressed this in a different way. He told me that his progress began when he suddenly realized that everything I had told him about practicing pertained to him specifically. As he explained it, he used to think that the concepts I had painstakingly worked out with him at his lessons were generalizations and not meant for him in particular. But after I guided him repeatedly through the process of practicing during each lesson, he eventually realized that all the suggestions I gave him were indeed applicable to him and to his individual talent. Only then did he gain the confidence to practice in the same way on his own. He wanted results and he deserved to have them. Guiding him through the process of practicing right there at his lesson helped him to deal honestly with himself. When he finally sounded on the piano the very musical feelings which he had always hoped to express, his regard for himself as well as for me increased immeasurably. In contrast to the care I offered Pupil No. III, the lack of concern shown to Pupil No. IV (The Cookie Jar is Empty) by the director of her school saddens me to this day. An insignificant mistake made by an eight-year-old child became in his estimation a threat to his reputation. A child's feelings and progress were evidently the least of his concerns.

The essential ingredient, then, in a teacher–pupil relationship, as in all relationships, is the sincere concern of one person for another. A teacher of music demonstrates this concern by really caring whether or not his pupils practice. If a pupil senses that his teacher has little or no interest in his progress, he is apt to care less about himself and others. This invites apathy. To prevent this condition from developing, a teacher must be alert to his pupil's needs, concerned about his progress and, above all, must be able to exercise extreme patience. For it may take a long time before such a pupil is able to respond in kind to his teacher's respect and affection. As these case histories demonstrate, the emergence of a pupil from a period of confusion and inactivity to a state of confidence and productivity is ample reward for any teacher's efforts.

You may assume mistakenly that your teacher, like your parent, is the sole dispenser of knowledge, advice, and direction. But when your teacher consults you on issues that affect your progress, a balance is achieved whereby you and your teacher interact as giver and receiver alike. Such an exchange requires verbal as well as musical communication. It will convince you, as it did my recalcitrant pupil of Chapter 1, that your teacher cares as much about you, personally, as he does about your musical talent. You in turn cannot help but respond to his caring by practicing. You thereby nurture your talent and satisfy to the fullest extent your human need to give and receive approbation. Moreover, when you practice, you are laying the foundation for self-reliance and freedom—the kind of freedom that begins with a strict adherence to accepted disciplines and ends in the confidence gained by mastering an instrument.

Finally, nothing acts as a greater deterrent to practicing than a sense of inadequacy. You may believe, for example, that you dare not practice and perform certain compositions simply because your playing is not on the level of the great artists. Pupil No. V (The Pianist from Wall Street) spent most of his adult life disproving this notion. Interestingly enough, it was only when he acted upon his right to express his artistic calling (even though it was not as soloist with the New York Philharmonic) that his playing actually reached the high standards of true artistry. Pupil No. II (The Commitment) has something important to say on this matter:

> The study of music is very different from other pursuits. First of all, I don't get paid for practicing a Beethoven Sonata. Practicing has nothing to do with dollars unless, of course, you get paid for performing. Before I became career-oriented, my teachers never encouraged me to perform. They thought that performing was the exclusive domain of the professional students—the ones who win contests and are striving for big careers. Some famous teachers in New York, for example, never allow any but the most gifted students to perform in their classes. Their main concern is to make the best possible impression on the other students and visitors. Therefore, if you're not a star, then you never get a chance to play. It never occurs to them that the experience of performing may be beneficial personally for a student even though he is not necessarily preparing for a career. Nevertheless, I discovered that if you sincerely want to play and search patiently, you will usually find places and audiences. And if you are well-prepared, you may either get re-engaged or even attract additional invitations. Of course, none of this was evident to me until I learned to practice.

Another deterrent to musical progress is the false notion that only career-oriented musicians deserve to practice seriously, to study with the best teachers, and to own the finest instruments. But a love of music and the desire to develop your talent do not require that you become a professional musician any more than a devotion to religion means that you must enter the priesthood or become a rabbi. It is not your goal that gives you the right to study seriously, but your genuine desire for musical knowledge. And this right belongs to everyone—including the aged. For the mind, as science continues to inform us, will grow so long as it is presented with challenge and stimulus. In short, nothing should hinder our course—nothing, that is, except the obstructions of our own making or those we allow others to impose upon us.

You may think that my concern for my pupils entails undue self-sacrifice, but this is not the case. The solutions I have been fortunate enough to find for them actually relieve my own distress at their possible failure. It is one thing to be moved by human suffering, but the degree to which you are moved is measured by the action you take. This holds for practicing, too. Good intentions mean little. Instead of making resolutions, demonstrate with your own two hands how you intend to realize those intentions. Not to do so shows a lack of regard for your teacher, for yourself and, above all, for the art of music. Not practicing makes you miserable; but continuing not to practice may indicate that you are not miserable enough. As you have seen in these case histories, a pupil may face the following conflict: "I am distressed because I cannot fulfill the promise of my talent. But I will be even more distressed if I lose my teacher and friend because of my negligence. I'd better practice."

It is not easy to practice properly. Because of this, there is a tendency in some individuals to use the unfortunate circumstances of their past as an excuse for being irresponsible to themselves and others. But once a pupil learns how to practice, he no longer has the time or even the inclination to dwell on his past. He is too busy fulfilling what he expects of himself and what others expect of him. What used to be an abhorrent task now becomes the prelude to joy and accomplishment. Pupil No. I (The Lifeline) summed up what practicing meant to him when he told me, "When I practice properly, I come to love myself, my art, and you." I could not help responding, "You're not the only one. When I practice properly, I love you, too."

3 Concentration

NATURAL AND DELIBERATE CONCENTRATION

If you master concentration, you will never have to be told how to practice. Concentration is a requisite for all tasks, especially those demanding a high degree of skill. Since nothing worthwhile can be accomplished without it, we had better determine how it can be induced. In order to concentrate, you must first direct your attention to something in particular. When practicing, for example, you need to have a clear idea of what it is you wish to accomplish. You must have a specific goal in mind. By focusing your attention on this, you will intensify your powers of concentration.

There are many activities in life in which you slip automatically into a natural state of concentration: a good movie, for example, can fascinate you to the extent that you are drawn involuntarily into the plot; being with someone you love inspires such an intense interest that you can often forget about yourself entirely; children at play can become so engrossed in a game that they may fail to hear their parents calling. In short, being interested and involved in what you are doing makes you concentrate in spite of yourself.

In the book *Gestalt Therapy*, a comparison is drawn between deliberate concentration and natural ("healthy, organic") concentration:

> In our society concentration is regarded as a deliberate, strenuous, compulsive effort—something you *make yourself* do. This is to be expected where people are forever neurotically commanding, conquering and compelling themselves. On the other hand, healthy, organic concentration usually is not called concentration at all, but, on those rare occasions when it does occur, is named attraction, interest, fascination or absorption.[5]

Although both types of concentration come into play in practicing, it is the latter that produces the best results. If by forcing yourself to concentrate you set up a barrier that impedes your progress, you can rob yourself of the vital energy needed for your best work. How then can you induce "healthy, organic" concentration when you practice? Needless to say, if you are not in the mood to practice, natural concentration is affected proportionately. To induce it, however, you can begin by practicing deliberately toward a specific goal at a predetermined time, whether you are in the mood or not. Thus, by adhering to a self-induced routine, you will eventually become so absorbed in what you are doing that your "deliberate concentration" will be converted into "spontaneous concentration." The one essential ingredient for bringing about this conversion is an unconditional love of the composition you intend to master.

SIGHT-READING

Few activities can capture a musician's interest more easily than sight-reading. For this reason, I would unhesitatingly choose the ability to read well as one of the most valuable assets a musician can have. Some have a natural talent in this direction. The more new repertory they explore, the greater their skill becomes. For me, sight-reading was never a chore but a pleasure. I remember at age fifteen visiting the Newark Public Library every Saturday morning and staggering home under a mountain of piano scores—original works and transcriptions of operas and symphonies. It was quite a feat to maneuver the stack through the bus door, but I certainly improved my sight-reading.

However eager some musicians may be to explore music, their deficiency in processing musical notation quite often deters them from doing so. I am convinced that the correction of this deficiency must take top priority in musical education, not only because sight-reading enables one to grasp a piece as a whole, but more important, because it trains the memory and sharpens the powers of concentration. I had never noticed this connection between sight-reading and musical memory until rather recently when I had to confront the problems of an especially conscientious pupil who simply could not read. Apart from the fact that he could not satisfy his curiosity by reading through repertory, he found his practicing to be a particularly agonizing process. For he could not even read through the pieces I assigned him. To deal with his problems, I began by restricting his reading to simple scores and having him adhere to all the standard approaches to sight-reading:

1. Before playing, study the music silently, taking special note of the key and time signatures.
2. Clap the rhythm.
3. For pieces in a distinguishable key (tonal), play the scale in which the piece is written to fix the tonality in your ear.
4. Keep your eyes on the score at all times.
5. Read from the bass upward.
6. Look ahead.
7. Move your hands only when necessary.

Although he followed this program faithfully, my pupil made little progress. From my close observation of his physical reactions to notation—in particular, the timing, or lack of it, between his eye–hand reflexes—I saw clearly enough the tendencies of a poor sight-reader. To help him, I had to find out what good sight-readers do. Watching the facile readers among my pupils, I looked for certain constant factors in their processing of notation. In every case, their eyes, I noticed, moved in slight anticipation of their hands; their hands knew the keyboard as one does the most familiar terrain. Yet, none of these good readers could tell me anything about their mental processes. "I'm not exactly sure what goes on in my mind," was the usual response. Or, "When I see the notes on the page, I just seem to feel them with my fingers. I never think of the names of the notes at all." It occurred to me then to wonder what I myself think of when sight-reading.

To peer into one's own mind as a disinterested observer is not the easiest of tasks. But what I discovered by making the effort not only helped my pupil, but also revolutionized my approach to teaching sight-reading. The instant I began to read, my mind framed a running commentary coincidental with the automatic movements of my hands. The absorption into my mind and retention of successive musical facts were triggering the appropriate responses of my hands. By drawing on a great store of information, gathered from years of experience, I was able to analyze complex musical situations at a glance and reduce them progressively to their simplest elements. Above all, I found myself able to anticipate what was to come, as, for example, repetitions of motifs, rhythms, and harmonic progressions. This ability to predict musical events, being the major skill for sight-reading, is rooted, as I realized from observing myself, in the power of retention. Thus, to know what is to come, one has to remember what has just transpired.

When my pupil arrived for his next lesson, I placed before him one of my own compositions in the intermediate grade:

Seymour Bernstein, *The Praying Mantis* (from *Insects*, Bk. 2). (Reprinted by permission of Alexander Broude, Inc.)

I allowed him eight seconds to reduce the first measure to the simplest theoretical and structural facts he could find. He was then to close his eyes and recite whatever of this information he could retain, as, for example:

The bass is held throughout the measure.
The soprano moves in contrary motion to the tenor.
The right hand begins with an augmented fourth.

I then allowed him eight seconds to play the first measure while simultaneously scanning the second measure for associative information. This meant, of course, that he had to take in the second measure with his peripheral vision while he was decoding the first. At the same time, his fingers had to find their way over the keys unassisted by his eyes. I then had him stop playing at the end of the first measure and recite only those facts absorbed from the second measure that were harmonically or intervallically related to the first measure. At this point he faltered, but with a little coaxing and a lot of encouragement, he finally reported the following:

The bass is tied into the second measure.
The soprano moves down three diatonic steps.
The last note resolves into a G major chord.

His assigning a pitch name to a chord for the first time encouraged me to have him play through the first two measures while scanning the third at whatever point he felt able. This time, he not only retained more specific information, but also began to draw upon his knowledge of theory, as his comments on the third measure showed:

> The bass, D, is a pedal point. The soprano, B, in the third measure resolves to an A, making it part of a D7 chord. There is a tenor B♭ in the final chord that is somehow related to the B♭ in the first measure. But shouldn't it be notated as an A♯ instead?

"If you can raise a question on enharmonic notation, then you are retaining more information than either of us thought possible," I was happy to observe. I now set the metronome at $\downarrow$ = 60 and asked him to read through the entire composition without stopping, even if it meant omitting notes. More important, he was to continue a running commentary of associative facts while he was playing. At first, his recitation comprehended a few notes only, but soon he was able to scan one or two measures in advance of his playing. As he grew more adept at performing these multiple tasks, he finally began to predict what was to come with greater accuracy. Though he could foresee at this stage only the obvious—such as simple cadences and melodic progressions that did not deviate from the established tonality—he was nonetheless calling upon his musical memory. That is, he was retaining a mental image of the melodic pattern he had just played long enough for it to make musical sense to him. And in the split second it took for his mind to absorb this meaning, three things happened: his ear responded to the tonality, his hands reacted to the signal from his mind, and his eyes were set free to look ahead. It was, of course, only a beginning. But it encouraged him to continue exploring unfamiliar scores. For me, it was proof again that the human mind, if presented with sufficient stimulus, is capable of performing far more difficult tasks than usually seems possible. For the sake of convenience, I have condensed the process of sight-reading developed for my pupil into an outline of essentials:

I. Preliminaries
   A. Identify key and time signatures.
   B. Identify all rhythmic values and determine how they relate to each other; for example, ♫ = ♩ ; ♪ = ♫
   C. Know your scales and arpeggios thoroughly, including all the forms of minor scales.
   D. Identify all intervals, recognizing how they are distributed over the lines and spaces of the staff. This facilitates visual comprehension:
      1. thirds, fifths, and sevenths extend from line to line or space to space.
      2. seconds, fourths, sixths, and octaves extend from line to space or space to line.

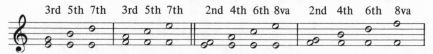

   E. Recognize chords and their inversions.
   F. Identify cadences—especially IV, V, I.

II. Sequential Steps for Memory Retention in Sight-Reading
   A. Set the metronome to a slow tempo.
   B. Allow it to tick for a full measure. Simultaneously, scan the first measure of the piece you are reading and recite whatever theoretical or structural facts you can absorb.
   C. Keep your eyes on the score.
   D. With the metronome ticking, begin to play the first measure, listening carefully to what you are playing. Simultaneously, scan the second measure for associative information. Recite your findings *before* you reach the second measure.
   E. Repeat this procedure, moving from the second to the third measure and so on.
   F. Repeat this sequence from measure to measue throughout the entire piece. Omit notes, if necessary, but try not to stop.
   G. Do this every day for at least fifteen minutes, always selecting an unfamiliar piece, and, above all, using your metronome as

a guide. In time, your memory will sharpen, your sense of the key-board will become more dependable and your aural experience of melodic patterns in various rhythmic and tonal contexts will assist you to predict musical events.

As my pupil progressed slowly but steadily in his sight-reading, I could not help recalling a wise saying in the Talmud: "From my pupils have I learned." For certainly, the events in my pupil's progress helped me to understand a fundamental factor in sight-reading—namely, that it enlists the musical memory far more than has been noticed even by musicians themselves. It is, in its highest stage of efficiency, a form of instant comprehension and retention—not only of notational symbols, but of everything on the printed page that represents music. All told, sight-reading serves three important functions: (1) it allows for a spontaneous response to an entire composition, which, as is discussed in Chapter 9, is critical in the initial stages of learning; (2) it assists the tactile and kinetic memory by developing a sense of the keyboard; (3) it activates the musical memory—that raw material from which all our responses, comprehension, and musical associations are fashioned. In short, the ability to group notes into patterns, to experience these patterns as musical events, and to discover in them a musical meaning enables a musician to probe to the heart of the music he plays.

INDUCING CONCENTRATION

Performing is a natural outgrowth of your love for music. No matter how much concentration is required in working toward this goal, the rewards far exceed the difficulties. The very steps that lead toward self-realization are to be found in the learning procedures that enable you to perform a musical composition for one or more individuals.

The first step in learning a new piece is to play it through from beginning to end even if it means making mistakes. Because your goal is to encompass the meaning of the composition as a whole, every impression you absorb, however fleeting it may be, is important at this stage. That is why it is so crucial that you be able to sight-read. Liszt, who sight-read perfectly, used to skip this process and begin a new piece by studying it slowly and in great detail. To a pupil, however, he suggested sight-reading every day so that she would learn to grasp a piece as a *whole* and not just in small details. Therefore, allow yourself to make mistakes. A fear of hitting wrong notes, causing you to stop and start again and again, hampers you from experiencing the music in its entirety. Freeing yourself from this fear will enable you to function far better than you anticipate. To your delight, you will end up making fewer mistakes. As a result, you will grasp the composition as a total structure, at the same time sensing its emotional content. It is not necessary to analyze during this preliminary phase. Just be receptive to your natural feelings about the piece without inhibiting those associations that may occur to you during the reading. Being receptive means, for example, that you welcome and enjoy any comprehension of form and content that is revealed along the way. But if this initial comprehension does not come about quite naturally, don't seek it out forcefully. Instead, allow the music to reach you unimpeded by analysis. Because of their extreme complexity, some contemporary works are very difficult to sight-read and for that reason cannot be approached in the way I have described. In order to grasp the content of such compositions, it is advisable that you study the details first before proceeding to read through the entire piece.

After you have gained a general feeling for a piece in its entirety, it is time to concentrate on smaller goals. Play the piece through again (you will already have played it through as often as necessary to satisfy your curiosity about it), but this time concentrate on the technically difficult measures. Bracket them in pencil when you have finished. These bracketed measures now become targets of still more intense focus. Study these measures carefully in order to find a comfortable fingering for your particular hand. Chopin thought that *everything* depends on a good fingering. Most performers agree that good fingering is the sine qua non in expressing music on an instrument, for it not only affords you ease and accuracy at fast tempos, but also comfort and control in slow passages. However, some instrumentalists consciously neglect to devise fingerings for music that moves at slow tempos, the feeling engendered by such music leading them to adopt whatever fingering "happens to come along." This, I believe, explains why these performers tend to suffer more memory slips when playing slow music than fast music. For if you use a different fingering each time you play the same passage, your reflexes are unable to store secure patterns that will fortify your memory.

Curiously enough, you won't necessarily arrive at a good fingering by practicing a difficult passage slowly. What may feel comfortable at a slow tempo may not work at all when you play it faster. Therefore, even though you can't negotiate a problematic passage perfectly when taking it up to tempo, try it faster anyway. Be daring! Even if you make mistakes, you will nonetheless find out whether or not the fingering in your edition or the one devised by you and your teacher will eventually work. Once again, do not be overly concerned if mistakes should occur. Remember that you are working in a process and that playing through a piece up to tempo, even with mistakes, is only one step in this process. Besides, when you anxiously try to avoid mistakes, you not only distract yourself from concentrating on musical values but also create tensions that are often hard to eliminate. Your goal is perfection and all of these procedures will lead you gradually toward it.

Once you discover a reliable fingering, you are ready to practice in greater detail. Be cautioned, though, to exercise great care since a more concentrated focus can easily divert you from your original intention—that of becoming absorbed in the emotional content of the composition. As you proceed to work through the various passages in increasingly smaller sections, repeating them in slow and fast tempos, keep in mind that mechanical practicing, if devoid of feeling, can produce accuracy but not musicality. For this reason it is necessary to abandon all detailed practicing from time to time and play the piece through in its entirety. After all, you will understand the musical significance of individual passages only when you relate them to the larger structures of which they are a part. Therefore, playing the piece through will reinforce not only your love of the composition, but also your sense of it as a unified whole. For it is specifically your desire to express this whole musical structure that motivates you to work on details with true concentration. Thus, you build up musical patterns note by note, the sum total of which represents your conception of the entire composition in much the same way as an architect converts his image of a large building into the detailed specifications of a blueprint.

THE AUTOMATIC PILOT

After constant repetitions of both small and large patterns, a magical process called *reflex action* takes place. This "automatic pilot," as a friend of mine aptly calls it, eventually becomes your mainstay when performing from memory. What happens is that while you are concentrating on specific goals, a storehouse of impulses is being fed into your brain—nature's most efficient computer. The period of time between the first encounter with a piece and the moment at which the "automatic pilot" takes over differs with each person. Knowing this can teach you patience. To help matters along, however, be sure to feed the *right information* into your computer. You could be tempted, for example, to circle around the preliminary phase of your work, that is, to sight-read indefinitely. But if, by doing this, you keep feeding haphazard fingerings, chance note patterns, and distorted rhythms into your computer for too long a period, you will actually be practicing mistakes, and the reflex action, true to form, will faithfully reproduce this confusion.

In Chapter 1, I stated that practicing is a process through which thoughts, feelings, and physical gestures become synthesized. Therefore, when your feelings are converted into muscular activity, your automatic pilot or reflex system is fed not only physical impulses but also the *feelings implicit within them.* This fact is of extreme importance, and understanding it will help you make the following resolution: never approach a passage in a purely mechanistic way; alway have, instead, an *emotional intention.* This does not mean that you should give free rein to your feelings. Rather, you must always strive for a *balance* between thought and feeling.

Many instrumentalists think they must practice dryly and mechanically to build a sound technique and that feeling is added at the end, like the icing on a cake. Concerning this, Liszt advised his student Valérie Boissier not to practice her exercises mechanically, "for the soul must always try to express itself."[6] When you synthesize musical feelings with each gesture during your practicing, you can depend upon your automatic pilot to reproduce beautiful playing.

The ultimate in concentration is your awareness of what you feel on every note you play. Such an awareness brings you into close accord with the composer's intentions. Just as feeling is fed into your reflexes via your muscles, conversely, the same is true of dry, mechanical playing. This explains the plight of the pianist who practices diligently with high, percussive fingers and succeeds only in conditioning his muscles to play unmusically. Finally, at a performance, his intention to project feeling is thwarted by his reflex system. How could it be otherwise? It is obeying, true to its nature, the commands it received from hours of dry, mechnical work. This explains why an awareness of feeling should be your primary concern, both at the piano and away from it. The next chapter is devoted exclusively to feeling.

A CLOSE LOOK AT MISTAKES

Most musicians agree that young instrumentalists of the twentieth century show a standard of excellence unparalleled in the history of the performing arts. You have only to hear one of the rounds of an international competition to realize just how high this standard can be. Recordings have even higher standards since the technique of splicing makes it possible to eliminate all mistakes from a performance. Because of this, music lovers who are used to hearing mistake-free recordings, are shocked when performers play an occasional wrong note at a concert.

Society teaches us that mistakes are unacceptable. This can be good or bad. There is a tendency, for example, to give the first prize in contests to a contestant who plays perfectly even though he does not show as much imagination as another, and to by-pass an imaginative performer who makes too many mistakes. But why should an imaginative performer make mistakes? Is he willing to sacrifice accuracy for sensitivity just as a meticulous performer strives for technical perfection as an end in itself? Neither extreme is desirable. Wrong notes get in the way of a musical message, but it is just as bad to sacrifice musical feeling for the sake of hitting every note correctly. Trying to play note-perfect without feeling is comparable to striving for a straight "A" average in school as an end in itself. One reason for pursuing perfection at all costs is to guard against the possibility of failure. After all, failure can have unpleasant aftermaths: a mistake on a test results in a lower mark; your parents may be disillusioned with you; your deficiency in meeting high standards may shake your confidence. In other words, failing to meet external standards can result in a rejection by others and a lower estimation of yourself.

If a performer plays "more wrong notes than there are fall leaves in the Adirondacks," as one critic sardonically said of a pianist's debut in Carnegie Hall, then his performance reflects a lack of preparation. Perhaps he miscalculated the amount of time it takes to prepare a program; perhaps the works he programmed were beyond his capabilities. He may, of course, have suffered debut nerves. When a performer recovers from the shock of a bad review or a student faces the reality of bad grades, he must answer his conscience: "Did I or did I not prepare my best?" Some musicians prepare inadequately either by cramming in their practicing at the last moment or by not practicing enough hours each day over extended periods of time. Others never learn to concentrate properly during their practicing and, as a result, end up making even more mistakes than when they began. Mistakes can also be symptomatic of your striving toward unrealistic goals. Suppose you have a friend who plays faster and more brilliantly than you do. Your performance sounds excellent as long as you play a little slower and softer; but your competitive nature makes you determined not only to match your friend's performance but even to surpass it. If you end up with "more fall leaves" than you imagined, it means that your goals were not commensurate with your abilities. In this case, mistakes are a sign that you are striving beyond your present level of attainment. Yet, a brilliant performance can challenge you by serving as a model to emulate. Experimentation can tell you whether or not your mistakes are merely transitory or whether your goals are, in fact, unrealistic. Sometimes overly ambitious goals are foisted upon you by others. A teacher or parent may expect you to conform to a standard that is conceivable to them but not ideal for you. You will then make mistakes.

When your fantasy audience hovers about you, symbolizing the highest musical standards, it is up to you to evaluate those standards relative to your own present ability. Such an evaluation will enable you to pinpoint not only the cause of your mistakes but also the limits of their acceptability to you and to others. For example, do your mistakes indicate a lack of serious practicing or do they derive from a suggestion to chance errors in the early stages of learning a piece? Do they distort the musical intention or are they merely insignificant slips that even a skilled performer is entitled to make? Assuming that you have practiced conscientiously, an occasional mistake should neither distract you nor your audience from your musical intention nor should it lessen your self-esteem. It is, in fact, your knowledge of having prepared your best that enables you not only to recover in seconds after making a mistake but also to play the following measures so beautifully as to dispel all remembrance of it. Being able to do this is proof in itself of your integrity and devotion to your art. Besides, such insignificant mistakes are usually more painful to you than they are to others.

I have an artist friend who has developed a method of drawing that is similar to everything we have discussed concerning the process of practicing. His chief concern, like yours, is to capture the whole feeling of his subject. Therefore, without taking his eyes off his subject, he makes a free, spontaneous sketch in his pad. Instead of examining this sketch, he tears it out and makes nineteen more. Finally, he looks at the twentieth sketch and then proceeds to focus on details—exactly as you have been advised to do in your practicing. By dispelling his fear of making miscalculations during the initial stages of his drawing, he preserves his artistic spontaneity and actually succeeds in sketching more accurately.

No one likes to make mistakes, no matter how insignificant they are. The kind of steps you take to eliminate them, however, will either lead you toward your ultimate goal of self-mastery or cause you to circle endlessly around meaningless details. You must constantly refresh your spirit by becoming one with the harmonious order of music, just as a painter does by contemplating the harmony in a Raphael painting. The perfection which you perceive in great music becomes the standard toward which you direct your own work. Having adopted such a standard, you are then willing to devote whatever preparation is necessary to do justice to a work of art. When you concentrate properly during your practicing, your sensibilities will become fused with the sublime order inherent in music. Ideally, such order does not admit of error. Nevertheless, we are only human and, provided that we practice properly, whatever mistakes we do make will be inconsequential in the light of true artistic achievement.

A CLOSE LOOK AT THE WHOLE AND ITS PARTS

One evening I invited some friends and pupils to meet the well-known composer, the late Alexander Tcherepnin, on the occasion of a newly released recording of his works. At one point during the evening, he went to the piano and played a series of chords, exclaiming, "I have just reduced the first eight bars of the *Jupiter Symphony* to a harmonic progression. But analyzing these chords will not bring us any closer to an understanding of the music."

Later, after our distinguished guest had left, I discovered what had elicited his somewhat dramatic remark: he had been discussing the importance of retaining an emotional response to music during all detailed analysis. It was not that he disapproved of harmonic analysis. On the contrary, he considered it indispensable and had even taught a course in it for many years. What he meant to convey by his striking observation was that our love for a *Jupiter Symphony* defies all rational analysis. It is specifically our emotional response to a composition as a whole that leads us to love it. In other words, we could not possibly come to love a composition or, for that matter, a person, through the process of analysis alone. For if details are analyzed as ends in themselves, they divert you from a natural acceptance of your love—whether it be for a work of music or for a particular person. As far as music is concerned, analysis, as I see it, has two primary functions: it facilitates memorization and it substantiates theoretically what we already feel. To put it another way, our responses to music antecede all else, placing analysis after the fact. Understanding the details of style and structure merely enhances that which you have experienced in its total form. But the manifold attributes of a work of art are like those of a human personality. Considered independently from the whole, they can enlighten you as to particulars, but they can neither explain your love nor lead you to love a composition or a person.

Keeping intact your love of a composition as a whole enables you to work on details creatively: you memorize the intervals within one motif while simultaneously absorbing the structure of similar motifs throughout the piece; your musical conclusions on one phrase are correlated with numerous other phrases. Your sense of the composition in its entirety also inspires you to find novel technical devices for expressing your musical ideas: you try a different fingering, a different pedaling, or a different angle of your elbow. In your constant search to find the sound that will communicate your musical feeling, you may experiment with various procedures only to return to your initial solution. Pupil No. IV (The Cookie Jar is Empty) reminded me of one such experimental session on the *Appassionata Sonata* by Beethoven:

> I remember a passage that wouldn't work. You suggested, "Try taking the top B♭ with your fourth finger instead of your third; try dividing your hands; try changing the right pedal on the first 16th note; now let me hear it once more with the long pedal and your third finger. Oh, that's much better. By all means, do it that way (see Illustration I).

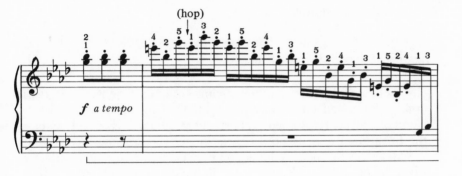

ILLUSTRATION I. Beethoven, *Sonata in F minor*, Op. 57 (pedal indication and fingering by Seymour Bernstein)

Susan Goldberg, pianist, offers the following facilitation:

In Konrad Wolff's book, *The Teaching of Artur Schnabel*, there is a beautiful description of this process:

> His [Schnabel's] method of practicing was experiment rather than drill. . . . His practice time was devoted to working out the exact articulation of a piece. He worked over each phrase hundreds of times to find the fingering, the hand position, the finger and arm movements that would secure the perfect inflection of melody, rhythm and harmony which he heard inwardly. To his pupils, he defined practicing as "passing the day at the piano with patience and serenity," and this, as far as I know, is what he did himself.[7]

A CLOSE LOOK AT FINGERING

There are endless possibilities for a good fingering. Schnabel's edition of the Beethoven *Sonatas*, to cite one example, is a treasure trove of creative ideas. His intimate knowledge of musical stresses and relaxations within a phrase determined his choice of the strong or weak fingers of the hand. This ingenious edition is a lesson in how to co-ordinate musical needs with physical resources.

The work scores of great instrumentalists show a striking difference between those who subscribe to a fixed, mechanical approach and those who are essentially creative in their practicing. One way in which you can recognize a creative approach is in an artist's choice of fingering. On a single bar of Sir Clifford Curzon's work scores, for example, you can see the intricate workings of an inventive mind—always malleable, forever actuated by the constant search for a fingering that will yeild maximum expression even to two notes. The score that follows is an awe-inspiring testimonial to musical truth as he perceives it. Each number, each line, each commentary graphically portrays his struggle to reveal this truth to us. The result: his inimitable artistry (see Illustration II).

In the book, *Landowska on Music*, there is a reproduction of one page of Bach's *Fugue in B Major* from the *Well-Tempered Clavier, Book I*.[8] This is another example of how a great musical mind approaches the dynamics of fingering. The photograph shows tiny bits of white paper pasted over holes worn into her music from constant erasures. She explains what prompted these constant changes: "Sometimes finding a solution for setting in relief a certain phrase demands a complete change of fingering and more

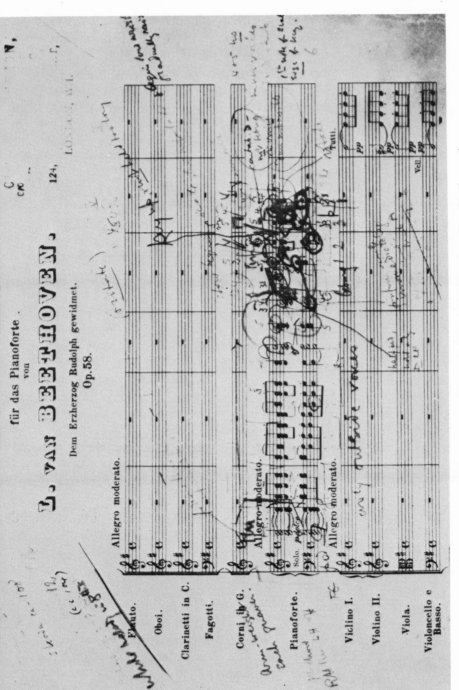

ILLUSTRATION II. Beethoven, Concerto No. 4 in G major, Op. 58 (from the work score of Sir Clifford Curzon)

work. All the better, as long as it will sound! One must never be afraid to start all over again as many times as it is necessary."[9]

Leschetizky once gave a pupil some memorable advice about fingering: "Play it with your nose if necessary, but make it sound right!" Making it "sound right" may, in fact, require a fingering that appears at first to be absurd. The choice of placing the thumb on the high F near the end of the *Harp Etude* by Chopin is a case in point. Interestingly enough, it will help you to play the high F with accuracy and control (see Illustration III). Old-fashioned notions

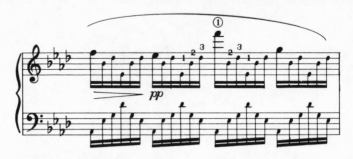

ILLUSTRATION III.   Chopin, *Etude*, Op. 25, No. 1

ILLUSTRATION IV.   Beethoven, *Klavierstück (Für Elise)* (Klinskly–Halm WoO 59)

ILLUSTRATION V.   Schumann, *Papillons*, Op. 2

such as "always change your fingers on repeated notes" have for years held back the art of piano playing. *Comfort* for the sake of musical expression and control of sound should be our primary concern—and not rigid rules (see Illustration IV). We also need to reappraise the fingerings of octaves. Keeping the hand in a mold and adhering to 1 and 5—even on black keys—will often produce free and, therefore, even octave passages (see Illustration V). Pian-

ILLUSTRATION VI. Brahms, *Trio in B major*, Op. 8

ists often resort to hand divisions to facilitate the playing of diffi-cult passages. Illustration VI—certainly one of the more extrava-gant "swindles" I have devised—once sent a colleague into gales of laughter.

There is a risk, however, in striving for a creative fingering. If, for example, you change a fingering too soon before a performance, your automatic pilot may not have enough time to absorb the new pattern. You may then be prone to memory slips. Therefore, it may be best to make do with your old fingering and practice the new one between performances until it becomes more reliable. In any case, the lesson to be learned from great artists such as Curzon, Schnabel, and Landowska is that true art never remains static. "Fingerings," as one artist told me, "may sometimes change as much as people do." Such changes should grow, of course, out of a tireless search for what is true and beautiful in life as they must in art.

ANTICIPATION—THE ARCH ENEMY OF CONCENTRATION

One of the most serious problems faced by the performer is *an-ticipating a note before it is time to play it.* One way of dealing with this problem is to concentrate on the *full length of each note value*—filling it out, as it were, to overflowing. When playing a long note, always try to keep in mind the shorter values pulsating throughout its length. The following exercise will demonstrate this important rule:

1. Choose any three notes on the piano.
2. Play them in whole notes—slowly and legato—with either hand, following the dynamic scheme:

3. The first time through, concentrate only on the pitches and the dynamics.
4. The second time, count aloud 1-2-3-4 on each note. As you count, make a crescendo with your voice to the second note and a diminuendo to the third note.
5. Count silently and imagine that each note is gradually increasing and diminishing in intensity. During the crescendo, move your body slowly forward at the same time gradually increasing the

pressure in your arm and finger. For the diminuendo, move your body slowly back to its original position while gradually decreasing the pressure in your arm and finger. (The increase and decrease in pressure thus coincide with the dynamic scheme.)

As soon as a piano string is set into motion, the sound begins to die. This explains why some pianists stop concentrating on long note values. Since they can't control the sound of a note once it is struck, they assume that there is no further need to concentrate on it. But beautiful piano playing results from knowing how to create illusions through a skillful manipulation of sound. To do this, you must first imagine crescendos, diminuendos, or a constant dynamic level on a sustained tone (see Chapter 5, where the illustrations demonstrate how this is achieved). Unless you imagine one of these three dynamic choices on any sustained sound, the following will result:

1. You will rob the *present note* of its full rhythmic value.
2. You will anticipate or delay the *next note*.
3. By allowing the first note to lose its musical impact, you will be unable to articulate the second note at the proper dynamic level so as to sustain the musical line.

Beautiful playing demands that each tone arrive at a specific time and at a specific dynamic level—no more, no less. To conceive a convincing dynamic plan for a particular note in a melody, you must think of the composition as a self-contained universe in which each note has a particular function. The choice of dynamics from note to note is ultimately determined by your comprehension of the entire piece and its overall musical content.

There is another kind of anticipation that interferes with your ability to concentrate. Most of us experience this at one time or another. For example, there are times when my desire to practice or write is so great that I resent having to perform various routine tasks of the day. This sort of resentment is then converted into tension which in turn robs me of the energy I need for my work. Thus, if while exercising I am worrying about my practicing, I am neither doing my music nor my abdominal muscles any good. But if I concentrate on my body and how it is functioning during sit-ups, I find myself feeling refreshed at the end of the exercise. I can then shift my attention to my work. If you allow too many tasks to occupy your consciousness at the same time, you cannot concentrate properly on any one thing. This applies equally to your practicing. If you practice one passage and at the same time worry about all the other passages in the piece that require your attention, you make it virtually impossible to concentrate on your immediate task. If this should happen, stop your work and take stock of the situation. Make a list of what you want to accomplish in the order of necessity and then focus on one task at a time. As though by magic, tension vanishes.

Performers who play from memory know that anticipation causes memory slips. Instead of concentrating on the natural flow of the music, a voice will suddenly ask, "What is the next bass note?" When this happens, the automatic pilot is sabotaged and a blowout occurs. Allowing the future to encroach upon the present is a sure sign that you are not concentrating. For when you really concentrate, you are concerned with *now, this moment, this note*—you are involved only in what you are doing at the moment.

Practicers who achieve optimum results from their work all agree that it takes a long time to learn how to concentrate properly. This should not discourage you. Sometimes you get immediate results; other times you have to wait for your rewards. Only children and immature adults expect immediate results. Once you realize that accomplishment is the offspring of patience, you will have taken the first step toward attaining your goals.

This book is a collection of ideas; it is not meant to take the place of your teacher but rather to stimulate you to new concepts and make you aware of the endless possibilities inherent in your art. It is to encourage you always to be responsive not only in your musical life but also in your personal life. I could never satisfy my curiosity about music with one composition any more than I could limit my associations to just one person. Being responsive does not rule out favorites in a hierarchy of interests, but it does offer unlimited possibilities in our search for knowledge and experience.

The thoughts of great artists can inspire you as you strive for perfection. Wanda Landowska, who writes about practicing with the same beauty and passion that characterized her playing, thus speaks to us all.

If everyone knew how to work, everyone would be a genius! I hate the word *practice*. Practice breeds inurement. Instead of discovering, of distinguishing traits that are deeply hidden or merely veiled, one ends seeing nothing anymore. One ceases to be aware.

To be aware, to be conscious at all times is what appears to me the worthiest in my thoughts and in my work. While interpreting, even at the most impetuous moments when a musical phrase overflows with passion, I want to remain conscious. I may forget a liberty I took at one place or another, but this does not change in any way my state of consciousness, which is always on the alert.

Awkwardness and mistakes in playing are always due to a lack of concentration.

I attach great importance to concentration because I was born into a family of undisciplined individuals. I had to kick and scold myself. But I believe that I have acquired the faculty of concentrating, and now I can teach it to my pupils.

I work best with closed eyes. Only then I see and I hear. How should one start to play? One has to concentrate and be entirely ready so that when the first note is struck, it comes as a sort of continuation of a soliloquy already begun. Too often the value and importance of the start in playing is belittled. And yet all depends on its being carefully prepared. Before I begin a phrase, between the preparatory gesture of the hand or of the finger and the first note, there is an infinitesimal period of time, always surprising because of its unpredictable duration and because of its expressive impact. The listener can never anticipate the exact dosage I apply to this rest.... Breathings and caesuras, especially those that precede a beginning, have a positive value equal to that of the notes themselves.

Similarly, the last note is never the last. It is rather a point of departure for something to come.[10]

4 Feeling

On June 7, 1783, Wolfgang Amadeus Mozart wrote a letter to his father in which he described the playing of Muzio Clementi, one of the great composer-pianists of the day: "What he really does well are his passages in thirds; but he sweated over them day and night in London. Apart from this, he can do nothing, absolutely nothing, for he has not the slightest expression or taste, still less feeling."[11]

Time and again we find the words expression, taste, and feeling in Mozart's evaluation of other musicians' playing. He sometimes interchanges the words, but the implications are always the same. Even a nonmusician, though lacking the informed judgment of a Mozart, can tell whether or not a performer plays with feeling. In voicing disappointment after a recital, a concert-goer may exclaim, "Well, his facility is remarkable, but he somehow didn't move me." Perhaps that concert-goer could not adequately describe what was lacking in the performance. To a serious practicer, however, feeling must never be thought of as indefinable. On the contrary. One kind of practicing produces communicative playing in which expression, taste, and feeling are recognizable to all; another kind of practicing results in "absolutely nothing." Our task is to determine what factors produce the kind of playing that communicates our deepest feelings to the listener.

Music is a language of feeling, the projection of which is the primary responsibility of the performer. It is, of course, impossible to express musical feeling without a sufficiently developed technical facility. But when an instrumentalist practices solely for accuracy and speed—both being important attributes of technical facility—he then by-passes feeling and loses touch with his musical intentions. The result is an unconvincing performance. To understand how this comes about, you have only to experience the sheer freedom and delight of technical mastery which you may then be tempted to exploit for its own sake. Therefore, as you practice to improve your technical facility, be aware constantly of your musical feelings and responses. It is specifically to give voice to these feelings that all your technical work is directed. In fact, by being in touch with your feelings during every activity at the keyboard, you can learn consciously to *arrest* your feelings temporarily, as, for example, when you examine a fingering, a physical movement or a dynamic sensation. Such analyses often require that you consciously suspend your emotional response to the music. Thus, by treating feeling objectively, you can gain control over your emotions both at the keyboard and away from it. But let us discuss musical feeling in greater detail and try to discover how it is expressed.

NOTATION

Feeling is a natural experience. All of us feel something during every moment of our lives. It is only when we attempt to communicate that feeling, when we try to verbalize it, define it, or write it down, that difficulties can arise. Knowing this must make us ever more respectful of musical notation, for it represents graphically the innermost feelings of the composer. Words, too, in a specific order, whether spoken or written, evoke particular feelings. Apart from the rules of syntax, what factors determine this order? An experienced writer has at his disposal a large and varied vocabulary. Yet, he may at times discover that there are relatively few words to express a particular feeling he wishes to convey. On the other hand, language offers him infinite possibilities for combining even those few words into novel and original sentences. This can discourage a writer if his feelings are thwarted by too many possibilities from which to choose. Ultimately, when a feeling is strong enough, when a writer or composer is filled with his subject, those possibilities are narrowed down and feeling itself inspires the choice of words or notes for a particular expression. Sometimes it may be necessary to rewrite innumerable times until the symbols—words or notes—match as closely as possible the feelings a writer or composer wishes to communicate. This process—the selection of the proper symbols to express what you feel—can be understood more easily in terms of language. If, for example, you wish to relate a profoundly moving experience, the intensity of your feeling will impel you to seek a natural and convincing flow of words. A composer, too, moved by a musical feeling, seeks the specific notes, rhythms, and dynamics to express this convincingly. However, no two individuals will make the same choices. Since each person is unique, his inner voice dictates only those words, those notes that express his *individual response* to feeling. Thus, writers and composers develop an original style simply by being themselves. The same is true for interpreting music. Even though two or more pianists faithfully adhere to the markings of a composition, each one's individual response to those markings will be unique. Like any other skill, interpreting music improves with practice. Being aware of your feelings motivates you to create a broader and more varied musical language with which to express those feelings. This is what makes you a convincing performer. In searching out the true meaning of a composer's statement, you will penetrate to the heart of the music when you realize that musical meaning is implicit in the very order of notes a composer has written. This, plus all the markings he has painstakingly recorded in his music, carry his message to you. For him, no other order and no other markings can adequately convey his feelings. For this reason, you must regard every mark in your musical score with attention and respect.

Sometimes, however, a composer does not notate all that he feels. In such a case, we are compelled to read between the lines, as it were. Bach, for example, left practically no expressive markings; Mozart wrote in an occasional *piano* and *forte* along with a few other interpretive indications. But with the development of the piano and its ever increasing capacity for range, dynamics, and sonority, composers began to notate with greater attention to detail. By the time Beethoven wrote his *recitativo* in the third movement of the *Sonata*, Op. 110, he used an expression mark and a tempo indication for practically every note. Moreover, he found the customary Italian indications inadequate and resorted to two languages—Italian and German. He was attempting by these means to bring the interpreter as close as possible to his own feelings.

There is another reason why composers started to pay closer attention to interpretive markings. As more and more instrumentalists began to play in public, it was not uncommon for composers to hear distorted interpretations of their own works. After all, not all performers had the capacity for expression, taste, or feeling, as

Mozart had observed. Beethoven was perhaps the first composer to leave as little to the imagination as possible.

Even with a wealth of expression marks at his disposal, a composer still finds musical notation inadequate. Despite these limitations, it is incumbent on every performer to be faithful to whatever a composer has written down. In other words, the inherent inadequacies of musical notation do not give performers the license to violate a composer's written statement. The composer has projected his heart and mind in the form of notes, slurs, expression marks, fingerings, and pedalings. It is your obligation to understand each and every one of them. The following experiment is helpful for this purpose.

Choose a piece you have never played before and take the music away from the piano. With a good musical dictionary on hand, go through the score and try to understand everything you see. Don't be disheartened if your ears aren't developed sufficiently to "hear" the music in your mind without sounding it. You can still see expression marks and distinguish melodic and harmonic patterns. Every time you come upon an expression mark, try to experience it fully. When you see the word *crescendo,* for example, try to find a corresponding physical sensation. Sound the rhythms aloud—tum, dee-dee-dum—or tap them on your knee. Absorb whatever you can of the emotional content without touching the keyboard.

BREATHING

All of us breathe to stay alive. Yet most of us breathe so poorly that it is a wonder how we manage to function. It becomes even more difficult to breathe properly when we are under emotional stress. Therefore, unless we learn to control our breathing, we will not only diminish our physical capabilities, but we may even inhibit our emotional responses to the music we play. "Feeling," says Dr. Alexander Lowen, "is determined by breathing and movement. An organism feels only that which moves within its body . . . holding the breath is the most effective way of cutting off feeling. This principle works in reverse, too. Just as strong emotions stimulate and strengthen one's breathing, the stimulation and deepening of respiration can evoke strong emotions."[12] In other words, feeling is heightened by breathing. It should be possible then to increase your capacity to feel music by breathing properly. Think of the human voice—the paradigm of musical instruments. It would not be possible to sing or even to speak effectively without developing a refined control of breathing. This control may be adapted to playing an instrument in the following way:

1. Take your music to the piano and sit with your arms relaxed and supported by your lap. In this position, your arm muscles release their tension. Part your lips slightly and allow your lower jaw to relax. Drop your shoulders and gently incline your head. Relax your neck muscles. Rigidity in the jaw, neck, and shoulders is a major obstacle to playing the piano. You have now taken the first step toward rectifying this problem.

2. Set the metronome at 60. Place both hands gently around your diaphragm. Close your eyes and inhale slowly through your nose. As you inhale, the abdomen inflates. Try to prolong this inhalation for eight ticks. Keep your mouth relaxed and your lips slightly parted. Now exhale through your mouth for eight ticks. The abdomen deflates. Be sure to expel all the air from your lungs. If it takes more or fewer metronome ticks to accomplish these two steps, make the necessary adjustments. Eventually, use the same number of ticks for each inhalation and exhalation.

3. Inhale for eight ticks; hold your breath for eight ticks; exhale for eight ticks; and finally, stay empty for eight ticks. Continue these deep breathing exercises for approximately five to ten minutes. If you experience dizziness, don't be alarmed. In time, the dizziness will vanish, leaving you refreshed and invigorated.

4. Open your eyes and fix your attention on the music before you. Try to scan a group of notes and organize them into patterns. Your aim is to convert these patterns into musical feelings and then to express these feelings through your muscles.

5. This is the most important step. Neither anticipate what you are about to feel nor worry about whether you are, in fact, going to feel anything at all. Be receptive, impressionable, expectant. Think of a negative in a camera—its function is to receive patterns and intensities of light. Your aim in this experiment is not to force your musical response, but rather to permit the music to affect you, to permeate you, as the light does a negative. Let the music find you instead of your trying to find it.

6. Take a deep breath and, as you exhale, begin to play the music before you. In your expectant and unprejudiced state, you will

respond naturally to the horizontal (melodic) and vertical (harmonic) structures, to the rhythmic patterns, and to all the marks of expression. Since the composition is new to you, its difficulties cannot be anticipated. Thus, each musical event will inspire spontaneous feelings within you so that your muscles will adapt as naturally as possible to the physical movements necessary to express feeling. If you keep breathing with each phrase and remain receptive emotionally and physically, you will execute technical difficulties with surprising ease. As the composition unfolds note by note, the feelings contained in the music will arouse similar feelings within you. You become one with the music.

One mark of a great composer is his ability to capture succinctly the feelings he wishes to convey. You respond to them because those feelings are awakened in you. Knowing that you can share a feeling that was experienced by a great composer establishes a unique rapport between you and him. Since breathing heightens this shared feeling, its importance in the interpretation of music cannot be overemphasized.

PHYSICAL ADAPTABILITY TO SOUND

To translate feelings into sounds requires muscular responses not unlike those experienced in daily life: the gentle cradling of an infant, the vigorous grasp of a friendly handshake, a farewell wave. Each is a physical response to an emotional stimulus. However, none of these responses demands a conscious intellectual control, and the same is true of a musical response. Many technical and/or musical problems could be prevented at the outset if you would allow yourself to respond naturally to music. As we have already discovered, anticipation can create emotional and physical difficulties at the piano. Problems can also result when you anticipate an interpretation before allowing the emotional content of the music to express itself through you. Therefore, focusing prematurely on interpretive details can rob you of spontaneity and foster additional obstacles. This is not to suggest that you should sit at the piano in a trancelike state with a come-what-may attitude. After all, musicians who play persuasively have defined for themselves not only what the music means to them but also how to express it physically on their instruments. Rather, I am suggesting that you may complicate your response to music during the first stages of learning by overanalyzing instead of allowing yourself to respond naturally. This does not rule out your need to examine a difficult section when the occasion arises. But in general, your grasp of the true meaning of a composition and your ability to articulate that meaning will be furthered by reading through the music freely and daringly.

When Pupil No. IV came to study with me, she confessed somewhat shyly to never having performed a Chopin *Etude*. She had been practicing a few of them slowly for six months, she explained. "Haven't you ever tried to play them up to tempo?" I asked. "I wouldn't dare," she replied. "It will take me a year to work out the difficulties at a slow tempo before I can even think of playing faster." I explained to her that playing slowly engenders one kind of feeling and playing fast another; that each tempo entails a corresponding physical organization. For this reason, practicing slowly exclusively will not necessarily enable you to play fast. Her primary goal was, of course, to avoid making mistakes. Assuming that slow practicing would reduce the risk of mistakes, she took the *Etudes* through endless hours of slow practicing without ever experiencing their emotional content. Although she tried to meet their technical challenges, she labored under the impression that the *Etudes* would persist in being physical impossibilities for the rest of her life. I was at the metronome in a flash, set it at 144 and opened her music to the *Etude* in F *major*, Op. 10, No. 8 (see Illustration VII). She blanched. Of all the *Etudes*, this one frightened

ILLUSTRATION VII. Chopin, *Etude*, Op. 10, No. 8

her the most. "Try it up to tempo," I suggested, "but be prepared to make mistakes. At all costs, let yourself be carried away by its exuberance." I also pointed out to her that although the physical difficulties are specifically in the right hand, the left hand must carry the snap and bounce of the musical motifs. Concentrating on this, she abandoned herself to the "tidal wave," as she called it. Thinking that what I had asked her to do was hopeless, she let down her defenses and thus performed the *F major Etude* note perfect and up to tempo. When she reached the final note, she turned to me, rather pale, and said, "I can't believe what's happened!"

You should not conclude from this account that slow practicing is useless. On the contrary. Nothing can take the place of slow, careful practicing. In fact, Pupil No. IV succeeded in playing the *F major Etude* well because she had practiced it slowly. But the experience proved to her that she had waited too long to try her wings and, as a result, never felt the true physical exuberance of the piece which only a fast tempo could convey. Moreover, she saw for herself that her gifts were sufficient to complete works of great technical difficulty far more quickly than she had been led to believe. This success provided her with the stimulus she needed. She promptly learned Beethoven's *Appassionata Sonata* in record time and played it up to tempo for my students. Shortly after that she performed it in public with great success.

Pupil No. II related a striking experience he had during one of his practice sessions. While working on a Beethoven Sonata, he suddenly had difficulty executing a scale passage. It didn't appear to be unusually hard, yet it sounded bumpy. He decided to stop working on the Sonata for a while and practice scales and arpeggios. The longer he practiced, the more uneven the scales became. Being exceptionally gifted, he felt humiliated at his failure to play an E flat major scale to his satisfaction. Recalling what I had told him about synthesizing feeling and physical attitudes, he decided to experiment by playing the E flat major scale passionately. Miraculously, all the bumps disappeared. Simulating a feeling of tenderness, he tried a scale in another key. Once again, he played it perfectly the first time. Just as I have noticed in my own practicing and teaching, many technical problems vanish instantly when musical feeling dictates the proper physical attitude. "In short," as Heinrich Neuhaus so aptly observed, "the greater the musical confidence, the less the technical insecurity."[13]

This sound advice must not be carried to extremes, however, for it doesn't mean that a receptive emotional state is a panacea for all technical problems. Most great instrumentalists have done their share of technical exercises; some more than others. Accomplished dancers, too, work at the bar many hours a day to condition their bodies to respond to feeling. Even when you work on exercises, try to approach them with a musical intention. Should you arrest your feeling for some specific purpose, know consciously that you did so. Because I know how important this rule is, I constantly remind my students never to do anything of a purely mechanical nature without being aware that they have arrested their feelings intentionally. Suppose that you wish to practice the D Major scale at 100 quarter notes to the minute solely to achieve evenness. You may set about your task without any musical intention at all, your purpose being to avoid accenting the thumbs while keeping your hand arched and your fingers slightly curved. You are encouraged to find yourself executing the scale quite evenly. But when you apply this skill to an actual musical situation—a Mozart Sonata, for example—you discover to your dismay that it sounds uneven again. As Pupil No. II found, even a scale must be supported by a musical feeling appropriate to the context in which it occurs. As such, it calls for a compatible muscular organization, and since you use one muscular attitude to play mechanically and another to play with feeling, an excess in either direction will always yield undesirable results. You must, therefore, strike a balance between emotional involvement and critical objectivity. In fact, it is exactly such a balance that has its applications to nonmusical situations.

There is a marked difference between instrumentalists who merely reproduce dynamics and those who experience dynamics. One pianist will play a crescendo by carefully making each successive note louder than the one before; his performance is recognizably cold and calculating. Another pianist will experience the crescendo emotionally; hearing him, you know that you have had a musical experience. Some instrumentalists think that they will bore the listener unless they make endless waves of crescendos and diminuendos. On the contrary. In many instances, the same dynamic maintained from note to note can produce one of the most beautiful of musical expressions. With this in mind, practice a four-octave scale keeping each note at the same degree of *piano*. The effect produced is anything but boring, for *piano* is not just a degree of sound—it is a specific feeling.

One of my pupils once played a late work by Liszt called *Nuages Gris (Gray Clouds)*—an eerie, atmospheric work containing only a few dynamic markings. She tried, therefore, to play almost wholly without nuance. When she performed it for my pupils she made the mistake of assuming that the same dynamic from note to note signified an absence of feeling. When I pointed out to her that the same dynamic denotes a specific emotion, her playing changed completely. A difference appeared both in her sound and in her physical attitude. She instinctively breathed more slowly—sometimes holding her breath—and her body became still. The result was that she was able to lower each key with a slow, controlled speed, drawing from the piano a ghostlike tone inherent in the music. She discovered how to convey the unearthly feeling of *Gray Clouds* through appropriate physical attitudes and was thereby able to capture its mystery, not only through a constant *pianissimo* but in the silences as well (see Illustration VIII).

Often, when there are technical inhibitions, a shift of focus to feeling can induce an unexpected freedom in performance. Such a case was reported to me by an amateur actress who suddenly found herself singing the lead in a production of *Finian's Rainbow*. For the first few weeks of rehearsal, everyone in the cast concentrated on the best possible voice production. Like the others, my friend was concerned primarily with her vocal technique. One day the director singled her out and stopped the rehearsal to say, "Forget about your voice and concentrate on telling me the story. Think of the *feeling* behind each word you are singing." As if by magic, her voice immediately took on a completely different hue. There was nothing unusual about her voice. Yet when it was supported by feeling, it became compellingly affective.

The ideal condition in every case is for true musical feeling to take over the body and select the proper muscular response for specific effects. To prepare the body to become a vehicle for musical feeling, a singer, for example, must give as much attention to spinal alignment as to the flexibility and position of the jaw and tongue. Some pianists, however, focus exclusively on their fingers without understanding that fingers are really extensions of the body. In other words, the fingers, arms, torso, and feet must all participate in expressing musical feeling on the piano. And, as we have seen, breathing is as important in playing the piano as it is in singing.

All the suggestions given thus far have pertained chiefly to your

ILLUSTRATION VIII. Liszt, *Nuages Gris.*

first encounter with a piece. You are now ready to begin the kind of practicing whereby you become conscious of everything you feel and do at the piano. But even while you thus objectify your feelings and your physical response to them, it is still necessary for you to remain open and impressionable to the music. This ability to be objective without inhibiting spontaneity is one of your chief goals as an instrumentalist. Play the piece through once again and this time be aware of how you breathe from phrase to phrase. There are many techniques of breathing, so you are free to choose the one which best suits your purpose. One suggestion is to breathe as singers do; that is, sing the entire piece through and mark the places where taking a breath seems natural. (A word of caution, however: if your voice is anything like mine, you may find it necessary to close the door of your practice room!) Another suggestion is to experiment with inhaling as you play one phrase and exhaling on the next. For soft passages or for the final note of a phrase, try *holding* your breath. Also, you will discover that difficult passages are facilitated when you inhale *before* you play them and exhale *as* you play them.

CONCLUSIONS

At every stage of your development, it is possible for you to give a truly convincing performance. You have only to harness your natural musical instincts to the service of the music you are practicing. The process begins in your inner world of musical intuition and reaches the external world of sound through highly coordinated physical gestures. Such a synthesis does not come without effort. Even the most gifted instrumentalist must practice arduously to perfect it. Although great artistry is vouchsafed to comparatively few, I always assume that everyone is gifted in his or her own way. Usually, your gifts will emerge when physical and/or psychological blocks are removed. But this takes time, repetition, and, above all, patience.

Physical problems are often the result of preoccupation with technique to the exclusion of emotional responses to music. Many technical problems can be eliminated, therefore, if you keep your musical feeling intact during all detailed work while allowing your body to find a natural means of expressing it. In this way, your entire body becomes an active force in producing the sound that will express a composer's intentions as you perceive them. When physical gestures occur naturally, observe them. Look in upon yourself as if you were your own audience. You will notice that each feeling has a corresponding movement and sensation: you choose high fingers to express one feeling and fingers close to the keys to express another; one passage seems to require wrist staccato, while another requires an arm staccato; other musical feelings cause your torso to swing forward, backward, and from left to right in various degrees and combinations; your feet, poised on the pedals, are synthesized with your fingers and your aural perception. All of these sensations are fed into your automatic pilot so that in time *your muscles are trained to reproduce feeling involuntarily.* A good teacher can induce feeling in you by teaching you the correct physical gestures. But the time it takes you to impart feeling and movement to your automatic pilot depends on how long you practice and on the level of concentration you maintain.

Your initial response to music occurs without intellectual analysis. Gifted children, for example, often project deep musical feeling without being aware of musical structure or historical facts. It is this kind of innocence from which adults can learn. Therefore, in practicing, avoid an excess of analysis and allow the music to reveal its own beauty—a beauty that is answered by something deep within you. Once you recognize your response to this beauty, you are ready to pinpoint everything that contributes to musical expression. Only then will you be able to control your feelings when you perform for others. Practicing helps to promote the receptivity and the capability necessary for this experience. Above all, do not be discouraged when musical or technical problems occur. After all, the music you practice needed time to be conceived and to be painstakingly notated. It therefore warrants your patience and effort to grasp its meaning. A Zen philosopher put it this way: "If you would paint a chrysanthemum, look at one for ten years until you become one!"

Great artists succeed in establishing a close identification with the music they perform. It is this capacity that sets them apart from other performers. Sir Clifford Curzon, for example, plays the *Fourth Concerto* of Beethoven with rare insight and a beauty of sound that is quite indescribable. It is as though he and the *Concerto* are one. If such transcendental playing were the result of talent alone, we might all feel defeated. On the contrary. He inspires us by demonstrating before our eyes the results of a lifetime of dedicated practicing. You may not ever be able to play like Sir

Clifford, but your response to his playing indicates that your potential is perhaps greater than you realize. If you have faith in this potential and practice diligently, you may "paint more chrysanthemums" than you would think possible.

Practicing is often looked upon as a boring activity. Discipline, too, is a word that carries a stigma of forced adherence to unpleasant tasks. But when the organizational aspects of practicing are directed toward the ultimate goal—the organization of the *self*—then one is more readily inclined to accept both self-imposed and externally imposed disciplines. Such a goal enables you to approach your practicing with infinite patience, a virtue which most children lack. A mature person, however, learns to wait for rewards, no matter how long they are in coming.

A striking description of discipline appears in the book, *Zen in the Art of Archery*. In the Far East, archery is practiced to master the mind (not unlike the ultimate goal in practicing the piano). The author describes the ordeals he endured in his attempt to master this art. For example, it took him more than five years before he was able to draw the bow in the manner prescribed by his Master. The rigorous disciplines often forced him to lose his temper, whereupon his Master would exclaim, "So let's stop talking about it and go on practicing!" Questions he usually asked his Master were almost always greeted by, "Don't ask, practice!" He did practice and he did succeed. He even learned to breathe as his Master had taught him: "I learned to lose myself so effortlessly in the breathing that I sometimes had the feeling that I myself was not breathing but—strange as this may sound—*being breathed*. And even when, in hours of thoughtful reflection, I struggled against this bold idea, I could no longer doubt that the breathing held out all that the Master had promised. . . . The man, the art, the work—it is all one."[14]

To carry practicing far enough is to free yourself of all physical limitations and *to be breathed* by the music. There will be transcendental moments when you will neither feel your fingers nor be conscious of your breathing—moments when your entire being will express that nameless beauty of which you are a part. Such feelings radiate from the great works of art that attest to man's rational nature. Musical literature, therefore, is a veritable history of universal emotions. To experience this through practicing establishes within you an order that binds you to nature and affirms your faith in mankind.

If you are a practicer, you are among the most privileged members of society. For you are given the opportunity to experience profound musical utterances. To be worthy of this demands a discipline of the highest order. Your reward will be the ability not only to express music with your own two hands but also to mold your entire life into an art form of its own. For discipline brings confidence; confidence gives you the freedom to explore other dimensions of beauty in a never-ending cycle of revelation.

Part II
The
Disciplines

5 Tempo–Rhythm–Pulse

Rhythm governs the universe. It is awe-inspiring to gaze into the heavens and contemplate the speed and the predictable course of each planet. In our more immediate environment we know when a tree will bear fruit, when birds will migrate. Farmers plant their crops in accordance with the rhythmic interchange of seasons; fishermen can predict the tides. Miraculously, our own body rhythms are, for the most part, regulated by nature. In the Western world, the idea of consciously governing your own body rhythm was, until quite recently, a concept associated with Eastern mystics. But science, through the technique of bio-feedback, is now teaching man to control his heartbeat and blood pressure (although yogis have been practicing such techniques for centuries). In other words, through a particular kind of concentration, you can actually exercise conscious control over certain body functions which hitherto were thought to be exclusively involuntary.

Even though they may not be aware of it, musicians often use the technique of bio-feedback. For it is this kind of technique that enables a performer to control various tempi and dynamics with predictable results—in spite of nervousness. Thus, while his heartbeat may be rapid, he must command himself to experience and execute a profound *adagio* when it is required. By concentrating on stillness, a performer actually can will his body to express it. Such control does not, of course, occur spontaneously at a performance; rather, after hours and hours of practicing, a performer's reflexes are conditioned to carry out his intentions successfully. This predictability insures the very mood that the performer wishes to express, no matter how fast his heart may be beating.

SOME DEFINITIONS

Rhythm refers to any regulated movement containing strong and weak pulses. This definition can apply to musical rhythm as well as

79

natural phenomena—as, for example, the ebb and flow of tides. Regulated movement is, of course, epitomized in the dance. Barbara Mettler, a dance specialist, thus describes rhythm as "the wavelike nature of the impulse, the alternation of activity and rest, which causes one movement to grow out of another, creating continuity and flow."

Pulse, on the other hand, is associated specifically with your heartbeat. In its strictest sense, it refers to a recurrent, vital movement and direction in musical performance.

Tempo is the organization of rhythm and pulse at a specific rate of speed. Thus, composers often use metronome indications to approximate their own conception of a tempo. To express a composer's intentions, you have only to set your metronome to the prescribed tempo and adjust your own body rhythm and pulse to it.

THE EFFECT OF RHYTHM ON YOUR BEHAVIOR

Drum beats have for centuries incited men to battle. Music also, as Congreve observed, "hath charms to soothe the savage breast!" Far from being mere poetic fancy, there is scientific evidence to support such claims. Studies have shown that the symmetrical pulse of march music, for example, produces an involuntary response in the body. Specifically, it is the thalamus, a brain center lying below the master brain that "is the main relay station of emotions, sensations and feelings. The thalamus is connected to the master brain by nerve pathways, and the stimulation of the thalamus almost simultaneously arouses the master brain. Once the master brain is aroused, it sends impulses back to the thalamus and so a reverberating circuit is set in motion."[15] This explains why children can respond to rhythm and emotion in music long before they are aware of its constituents. It is not surprising, then, why music has become a major factor in treating certain mental disorders. Patients who cannot be reached through the spoken word respond to music. This knowledge led to an experiment in the ward of a mental institution: when march music was piped into the ward through speakers, the patients, it was discovered, cleaned up their areas in half the time. Many were seen tapping their feet, swaying their bodies, and nodding their heads. Such responses, known as thalamic reflexes, became the basis for music therapy which is, in essence, a study of the effects of music on behavior. Imagine then what you experience during an average practice session. It would be reasonable to conclude, therefore, that your emotional responses to music can influence your total behavior. Even your choice of repertory can affect your behavior. For example, an abundance of fast, loud pieces will tend to make you emotionally charged; on the other hand, a preponderance of slow, introspective pieces will produce the opposite effect. For music—like life itself—necessitates your constant adaption to every kind of tempo and every nuance of emotion. It is exactly in this area that practicing can be of immeasurable help to you, for a truly musical performance calls for your conscious adaptability to and control of innumerable rhythmic and emotional subtleties.

One of the most significant factors in practicing is your ability to control tension and thus express through your fingers a specific tempo and a feeling engendered by that tempo. For instance, a passionate feeling causes an appropriate tension in your body. But if this tension should mount beyond your control, the passion you feel cannot be expressed. Similarly, fast playing requires a degree of tension which, if allowed to exceed the optimum limits, can actually hinder speed. Before we discuss how to exercise conscious control over your muscles for various tempi, let us consult the great composers on the subject.

HOW FAST IS FAST? HOW SLOW IS SLOW?

Ever since composers began to write tempo indications in their music, *allegro* has come to mean fast. Seeing an *allegro* at the beginning of a Beethoven Sonata, you then have a right to ask, "How fast is *allegro*?" Beethoven himself pondered this question. In fact, in 1817, he wrote a letter to Ignaz von Mosel, a music critic in Vienna, expressing discontent "in regard to the terms designating the measure of time that were handed down to us when music was still in an age of barbarism. For instance, what could be more meaningless than Allegro, which definitely means *merry*."[16] Beethoven's reluctance to confine himself to a fixed tempo is further illustrated by the following incident. Ferdinand Ries, Beethoven's pupil, purchased a copy of his master's symphonies in London. Ries then wrote to Beethoven asking for metronome markings for the various movements. Receiving no reply after waiting an unusually long time, he sent Beethoven another request. Subsequently, two copies of the metronome marks arrived—one completely different from the other! When Ries later presented this discrepancy to Beethoven, the great composer exclaimed, "Let us not have any metronome numbers at all!"[17]

Brahms, too, was reluctant to supply metronome markings for his *Intermezzi.* "Do you think I'm such a fool," he exclaimed, "as to play them the same way every day?"[18] The inference is that each feeling suggests a particular tempo. It would follow, then, that a change of mood from day to day would have caused Brahms to play his *Intermezzi* at different tempi. That is why most composers refuse to be confined to metronome markings which set an arbitrary tempo for everyone. In fact, as we have seen, they often change their own minds about tempo indications. And since each person has a different emotional and physical disposition, it is understandable why a tempo indication or a metronome number should not be taken literally unless, of course, it suits your temperament. Composers in the twentieth century have been open and realistic concerning tempi. Accordingly, they use the term "circa" (abbreviated, ca.), meaning "about" or "approximately," to qualify metronome indications.

On the other hand, ensemble playing calls for a tempo mutually agreed upon by the musicians. That is, the instrumentalist who begins a chamber music work is expected by his colleagues to set what I call *absolute metronome.* Thus, a specific tempo can actually be memorized. It is a good test of discipline to see if you, too, can memorize a tempo and duplicate it each time you play—or, at least, come close to it.

Try the following:

1. Go to the piano and find your own metronome number for a piece you are studying. Write it down at the beginning of the piece.
2. On the following day, play the piece without the metronome and try to remember the tempo of the previous day. Check yourself with the metronome when you have finished playing to see if your tempo has matched it. If it hasn't, keep trying. With patience you will eventually come close to remembering your tempo. After you have mastered this discipline, you then have the right to change your mind.

Your ability to approximate your own tempo assures greater control in a performance. Nervousness may cause you to exceed the tempo at which you practiced; your fingers, trained to function best at M $\quartnote$ = 116, may lack efficiency at M $\quartnote$ = 126. Conversely, it is possible to exercise too much caution and end up playing too slowly. Therefore, unless you memorize a tempo, you may not be able to maintain a steady pulse so necessary for a convincing performance. Your ultimate achievement will be your ability to take advantage of that heightened feeling during a performance and consciously play either faster for *allegros* or slower for *adagios*. This flexibility of tempo and pulse is one of the attributes of a true artist.

Practically every activity in life requires a tempo that is as personal as it is functional. For example, some individuals read quickly without sacrificing comprehension. I, on the other hand, tend to mull over what I happen to be reading. It therefore takes me a relatively long time to complete an average book. Sometimes, as in the case of Pupil No. IV, we are able to function faster than we think. In general, though, it is not wise to play any faster than your technical ability allows. Although Pupil No. IV was indeed ready to play faster, another pianist may not have been so well-equipped technically to play that fast. I once had a pupil whose tempo invariably exceeded her capacity to play musically. My chief concern was to convince her that she played beautifully at her own tempo—a tempo that was slower than mine. But being a conscientious student, she felt obliged to adhere scrupulously to each metronome indication. I had to remind her constantly that these numbers were merely guidelines around which she might fluctuate according to her own capacities. Finally, the best advice I could give her was, "When the tempo is right, your message will be clear."

Our consideration for others motivates us to re-evaluate the tempo at which we function—both musically and personally. For example, if anxiety causes you to rush in a performance, then it should be your regard for the music and the audience that enables you to take whatever measures are necessary in order to exercise control. Thus, a lecturer who speaks too fast may show as little concern for his audience as a pianist who plays too fast. Even a routine activity such as walking puts your sensitivities to the test. I enjoy walking rather briskly, but I adjust my pace when I walk with a friend whose tempo is slower than mine.

PHYSICAL RESPONSE TO SLOW AND FAST

In playing the piano, various tempi require different movements, especially from your arms and wrists. The following experiment will bear this out:

1. Set your metronome at 60. Play a C major scale *forte* with both hands—up one octave and down again. *Keep your fingers taut* (see the explanation on taut fingers in Chapter 7). Play one note per tick.
2. Play the scale again. Inhale before you begin and exhale as you play the scale. At this slow tempo, you should make large movements with your wrists, lower arms, and upper arms. That is, your arms swing up for the preparation of each note and roll down as your fingers lower each key.
3. Now set the metronome at 132 and play sixteenth notes (four per tick), still *forte*. Exhale as you do so. Try to maintain the same exaggerated wrist and arm gestures at this faster tempo. I am sure you will agree that it is nearly impossible to do so.

From this simple experiment we can conclude the following:

1. A slower tempo invites larger motions.
2. The law of economy insists that the faster you play, the smaller the motions.
3. When you play slowly, your body, arms, and wrists are more relaxed. (But not your *fingers!* Remember that they are always *slightly stretched* or *taut.*)
4. For faster tempi, contract your muscles to make your body, arms, and wrists more stable.

ADAPTATION FOR FAST PLAYING— THE JOINTS OF STABILIZATION

I have demonstrated the following exercises to large audiences. Although most people do them reasonably well even the first time, some look as though their hands and arms are stuck in a block of cement. If you have never before exercised conscious control over your muscles, try these exercises at a moderate tempo. Be sure not to overcontract your muscles in order to stabilize a joint.

The Wrist

1. Sit in a chair. Hold your arms in front of you, elbows slightly bent and palms facing away from your body. Keep your arms and wrists as relaxed as possible and your fingers slightly stretched (taut).
2. Wave your hands up and down, ten times, from your wrists. Pretend that you are waving goodbye to someone at a rather slow and easy pace.
3. Now do the same thing as fast as you can. Be cautioned, however, not to go too fast! For this exercise requires that your hands move as far up and down from your wrists as possible.
4. Now *gently tighten* your elbows and wave goodbye fast and vigorously, moving your hands up and down as far as they will go. You will notice how much easier it is to do this with tighter elbows.

The Elbow

1. Relax again. Move your lower arms from the elbows to your fingertips up and down slowly, tracing a distance of about ten inches.
2. Keep relaxed and do it faster without changing the distance.
3. Now, with your spine erect, brace your shoulders by gently sloping them down toward the floor. Keeping your arms bent at the elbows, move them up and down vigorously. Easier with tighter shoulders? I should say so.

The Shoulder

1. Hold both arms straight out, palms facing the floor.
2. Keeping your palms parallel to the floor, move your arms toward you with bent elbows; then move them straight out again. Do this ten times. Keep relaxed and do the same thing faster. You will notice that this makes your head bob up and down. Now tighten your waistline and your abdominal muscles and try it fast once again. Notice that your head is now stable.

These exercises demonstrate the following:

1. Every joint of *movability* must have a corresponding joint of *stability*.

2. The faster you move, the more firm you must be in the joint of stability.
3. The joint of stability is always one joint removed from the joint of movability. The combinations are as follows:

   a. If your wrist moves quickly, your elbow remains firm.
   b. If your elbow moves quickly, your shoulder joint remains firm.
   c. If your shoulders move quickly, your waistline remains firm.
   d. If your fingers move quickly from the knuckle joints, your wrist must remain firm. Try the C major scale once again at a fast tempo and notice that your wrists must be more stable the faster you go.

The whole idea of a moving joint being dependent upon a stable joint stems from sound physiological principles. Rooted as these suggestions are in natural biological function, they will bring you an immediate sense of freedom whose application will appear obvious to you. Once again, you are called upon to be objective as you experiment with the above suggestions, for it is important that you pinpoint the sensations resulting from movability versus stability. You can do this best by observing yourself in a mirror. *Listening* to your sound, *feeling* economy of movement, and *seeing* it as it actually occurs will be all the evidence you need to make these principles a necessary part of your practicing. The task is now before you: to master the piano, you must be able to move one joint and stabilize another simultaneously. It may appear difficult at first, but it can be done. All of these movements are used independently or in various combinations when playing the piano. You will facilitate your task if you learn to control them away from the piano.

LONG NOTES

The Illusion of a Crescendo on Long Notes

Long sustained notes present a difficult problem for the pianist—one which occurs in both slow and fast passages. Almost all instruments, with the exception of the piano, are able to sustain a specific dynamic on a single, held tone. The human voice is a perfect example. When you sing, you can either maintain the same dynamic or vary it in any degree you wish. Alas, a piano tone begins to die the instant the hammer falls away from the strings. However, there is a way to compensate for this deficiency in the piano. With a clever manipulation of accompanying figures, you can actually sculpt a single tone, creating the illusion of a crescendo. Here is an example of how this can be done:

Play the following four-bar theme as expressively as you can.

Mozart, *Sonata*, K. 332

Now play it again, adding the left hand.

Play the passage once again, making a slight crescendo in the left-hand figure, measure 2.

You have just created the illusion of a crescendo on the half note in the right hand melody. Try it again, this time making sure you have the right hand sing over the left-hand accompaniment.

Before we leave this theme, I would like to point out some important musical principles which can be applied to similar passages:

1. When you play a large interval on the piano, you can often achieve a beautiful effect by playing the highest note softer than the previous note (see bar three, B♭ to G). Think of a vocal slide

or imagine a string player approaching the high note of a large interval. Large intervals are difficult to sing and to play on practically every instrument but the piano. For example, try to sing a sixth from B♭ to G. When you play it on the piano, simulate this tension so that you seem to rise with difficulty toward the G. Rising with difficulty implies that you not only play the highest note softer, but that you also delay it slightly. This is not to suggest that all large intervals are to be approached in this way. The musical content is, of course, the determining factor.

2. The musical direction for most four-bar themes is toward the third bar, as in the example given above. A certain tension is created either through loudness or softness in this directional bar. The same principle holds true in a melody that has four *phrases*.

Beethoven, *Sonata*, Op. 10, No. 3

3. One of the chief requirements for producing a beautiful tone is having the dynamics properly balanced between your hands. The sensation is as follows: there is pressure in your right hand and arm which projects into the keys through your fingers; at the same time, the pressure in your left hand and arm is minimal. In many instances you achieve a singing tone by depressing the left pedal (soft pedal) and "digging" into the key bed with your right hand fingers (more about the soft pedal in Chapter 7).

4. Accompanying figures usually sound more beautiful when you treat them polyphonically. This applies especially to Mozart. As a young student, I would often be reprimanded by my teachers for holding down my left-hand fifth finger on Alberti basses and all broken chord figures. In time, I discovered that my instincts were in fact correct. Mozart wrote the opening bar of his *F major Sonata* this way.

It is advisable to play it as follows:

You thus get a polyphonic effect by creating two voices out of one: the first F is played piano, or even mezzo-piano and held throughout the measure; the following five eighth notes murmur softly out of the initial impulse. The softer they are played, the better. Imagine a cello playing the F and a viola filling out the rest of the bar pianissimo. If I were to play this Mozart *Sonata*, I would hold the first note of the next three bars in the left hand in a similar fashion, and then make a slight crescendo on the second bar.

5. The slurs that appear in both the right and the left hand mean specific things. Yet they can be a source of great confusion. In Mozart and his contemporaries, such slurs were actually bow marks borrowed from the notation for stringed instruments and adapted to keyboard music. It would be wrong to assume from the slur marks in the Mozart *Sonata*, K. 332, that you should separate measure 1 from measure 2, any more than a violinist would allow a cessation of sound at this point for a change of bow. It is also wrong to assume that the second note of a slur must always be softer than the first (see measure 2 in which a crescendo appears on the second note). The subject of slurs is discussed in greater detail in the definitive book: *Interpreting Mozart on the Keyboard* by Eva and Paul Badura-Skoda. Chapter 3, entitled "Articulation," will help you understand how to interpret slurs and other signs of articulation in Mozart.

The "Kuh-Kuh-Kuh's" on Long Notes

Most musicians have their own methods for subdividing long notes, but often they forget to think consciously of them during a performance. One of my pupils fell prey to this fault in the third movement of the *Sonata*, Op. 109, by Beethoven. So long as she had a metronome ticking during her practicing, she was able to keep an even pulse during the quarter notes. But with the excitement of a performance, this lofty theme began to rush, at first imperceptibly, and then quite noticeably. This is what I finally had her do throughout her practicing and performing:

Beethoven, *Sonata*, Op. 109 (third movement)

Andante molto cantabile ed espressivo

kuh - kuh - kuh - kuh   kuh - kuh - kuh - kuh   kuh - kuh - kuh - kuh

kuh - kuh - kuh - kuh   kuh - kuh - kuh - kuh   kuh - kuh - kuh - kuh

She performed it for some of my students a few days later, saying her "kuh-kuhs" to herself. The theme was controlled for the first time. Her whispered "kuh-kuhs" were heard by no one, not even by those sitting only a few feet away from the piano. If you too have a tendency to rush, you will find this technique a useful corrective. The same obtains for filling out all dotted notes.

I am sure that you would have arrived at the following solution:

kuh - kuh - kuh–kuh–kuh-kuh-kuh-kuh

Follow this suggestion for all dotted rhythms and for all long notes. Fill them out either with unspoken or audible sounds, depending on the situation in which you find yourself. You can, of course, choose any syllable to serve the same purpose. I happen to like the sound of "kuh" and the articulate feeling it gives me in my throat. If you are subdividing long notes at a fast tempo, you might try *tuh-kuh,* a combination which flutists use for double-tonguing.

The opening measures of the *Sonata in F*, K. 497, for four hands by Mozart presents one of the most difficult ensemble problems in the repertory, as I discovered when I performed it at a Mozart Festival at the Kennedy Center in Washington. The first five bars require four hands to come together precisely on quarter notes marked *adagio.* Troublesome? Not when you employ the "kuh-kuh" method. Since I sat at the treble, I could turn my head away from the audience and toward my partner to whisper four "kuh-kuhs" on each quarter note for five whole bars. Everything went splendidly at the rehearsals, but during the performance I suddenly ran out of breath in the middle of the second bar. I felt my face gradually grow paler as my "kuh-kuhs" grew fainter and fainter. The incident made me realize how important breath control is to a performer. Fortunately, I was able to take advantage of my solo in the third bar for a quick catch-breath in time to continue my "kuhs." The passage was saved and the color returned to my cheeks (see Illustration IX).

Illustration IX.   Mozart, *Sonata in F major*, K. 497 (For Four Hands)

For best results in ensemble playing, give a measure of "kuhs" *before you begin* so that you and your partner arrive on the down-beat together. You can use this counting technique to begin any four-hand piece—unless you and your partner have found an equally effective way to synchronize your opening measures.

DON'T RUSH WEAK BEATS

On one occasion at Fontainebleau, Nadia Boulanger gathered us together to discuss problems shared by all musicians. One concerned the last beat of a bar going to the down-beat of the following bar. She asked us to walk through the room clapping 1-2-3-4. Each time we reached 4, we were to emphasize it by thrusting our arms forward and speaking louder. The point of the exercise was to go from 4 to 1 *without rushing.* You know, of course, that in a 4/4 bar, 1 and 3 get the natural accents. Of all the beats, therefore, 4 would normally be the softest. But in this experiment it became the *loudest,* drawing attention to a natural tendency to neglect the final beat in one measure and thus to anticipate the downbeat in the following bar. We subsequently tried this technique for 3/4 time, emphasizing 3 to 1.

RHYTHMIC CONTROL IN CRESCENDOS AND DIMINUENDOS

"Anyone who races during a performance cannot have a career in music!" These harsh words were directed at me by a famous violinist. The occasion was my first chamber music class at a well-known conservatory. I was nineteen. Such a pronouncement would have been grossly unfair in any context, but it was even more so considering the circumstances in which it was delivered—I was *sight-reading* the Mozart *G minor Piano Quartet* and rushed during a crescendo. At the time, I thought that my tendency to rush was an exclusive fault of my own—one which most musicians did not have to contend with. Subsequently, I discovered many musical problems that are shared by most musicians, one of which is a tendency to *rush on crescendos* and *slow down on diminuendos.*

Set your metronome at $\quarternote$ = 80. Allow it to tick for a while and imagine sixteenth notes running up and down the piano. As soon as you think you have the tempo, *turn the metronome off.* Play a four-octave scale, hands together, with the following dynamics: start *pianissimo* and make a crescendo to the highest note. On the way down, make a diminuendo. Try it two or three times, remembering to exhale during your playing. Allow your body to move laterally along with the scale. As the crescendo increases, move your upper body closer to the keys. (Some pianists move their bodies *away* from the keys for crescendos since a greater arm length sometimes gives a better control. Try it both ways.)

Now—if you are sure not to feel defeated by the following—set the metronome once again at 80. But this time try the same experiment *with the metronome on*. Don't be surprised if the metronome makes you go *slower* on the way up and *faster* on the way down. Practically every musician tends to do this. With practice you will eventually learn to feel a crescendo without speeding up, and a diminuendo without slowing down. This exercise can also be reversed: start *pianissimo* on the highest note, making a crescendo on the way down and a diminuendo on the way up. You may find this troublesome, for the natural tendency is to grow softer as you descend a scale and louder as you ascend.

BALANCE AND CONTROL

Paradoxically, the most artistic playing occurs when a performer judiciously defies the strict symmetry of pulse. But just as the ability to control a *pianissimo* comes from a position of technical strength, so, too, this artistic flexibility or rubato can be understood only when you have learned to adhere to a strict pulse. For this reason, beginning students are repeatedly cautioned not to hold long notes too long and not to play fast notes too fast. Advanced students, however, are advised to try the opposite—that is, to concentrate on the real meaning of rhythmic values—for long notes can be somewhat longer and fast notes can be somewhat faster. This means that there are intrinsic feelings associated with various rhythmic values, just as there are with different dynamics. In other words, rhythmic values and dynamic indications are symbols that represent feelings. This holds true also for accelerandos and ritardandos. A performer who has not the "slightest taste or expression" makes getting faster or slower a simple matter of calculation; a communicative performer, however, *feels* an accelerando or a ritardando. But you must be forewarned to avoid exaggerating ritardandos, especially when they coincide with diminuendos, for this can easily make a piece fall apart. Suppose, too, that you have been told not to rush on a crescendo and not to slow down on a diminuendo. When you finally learn to control this tendency, only then may you throw all caution to the wind. For, in fact, growing louder excites you and growing softer calms you.

To express all of this artistic freedom with good taste and discretion necessitates your ability to have full control over your musical pulse. In other words, you will arrive at just the right amount of musical flexibility when you can play in time. It is yet another example of how musical freedom, like personal freedom, flourishes within self-imposed guidelines. Many of us, for example, will do our best work within a restricted time span. Thus, having to meet a deadline wrests from us our most concentrated efforts. Similarly, most practicers do their best work when committed either to a music lesson or a performance. When interpreting music, a restricted time span will make convincing the placement of a single note—especially the final note of a slow, soft piece. Should we arbitrarily delay this note, we may then lack the sheer physical momentum to make it sound (a dropped note). Disciplining ourselves, however, to sound this note at a predetermined time— no matter what the consequence—usually assures our success.

All these examples prove what has already been discussed— namely, that discipline results in freedom. Rooted in *biological time*, our life processes require a constant organization of time sequences that determine the success or failure of our every action. Far from being an inhibiting factor, self-imposed timing initiates our most spontaneous thoughts and actions. In this respect, practicing teaches you to harness the very pulse within you, and, through concentrated effort, to place it at the service of your art. Thus, to unleash the well-spring of artistic energies within you is in itself liberating to the fullest extent. The skills derived from your art will radiate out to all other aspects of your life.

EURHYTHMICS

Emile Jaques-Dalcroze, the Swiss-born musician, pioneered a unique system of music education known throughout the world as *Dalcroze Eurhythmics*. After years of research during which he observed students with good and bad rhythm, he concluded that what students really needed was "a special training [program] designed to regulate the nervous reactions and to effect a coordination between muscles and nerves; in short, to harmonize mind and body."[19] Thus, the special training proposed by Dalcroze results in a harmony and balance similar to that which we seek in practicing. Moreover, an earlier suggestion to approach a new piece spontaneously also bears a striking resemblance to his method. Dalcroze attempted to inculcate in his students an instantaneous response to sound and rhythm. Each student's performance is encouraged—even those with imperfect control. Every response is regarded as a direct and honest reaction to sound and feeling. "Later on, when their sensitivity to aesthetic values of musical composition finds an intuitive echo in their minds, their movements will express their own artistic tendencies, and not those of their teachers."[20]

Dalcroze believed in starting this training at the earliest possible age. Thus children of two and three were taught to express rhythmic patterns by using "their limbs as instruments," the goal being to train the entire body to respond openly and naturally—like a tree moving in the wind. Since I was interested in all I had read and heard concerning the Dalcroze method, I was eager to explore these principles with respect to my own body. I therefore enrolled in a course offered by Katya Delakova who has herself developed a method of teaching body movement. Many of her ideas are similar to or influenced by Yoga, Dalcroze, and the dance. The class was comprised of adults representing a broad spectrum of professions. But as the course subsequently proved, all of us were strangers to our own bodies. Soon, though, as we shed our inhibitions in regard to natural body movements, we simultaneously liberated our feelings. Most of the instruction was centered on eliminating tension around the neck and shoulders, the techniques of which had a remarkable influence on my own playing and, in turn, on that of my pupils. Correct breathing was stressed throughout each class session, and this, of course, enabled us to liberate our feelings more readily. By teaching us to be receptive to instinctual response—such as the simplest movements of our arms and legs—Katya helped us to know ourselves more intimately. This led naturally to an appreciation of the unique capacities for expression in each other, for no two pupils in the class expressed themselves in the same way.

THE CHILD IN US

The following experiment is designed to help you let go of your inhibitions and recapture the spontaneity of the child in you. Try it alone at first. Later, as "letting go" becomes more natural, you can invite your family and friends to join you:

1. Put on your favorite record or turn on the radio to some music that appeals to you.

2. Lie on the floor letting your arms and legs sprawl wherever they happen to fall.
3. While the music plays, keep your eyes closed and breathe deeply. At this point in the experiment, you will notice a fluctuation in your breathing pattern, influenced, of course, by the kind of music to which you happen to be listening. Also, the music will affect various muscular responses throughout your body. Do not inhibit them; rather, allow the music to inspire unconscious feelings and movements.
4. As you continue to lie there with the music flowing through you, the following may occur: your right arm makes a circular motion in the air as the melody climbs higher and higher; a persistent rhythm causes your toes to move up and down seemingly of their own volition; suddenly, your left knee bends in response to a musical climax; before you know it, you roll to one side, resting on both knees, body erect, with your arms weaving in and out like seaweed undulating in the tide.

In other words, this experiment unleashes within you a torrent of instinctual responses culminating in improvisational body movements. If you were a choreographer, you would probably have been objective throughout but without inhibiting your spontaneity. Then, no doubt, you would have extracted some of the movements and organized them into a dance form. But as a mere listener, you engaged in such an experiment solely to recapture the child in you—that wide-eyed sense of discovery and exhilaration. As you dare to let go more and more, you will surprise yourself repeatedly by doing something totally new. Practicing affords you a similar delight, for through it you can learn to accomplish feats which you hitherto thought impossible. Even though you may have the potential for such accomplishments, you still must set the stage for discovery and revelation. You can begin by giving up the false notion that it is too late to do so. For, as Dr. Helen Boigon, a noted psychiatrist, once told me, "The most important element in any learning process is the emotional capacity to relax and be innocent, no matter what your age." Children in their innocence expect good at every turn. They imagine they can achieve anything—and they often do. Thus we learn from children that being open and innocent allows the best to come from us.

All the skills you gain from practicing enable you to keep your curiosity and enthusiasm alive. "Start over again each day!" one of my teachers advised me. Children do this naturally. The possibilities awaiting them, the exhilaration of the unknown, supply them with the momentum necessary for achievement. In this respect, practicing teaches you to replace innumerable obstacles with predictable ends. Armed with confidence and security derived from such achievements, you can approach each day with the optimism of a child and the wisdom of an adult.

SLOW OR FAST PRACTICING?

One of your responsibilities as a practicer is to decide when to practice slowly and when to practice fast. Since your progress depends on carefully balancing the two, it is necessary that you weigh the factors governing this choice. You may begin by strolling lazily through your room. Walk at a slow pace and enjoy the comfort of centering your body weight on one foot at a time. Allow your arms to swing as your body moves from side to side. Observe the rather large motions you make during this slow pace. Now start to walk faster. At this pace, you will notice that your feet are closer to the floor. Also, your body no longer moves from side to side as it did when you walked slowly. Notice, too, that your arms stabilize your body by swinging to and fro from your shoulders. Moreover, the energy source which moves your legs now seems to originate in your hip joints. In relating these observations to playing the piano, we can postulate the following: *the energy resulting in fast, loud playing originates in an area as far away from the keys as possible—namely, the shoulders.* This holds true even if your fingers remain on or near the keys. All of this bears a striking similarity to swinging a golf club. Suppose you wish to drive a golf ball a great distance. In order to generate enough speed, your club must start its swing far enough away from the ball. The opposite obtains if you send the ball a short distance; in this case, your club need not be more than a few inches away from the ball. In short, *the greater the distance, the greater the speed.* Now, suppose someone challenges you to drive the ball as far as you can while still keeping the club relatively *close* to the ball. Undismayed, you brace yourself for the task, fully determined to generate a greater speed within a shorter distance. To your astonishment, you actually succeed! Restrictions considered, you do send the ball a greater distance than you thought possible. This *speed–distance* principle has a direct bearing on playing the piano. For example, every dynamic requires a particular speed with which the hammers swing toward the strings:

1. If you wish to play softer, you must generate less speed to the hammers (the keys are lowered more slowly).
2. If you wish to play louder, you must generate more speed to the hammers (the keys are lowered more quickly).

Obviously, the distance the hammers travel toward the strings is fixed by the mechanism of the piano. However, the distance between your finger and a key is variable; that is, you may initiate a tone by starting your swing far above the key, or by keeping your finger on the surface of the key before depressing it. One approach may be more efficient than the other, depending upon the particular grouping of notes and on the effect you wish to convey. But fortissimo chords require your special consideration. If your hands start two feet above the keys, you risk making a percussive sound caused by (1) the friction of your fingers striking the keys; (2) the "thud" of the keys striking against the key beds; and (3) the noise produced by the hammers flying too quickly to the strings. All of these extraneous noises result in banging. In fact, as an expert tuner once told me, hammers accelerating beyond a certain speed will actually displace the strings. This displacement causes the hammers to linger slightly on the strings, thus hampering the full amplitude of vibrations. The penalty for this is not only wasted energy, but also a *softer* sound! Therefore, to prevent this sudden acceleration of the hammers in loud playing, you must stay as close to the keys as possible. As in the experiment in which you were challenged to drive a golf ball a great distance with a short swing, loud playing demands that you stay close to the keys. Your entire body must be mobilized; the impulse begins at your feet and travels throughout your body, terminating at the strings. This necessitates a contraction of your back and abdominal muscles. Remember, too, that when you feel the dynamics, your body will assume the correct physical attitude. However, should your muscles not respond naturally, you must learn to contract them consciously. Be careful, though, not to allow your muscles to contract beyond what is necessary—otherwise, a desired flexibility can easily give way to stiffness. You will understand this better if you try the following experiment:

Leave the piano and walk slowly across the room. Take note of the corresponding sensation in your body. Now start to walk faster. Once again, observe your physical attitude. You will notice that various muscles will contract automatically—but only to the degree necessary for body stabilization.

Playing loud, fast passages on the piano requires a similar marshaling of energies; that is, the proper muscular contraction will *free* you. Your awareness of the muscular sensations within your body is, in fact, necessary for all activities requiring physical exertion. For example, if you are unaccustomed to intense exercising, a sudden, long hike will cause aches and pains in various parts of your body—an indication that your body is not conditioned properly for the stress placed upon it. Similarly, slow and soft practicing will not condition you for the demands of fast, loud music. Loud and fast playing necessitates a physical involvement above and beyond that required for soft, slow playing. However, practicing loud and fast continually will exhaust you both physically and emotionally. After all, your ears and nervous system can take only so much loudness before they rebel. Productive practicing, therefore, requires that you be practical. As you remember, Pupil No. IV was impractical in that she assumed it would take her a year of slow practicing to play Chopin *Etudes* up to tempo. Two examples of being practical are to adapt fast–loud playing to your individual needs and to choose repertory that contains a wide variety of musical and technical challenges. It is impractical, however, to practice pieces with a preponderance of chords and octaves requiring you to keep your hands extended for long periods of time, or to plunge into loud, passionate passages after not practicing for several days. Both tendencies, not uncommon among instrumentalists, can lead to muscle strain, a precursor of tendonitis. In the first instance, it would be wise to add some Bach and Mozart to your Brahms and Liszt (and vice versa); and in the second, to begin your practicing with stretching exercises (see p. 170), remembering of course to relax your hands intermittently by playing chromatic or diatonic five-finger patterns. In short, treating your hands with the care and respect they deserve by alternately extending and contracting them through a balanced diet of pieces and exercises will keep them flexible and strong.

In the chapter on concentration, you were advised to begin a new work up to tempo in order to get an overall impression of it. Now it is time to examine this kind of practicing in more detail so as to get the greatest benefits from it. But before we begin, the obvious must be stated. And that is that all practicers are different: some have a remarkable reading facility, while others experience anxiety when they look at a score; some have hands that adapt to all technical requirements—others have to develop flexibility (and often end up playing just as well or even better than those more favorably endowed); some can learn a new composition away from the piano, while others depend solely on a tactile sense to absorb the musical content and technical demands of a piece. Considering all of these variables (and there are many more), it is not possible to prescribe a method for fast-slow practicing that will be suitable for all musicians. In other words, the time span necessary for the assimilation of musical information not only differs from person to person but also fluctuates within each of us. It is no less variable than the maturation point of different plant species. In light of all this, it would be best, therefore, to experiment. If you are in doubt about whether to practice slow or fast, simply start to play without any preconceived notions and listen *objectively* to the results. Your sense of discrimination will tell you all you need to know—namely, whether you are ready to play a piece up to tempo or whether you must still exercise restraint over your ambitions.

Your teacher is, of course, indispensable while you are experimenting with choices of tempi. He knows your potential even as you yourself are striving to express it. In his desire to guide you, he not only points out your weaknesses, but he also shows you how to overcome them. Let us hope that he will not forget to praise you for your strengths. In truth, though, he can hardly be all things to you. However, some teachers (and they are extremely rare) are sufficiently developed both musically and personally to answer most of your needs. When a teacher is secure in his own abilities, he will often urge his students to consult with friends, colleagues, and even *other* teachers, for he knows that music is too vast a subject to be the exclusive domain of just one pedagogue. Your own teacher, however, must serve as a "clearing house," so to speak, with whom you pool all the information acquired from other sources. Having been helped to assimilate innumerable facts and suggestions, you may then approach your practicing with the confidence and determination of a true student—that is, one who is patient and ever willing to experiment indefinitely for the sake of one's art.

COPING WITH DIFFICULTIES

There is something miraculous about awakening to a new day and to a sense of unlimited energy that awaits your bidding. For the most part, two factors determine the way in which you will harness this energy: (1) a realistic view of your own potential; and (2) the degree to which you would like to develop that potential. With perfection as your goal, assume that a proper approach to practicing will resolve all difficulties—provided that you work at your own pace. What if it takes you ten years to paint a chrysanthemum! After all, Brahms waited thirty-six years before he rewrote the final version of his *B major Piano Trio*. Being aware of your own working tempo actually enables you to attain your goals much sooner than you might anticipate. But don't be too easy on yourself since a good challenge serves to propel you into areas where until now you may have been reluctant to go. If you have always learned slowly, it is now time to be daring and act on faith alone. First, be convinced that every moment of your practicing leads you closer to perfection. Knowing this will infuse you with confidence to move at a faster pace. Your feelings, your thoughts, and your physical sensations all will indicate whether or not your pace is realistic. It is certainly true, as a pupil once told me, that "physical difficulties are usually a symptom of unclear thinking." Therefore, be sure to analyze a difficult passage in musical as well as in theoretical terms. And, of course, double-check your fingering. When a passage does not feel comfortable, stop practicing temporarily and try to discover the cause of your unpleasant sensation. Better to do this than to continue feeding uncomfortable sensations into your automatic pilot. As long as you search constantly for a more efficient way, you will approach the standard of artistry exemplified by music itself. Being more efficient as an instrumentalist means finding a connection between your feelings and your physical gestures. For example, loud, passionate playing demands strong, steely fingers. It would be counterproductive, therefore, to have your fingers simulate the consistency of overcooked noodles. Needless to say, an awareness of physical sensations at the piano can be applied to various other activities involving muscular coordination. With this in mind, you will eventually learn to function economically in all that you do—musically and otherwise. For further discussion on this point, see Chapter 7, pp. 130–133, in which the significance of natural tension is explained.

During the first stages of practicing a new piece, your eyes encompass a series of notes and you spontaneously respond to them. As you become more familiar with the music, however, you may lose that spontaneity and begin to anticipate difficulties. "Here comes that passage in broken thirds," you may say. "I'd better brace myself for it." The trouble is that you are anticipating the difficulty four bars before it actually occurs! No sooner do you do this than two things happen: first, anticipation causes your muscles to contract involuntarily; second, by the time you reach the passage in question, anxiety diminishes the possibility of your executing it clearly. A countermeasure is to concentrate on the full value of each note you are playing *without anticipating what is to come.*

The next time you are stumped by a difficult passage, try the following:

1. Analyze the passage in every way possible: identify the key; determine clearly which notes outline a chord and which notes are purely decorative; pinpoint the notes in the passage of one hand that fall together with those of the other hand; choose the dynamics with which you wish to express the passage—write them down in your score; be sure you have found a comfortable fingering; *choreograph* the passage (see Chapter 8).
2. After analyzing the passage as suggested, play it in the context of the larger sections in which it appears.
3. Should the difficulty persist, isolate the passage once again and consider one or more of the following remedies: change the fingering; return to the original fingering; go back and forth between your original and the new fingering; try the passage at different speeds; be aware of the muscles involved in playing the passage; have clearly in mind how the joint of movability and the joint of stability are working in combination; involve yourself emotionally during all repetitions; shift your attention back and forth from the passage to the entire composition.

After you have exhausted all these possibilities, you may discover that the passage itself is in fact not the source of the difficulty. Rather, the problem may derive from the measure or measures preceding it. As an example, suppose that there are four bars of *forte* chords which are awkwardly written for your hand. The fifth bar, a passage in runs, always resists you. Yet, whenever you isolate this passage, you play it perfectly. It would be fair to assume in this case that your arm muscles overcontract on the measures with the chords preceding the runs in the fifth bar. Thus, by the time you arrive at the passage in runs, stiffness overcomes you—a musical rigor mortis of your arms and fingers, as it were. In such a condition, clear finger articulation is, of course, impossible. It would be far better to ease your execution of the chordal passage by doing stretching exercises. Once the chords feel comfortable, you will approach the difficult passage in the fifth measure with an ease necessary to assure its successful execution. Now, let us examine some other ways in which to practice difficult passages:

1. Practice the passage pyramid fashion: that is, start to play a few measures before the difficult passage begins and stop on the first note of it; start once again from the same place, but this time stop after the second note; continue to add one note at a time until you have played through the entire passage. This is perhaps one of the most useful approaches to mastering a technically difficult passage.

2. Play the passage backward: start on the last note, then play the last two notes, and so on, until you have worked through all the repetitions in their turn.

3. Set the difficult passage in its context: start one note before it and continue on through the passage to its completion; now start two notes before it and continue in the same fashion until, note by additional note, you have built a strong bridge to the difficult passage.

4. If, for example, the difficulty is in your right hand, play the same passage simultaneously with your left hand one octave lower. You will discover that one hand will influence the other, thereby affording you a fresh approach to what has been thus far resisting you.

5. Do the same thing, but this time cross your hands. First, try the left hand over the right and then the right hand over the left. A finger–arm twister, this method of practicing greatly improves your coordination.

6. We have already discussed how clear thinking influences your physical approach to the piano. Therefore, assume the following: *fast passages are slow passages played faster.* In other words, while you are playing fast, *think slowly.*

7. Practice at a tempo that is neither too slow nor beyond your present ability. Rather, choose a tempo that is only slightly faster than your ability to execute the passage perfectly. This faster

tempo challenges you to concentrate to the fullest extent, thereby inducing your best efforts and, as is often the case, your best playing.

When trying these suggestions, always remember to breathe properly. This assures an unimpeded flow of your energy—an energy that is rooted in musical feeling. Also, invent your own methods of surmounting difficulties. If you discover an approach that improves your playing, record it in your score. When you return to a piece at some future date, the evidence of your constructive thinking will be there to guide you during your practicing. This storehouse of accumulated information will aid you considerably should you decide to teach.

We have already discussed the vital necessity of repetition in your practicing. We have also seen how repetition can easily induce boredom. But practicing difficult passages in the ways that have been outlined not only aids you in your musical and technical progress, but also promotes the concentration that dispels boredom. The key, of course, is to discover techniques of practicing that arouse your interest and fascination. And you can do this best by tackling difficulties in a variety of ways. But you cannot do it alone. As this book has stressed all along, there must be a correlation between practicing, that is, working alone, and performing for others. For this reason, it is necessary that you test the validity of your findings as you change from one practicing technique to another. Through a verbal exchange with others and by performing for those whose opinions you respect, you can piece together a true picture of your artistic development. Such an exchange serves to bring you ever closer to your own realization of the music.

The response of others to your playing will reflect the way in which you have practiced. If, for instance, a defeatist attitude has prevented you from practicing a fast piece up to tempo, your audience will no doubt recognize this and respond accordingly. It signals the time for you to pluck up your courage and force the speed of the piece, and to persist until your body adapts to the faster tempo. In other words, abandon your reticence and try something that you have never before dared to attempt.

You may assume, as I used to, that practicing soft, legato passages with the right and left pedals makes you dependent on them and therefore constitutes bad habits. One day, however, I decided that it was not at all for dependency's sake that I used the

pedals, but rather to enhance the skills I had already a-
chieved—namely, playing legato and playing softly. Moreover,
since the pedals are used to create the ultimate in coloristic effects,
their use is indispensable during your practicing. Once having
discovered this, I discarded all sense of guilt—a guilt shared by
many pianists—and began using both pedals from my first encounter with a new work. As a result, I progressed much faster.
You may not, of course, be able to implement a new approach to
your practicing instantaneously. But the courage to try can be
found by remembering the ultimate goal in practicing—to liberate
yourself musically and to free yourself in all respects. It is what Edward Albee meant when he said, "I write to unclutter my mind."
The right kind of practicing will unclutter your mind, too, enabling
you to reach musical heights and personal mastery far beyond what
your present abilities promise.

The effectiveness with which you overcome difficulties, whether
in practicing or in life, depends upon your determination to succeed. When you are truly determined and fully committed to a
goal, you somehow find the means to achieve it. Let us say, for instance, that you are suffering from a sprained ankle and that you
have laboriously hobbled up three flights of stairs to attend a lec-
ture. You find the speaker stimulating and you are thus deeply
engrossed in his presentation. Suddenly, someone shouts "Fire!"
and the entire room is thrown into a panic. In a flash, you are on
your feet, sprained ankle notwithstanding, and you fairly leap down
the very stairs that you mounted so feebly only moments before.
Clearly, the overwhelming necessity to save yourself instantly triggered a mobilization of all your forces enabling you to harness
strengths as remarkable as they were surprising. I have seen practicers perform musical feats no less astonishing because they were
spurred on by a love for music and a determination to use their
musical accomplishments as a model for personal growth. Thus,
practicing teaches you to conquer difficulties and to view nothing
as insurmountable. The decision is yours, as it is in so many situations in life: that is, you may exercise your determination to succeed or you may hinder your own growth. It is commonly thought
that only the most gifted musicians are able to discipline
themselves—that talent and the capacity to work are synonymous.
However, I have taught individuals who appeared at first to have
little talent but whose capacity for work was enormous. Others who
showed amazing gifts often had little capacity for work. It is not un-

common for the former to surpass the latter in achievement, building to impressive heights what had appeared to be a modest talent. Therefore, we have no right to view anyone's talent—or anything, for that matter—in finite terms. Surprising revelations, musical and otherwise, can await us at every turn. Practicing uncovers a profound source of beauty within you. Seemingly hidden, its depths are revealed through your talent; its rewards, through your accomplishments. It is through practicing that you define your very nature; that you are able to view yourself and your environment with confidence and optimism. Sensing this process unfolding within himself and feeling a need to share it with me, a pupil wrote the following letter:

> I don't know whether you will be happy or distressed to hear that in your absence I have made remarkable progess. But knowing you, I am sure that you have already anticipated this. Being made to practice on my own has forced me to come to grips with some problems that have plagued me for a long time. One is that all these years I have been practicing at the wrong pace, a pace that was simply too fast. It appeared as though someone else's standards were being foisted upon me. Even though you often warned me about this, I still felt as though a false standard pervaded my work. Now that you are on tour, I am forced to create my own pace. This doesn't rob me of my desire to please my teacher. It's just that I always lacked the confidence that you seemed to have in me. This lack of confidence manifested itslf in several ways: I didn't take pride in fixing up my new apartment and I also resented my job. In fact, I felt that I didn't even deserve to have pleasure from the one or the other. You cannot imagine how much practicing has helped me overcome these false notions. I am now able to have a positive image of myself that influences all the other areas of my life.

SUMMARY

1. Use larger motions for slow playing and smaller motions for fast playing.
2. Every action at the piano demands a degree of muscular contraction. Slow, soft playing requires less contraction than slow, loud playing; fast, soft playing requires less contraction than fast, loud playing. But in all these cases your fingers must always remain *taut*.

3. In playing the piano, there is always a joint of movability and a joint of stability working together:
   a. Finger action demands a firm wrist.
   b. Wrist action demands a firm elbow.
   c. Lower arm movements from your elbow demand a firm shoulder joint.
   d. Upper arm movements from your shoulder joint demand a firmness around your waist.
4. Always subdivide long notes into shorter values. The same obtains for dotted eighth notes and their equivalents.
5. Be careful not to rush from the last beat of one measure to the first beat of the following measure.
6. You can create the illusion of a crescendo on a long note by adjusting the dynamics of the other moving voices.
7. Crescendos tend to make you play faster; diminuendos tend to make you play slower. Compensate accordingly.
8. Feel the full length of long notes; feel the excitement of fast notes.
9. Accept the symmetry of pulse and allow it to activate your body. Then take rhythmic liberties in response to your musical feelings.
10. Never play faster than your ability to play musically.
11. Although your fingers may be on or near the surface of the keys for fast, loud playing, all your impulses must originate in your shoulders or in your torso.
12. The degree of muscular contraction is proportionate to the intensity of the sound. Loud playing demands greater muscular contraction.
13. Don't anticipate difficult passages.
14. The cause of a difficulty with a passage may originate in the measure or measures preceding it.
15. Practice fast pieces or fast passages at a tempo slightly beyond your technical proficiency. This forces you to concentrate at full capacity.
16. Do not neglect to balance your practicing of fast pieces with slow, careful work.
17. Nothing takes the place of repetition over a long period of time. The following experiment will prove the effectiveness of this: Choose a difficult passage and repeat it twenty times a day at various tempi. For example, alternate between a tempo that

is half as fast as the final tempo and one that is slightly faster than your present ability. Finally, try the passage up to tempo, even if you feel that you are not quite ready to do so. Practice the various repetitions at the exact dynamic required by the music. Do this every day for a week. Positive results are assured.

6 Listening

In practicing, all activities relate to one another. For example, technique influences rhythm, and rhythm, technique. You may isolate any one of the innumerable factors that combine to make up a musical performance; but at the same time each one of these factors must harmonize with your total concept of a composition. And that concept is ultimately influenced by the way in which you *listen* to your practicing.

Rhythm permeates the universe; so, too, does sound. Certain sounds in nature are textured, their pitches composite, as in the swooshes of crescendos and diminuendos of the sea rolling against the coastline, or in the crackling boom of thunder. Other sounds comprise exact pitches. A bird can be recognized by its pitches and rhythms; the wind whistles on a high pitch and slides down to a lower one; a rain drop falling on a stone can produce a particular pitch. According to the Pythagoreans, even the heavenly bodies "produced sounds whose pitches were dependent necessarily on their size, speed and position and, moreover, corresponded to the mathematically determined notes of a musical scale."[21] This poetic notion of a celestial scale has appealed to mankind for centuries, for it assumes a real connection between earthly and heavenly harmonies.

LISTENING NATURALLY

The Occidental music to which you have been exposed all your life is composed of pitches that not only form melodies but also harmonic sequences. In fact, almost all the music you hear on the radio, television, or in public areas is based on the pitches of our major and minor scales. Constant exposure can so accustom you to certain melodic and harmonic sequences—some familiar enough to have become musical clichés—that you can easily recognize a wrong note in a piece you may never have heard before. Even though you cannot name the note, you know it is wrong. If you had been exposed frequently to electronic music, let us say, or even to Korean court music, you would in time have become just as familiar with those sounds as you are with traditional Western music.

Like many cultural traditions, music can be passed on from one generation to another as a kind of folk heritage. A writer, compiling a book of American folk songs, happened one day to be walking through the hills of Tennessee. Eagerly in search of new materials, he was excited to hear a woman's voice coming from a ramshackle home. She was singing one of the most appealing songs he had heard in his travels. Not recognizing it, he questioned her about it. "I learned it from my father," she told him, "and he learned it from his mother. But none of us ever learned to read a note of music!" Like our folk singer and her relatives, some individuals by-pass formal instruction and through a day-by-day exposure, or by sheer inventiveness, learn to sing or even to play an instrument.

Some musicians have reported unique musical experiences that appear not to have been influenced by or associated with any objective happenings in their environment. I remember having had such an experience at the age of seven. While sight-reading through a new book my teacher had given me, I discovered a piano arrangement of the *Serenade* by Schubert. The music touched me so deeply that I was actually moved to tears. On the following morning, I awakened with an uncontrollable urge to play my beloved *Serenade*. It was Sunday and my parents and three sisters were sleeping. I tiptoed down the stairs so as not to disturb them and began to play as quietly as I could. Once again, the beauty of the melody and harmonies was so overpowering that it made the tears stream down my cheeks. Awakened by the sound of the piano, my mother rushed downstairs, startled to find me weeping. As she comforted me, I told her, to her relief and delight, that the *Serenade* was the most beautiful piece I had ever heard.

We can easily account for our folk singer's ability to sing her song; after all, her father had sung it to her for the first fifteen years of her life. My experience, however, defies rational analysis. First of all, I had never heard music in my home, nor did I attend a concert until I was twelve (it was a piano recital by Rudolf Serkin). Moreover, I had never heard the Schubert *Serenade* before nor, in fact, had I ever heard of Schubert. Why, then, did the music seem so familiar to me?

Great thinkers have pondered such questions for centuries. Psychologists, philosophers, and neurologists have come up with impressive evidence and provocative theories concerning the origin of talent and the effects of music on behavior. Curiously, the least persuasive information on these subjects comes from musicians themselves. That musicians and scientists have not to this day unanimously accepted a single theory affirms dramatically the elusive nature of music. Nevertheless, several theories are extremely provocative and even inspiring. For example, Jung's theory of the Collective Unconscious captures, in my opinion, the essence of my childhood experience. Although Jung's theory has aroused considerable controversy among students of psychology, it adds greatly to those more generally accepted theories that refer behavior exclusively to the effects of experience or environmental influences. Whereas Freud and Adler formulated a "psychology of the person,"[22] Jung, on the other hand, conceived a "psychic system of a collective, univeral and *impersonal* nature [italics are mine] which is identical in all individuals. This collective unconscious does not develop individually but is inherited."[23] Jung further explains that these inherited characteristics not only determine how we will react to life's experiences but also determine the type of experience we might have. It is his opinion that the collective unconscious links us to a past that includes the entire evolutionary scale—namely, our ancestors as well as animals. Jung believed that a work of art has its source in "a sphere of unconscious mythology whose primordial images are the common heritage of mankind."[24] In describing the artistic experience, Jung said, "It is as though chords in us were struck that had never resounded before, or as though forces whose existence we never suspected were unloosed. . . . At such moments we are no longer individuals, but a race; the voice of all mankind resounds in us."[25] Was my own transported state at the age of seven a manifestation of these forces? Was the Schubert *Serenade* the catalyst that awakened a well-spring of inherited musical tendencies waiting to be released?

After years of research, science has now pinpointed the area of the brain—namely, the right side—where, it is believed, our musical talent resides. To corroborate this theory, a team of neurosurgeons performed autopsies on both musical and non-musical people. The results were truly startling: the brains of unusually gifted musicians clearly showed an enlarged right *planum temporale*. It was further concluded that this special development in the brain was present at birth, suggesting therefore that musicality is inborn and not simply "a matter of experience and practice." Thus, science had at last discovered a "structural counterpart [to talent] in the enlargement of the appropriate area of the temporal lobe."[26]

But even though an individual may be born with this highly developed area of the brain, such a potential remains dormant unless musicality, already programmed, finds its way to consciousness. And that, specifically, is the function of your teacher, your parents, or any knowledgeable person who can "lead out" your talent by educating you. For "educate" is, in fact, related to "lead out" (from Latin *e-duco*). A good teacher who has developed his own musical potential knows how to educate yours. He does this by actually practicing with you at your lessons, thereby revealing principles which you either grasp immediately or come to understand in your own time. The way in which you respond to your teacher's suggestions gives evidence of the musical potential that was already within you. Your teacher simply "educed" it. Your musical performance, therefore, not only reflects your capacity to feel, think, and express your musical convictions, but it also enables you to realize the potential with which nature has endowed you. Moreover, it establishes a link between you and your teacher—and, in fact, with all musicians who practice. You become a member of a family of achievers—all dedicated to the noble art of music. Since your teacher plays such a vital role in your development, he understandably occupies a special place in your hierarchy of relationships.

Still, the question of why one person succeeds over another hangs in the balance; that is, does success depend exclusively upon inherited potential, on educational influences, or, perhaps, on both? Plato had explicit views on this subject. Nowhere, it seems, has the significance of a master–pupil relationship been more vividly portrayed than in his *Meno*, one of the bright jewels among philosophical writings. In this dialogue, Socrates, the chief speaker, suggests to his friend, Meno, that "seeking and learning are in fact nothing but recollection." Thus, according to Socrates, the true function of teaching is to *awaken* knowledge and not to implant it. To demonstrate how the teacher helps a pupil to recover the knowledge that is already in his mind, Socrates summons one of

Meno's slaves, a young boy who is totally unschooled in mathematics. Through carefully phrased questions, Socrates then leads him to solve a mathematical problem—namely, how to square a square. The slave, though ignorant of the facts of mathematics, was shown by Socrates to have in his mind the capacity to grasp its principles. But it took Socrates' virtuosic handling of a pupil to prove that ignorance of a subject does not rule out the capacity to reason and finally to understand. My own experience in teaching bears this out. For over and over again I have discovered that pupils are far more gifted than they seem to be. The right question, the right kind of caring and, most important, the right challenge wrests from the student surprising responses, no matter what their age or experience, provided only that they listen carefully to verbal explanations and musical demonstrations. This is not to say that teaching alone can produce a Rubinstein, a Horowitz, or a Curzon. For, as Socrates' striking success with the uneducated slave indicates, the potential must be there waiting to be coaxed into consciousness.

I do not think, though, that my own childhood experience with the Schubert *Serenade* was attributable to my early training alone. It is more probable that factors in my environment, quite apart from my teacher's influence, set the stage for this event: I had access to a piano even before I was given lessons, and, most important, I grew up in an atmosphere of love. Although my parents and sisters were deeply interested in my progress, they somehow sensed that music was to be my exclusive province and that I would not brook any interference on their part. Thus, I was given the freedom to explore music on my own (which, as you will subsequently discover, is not always the most desirable course to follow). Sensing my need to be alone at the piano whenever I wished, my mother sympathetically and skillfully drew the activities in our home away from the room where I practiced. The luxury of solitude, the chance to experiment with musical sounds and even the right *not* to practice, were all gifts from my mother—gifts for which I shall always be grateful. In short, my mother created the conditions which enabled me to respond to Schubert's voice.

SUPERVISION

Yet, even when a talented person is exposed to favorable environmental conditions and to stimulating teaching, he may not be sufficiently disciplined or motivated to benefit from the one or the other. In other words, he may not have learned how to process such influences and convert them into personal gains. To be able to do this is, in fact, to know how to practice. We do know, however, that daily exposure to subjects in school (supervised education) compensates for a child's inability to study properly at home. Thus, children having low to average intelligence learn to read and write and multiply numbers. But think, if you will, what we are asking of an average child who takes piano lessons. Trying to unravel the complexities of one of the most challenging of disciplines, he is left to fend for himself with only one lesson per week. It is unreasonable, then, to expect him to practice efficiently—no matter what his gifts. For these reasons, I strongly recommend supervised practicing until that time when a child learns to concentrate on his own. Unfortunately, the disturbing psychological overtones existing between some parents and their children have placed a stigma on any kind of supervision. Whether or not this is warranted, the fact remains that parental supervision should in any case be subject to the watchful eye of the teacher. In many instances, it would be far better to forfeit a child's musical progress than to have his practicing force-fed at the hands of a neurotic parent. But it may just as often happen that such supervision can assist a relationship between a parent and child, establishing a bond between them that goes beyond the practice sessions. Whether supervision is done by a parent, another adult, or even a teenager appointed by the teacher, it can offer immeasurable help to practicers of all ages. As we have seen, the secret of productive practicing is to listen to yourself objectively; to compare the sounds of your instrument with your own musical concept. Being too young or inexperienced to do this alone, a student must then rely upon another person who will listen for him until he is able to listen to himself. As a symbol of emulation, the supervisor becomes the idealized image of the student's best self. Functioning for the musician as Homer did for the poet, the supervisor sits beside the student and symbolizes the correct way to listen.

TUNING IN AND OUT

Have you ever stopped for a moment to listen to the world around you? The city, the country—each is filled with its own sounds. Wherever you happen to be, take a paper and pencil and jot down everything you hear. You will be astonished to note the variety of sounds that fill an average day: there is the sound of a car, footsteps, a creaking board, all the sounds of nature—even your own breath. Music, too, appears to be everywhere—in elevators, restaurants, airports, hospitals. This kind of music, though it intrudes on our privacy, hardly ever demands our attention, primarily because it remains on the same dynamic level and circles around predictable harmonies. In other words, it is most noticeable for its lack of novelty and originality. In fact, such music seems to be designed specifically to lull us into unconsciousness. We may also be unaware of background music for films, even though such music is often of a high order. On the rare occasions when I attend a good film, I become so engrossed in the plot that I do not consciously hear the music at all. My reaction may in fact be a tribute to the composer; for when a musical background is skillfully composed, it is completely synthesized with the film into a combined art form.

All of these background sounds, musical and otherwise, may somehow have escaped your notice. But when you practice, nothing must escape you. For if your practicing is to be productive, you must be aware of every sound you produce. Moreover, you can train yourself to listen *inwardly* to sounds which originate in your mind's ear. Tuning in to them, so to speak, enables you to improvise and, eventually, to compose. All of this, of course, demands the greatest concentration possible. But when simple environmental sounds intrude on your practicing, it is a sign that you are not concentrating properly. You should not be defeated by this, however; rather, concentrate on the distraction itself and try to identify the sounds that have interrupted your practicing. Then, challenge yourself once again to see how effectively you can switch off those sounds by directing your attention back to the music. It may be, however, that your inability to listen properly is a sign of fatigue. After all, everyone's span of concentration is different—you may simply have been working too long. In that case, listen to the environment for a while and relax in its presence. You may also try to focus your attention on something quite different, such as a good book, a conversation with a friend, or a visual stimulus. Or, try simply to lose yourself in your imagination. When you finally return to your practicing, rest assured that environmental distractions will no longer interfere with your concentration. When you develop the technique of tuning in and out, you will exert a conscious control over your ability to listen.

A MUSICIAN LISTENS

Our parents and teachers have always taught us to think before speaking. Taken literally, this means that you should comtemplate what you are going to say before you speak aloud, the purpose being to consider the effect your words will have on others. In practicing, it is also necessary to listen before you play. Unless you do this, you will not be able to articulate your musical concept with any degree of predictability or conviction. This is not to be confused with an earlier suggestion in Chapter 3 that is applicable to your first encounter with a piece. In that case, you were advised to read a piece through from the beginning to the end *without* preconceptions so that you could sense the emotional content of the work as a whole. But once you have done this, you are ready to analyze everything—structure, sound, phrasing, rhythm, fingering, pedaling. Nothing must escape your attention. You will preserve your initial spontaneity if, from time to time, you play the piece through in its entirety. In this way, all the details will relate to the whole composition. Listening to details in relation to the whole is like reducing a musical universe into its parts. A photographer keeps this technique in mind when he works with a zoom lens. While zooming in on a detail, he retains in his mind an image of his subject as a whole. Just as a camera records permanently everything that it sees, your memory too, can be trained to absorb the innumerable details of a musical composition. You may then recall all or any part of this information whenever you wish.

To listen properly during your practicing is an art and, like all arts, it presents you with various choices. For example, some musicians often ponder the interpretation of a musical phrase in terms of dynamics. Yet, it is surprising how often others will instinctively arrive at the same conclusions. They will all agree that a phrase must go to this or to that note. "But how do you know this?" you may ask. "The music tells you so," is the only reply you will receive. Such a response acknowledges the existence of a logic in music—a logic to which musicians respond. Although their interpretations may vary considerably in respect to details, musicians' responses to the overall stresses and relaxations within the phrase are strikingly similar. It is much the same when we speak our native language. Most people will intuitively emphasize the same word in a given sentence. If you tell someone, "The meadow is brimming over with clover," your voice will rise to its highest pitch and loudest dynamic on the word "brimming." Why is this? The meaning of the sentence determined your choice, just as the meaning of a musical phrase determines that of the musician.

There is an intrinsic feeling within a musical phrase that has a mysterious element all its own which seems to transcend what we have come to accept as theoretical rules concerning musical interpretation. For example, an analytical musician will usually stress down-beats and also make a crescendo to a high note. Yet, the most poetic playing occurs when down-beats are softer and high notes are approached by a diminuendo. In language, too, the laws of natural word accent require us to speak certain words louder than others. To return to the sentence, "The meadow is brimming over with clover," the word "clover" should, theoretically, be the accented word. But the poetic image of the line would justify the placing of a stress on the word "brimming." This deviation from the rules of natural word accent is not unlike the avoidance of a stress on a down-beat in a measure of music. Such stress on a *directional* word requires the adjustment of dynamics on all the other words in a sentence; the same applies to the interpretation of a musical phrase. Your choice of dynamics—even for a single note—is governed by this principle. And since music is a sequential art—that is, it comes to you one note at a time—each tone functions in a specific way, fulfilling its part of the whole concept. Therefore, it is futile to contemplate the dynamic of a single tone without listening to the phrase of which it is a part. Just as you modulate your speaking voice to convey feeling, as a musician you must also consciously arrive at a specific dynamic for every note you play. Otherwise, you cannot convey your musical feelings to another person. The following experiment will lead you, step by step, to a predictable performance of a single tone:

1. Sit at the piano with your hands resting in your lap. Breathe deeply.
2. Imagine the sound of the first phrase.
3. Listen inwardly to the first note of this phrase in terms of its exact dynamic and quality of sound.
4. As you conceptualize it, be aware of your feeling.
5. Your feeling expresses itself in a muscular sensation.
6. Your finger, wrist, arm, and entire body should be imbued with the feeling of the note you are about to play.
7. Your muscles must be in a condition of natural tension in order to express this note.

8. As your arm rises, your finger becomes imbued with the sound you have imagined. In this sense, *the sound has already been assimilated by your finger.*
9. Take a deep breath; then, while exhaling, sound the note.
10. Listen to the sound and enjoy the realization of your musical concept.

If, by chance, the sound did not match your image, you may have overlooked one or more of the following requirements:

1. You must have a clear image of the dynamic *before* you play the note.
2. You must consciously feel the dynamic.
3. You must balance your mental image with your feeling by being neither too analytical nor too emotional.
4. Allow your feeling to express itself in natural body movements and sensations. Don't inhibit them.
5. Your physical co-ordination must be sufficiently developed to adapt to your feeling and perception. Only adequate and consistent practicing can make this possible.

In short, playing the first note of a piece is, in reality, a transference of an image that was preconceived in your mind's ear. As Wanda Landowska said: "One has to concentrate and be entirely ready so that when the first note is struck, it comes as a sort of continuation of a soliloquy already begun."[27]

As your body responds naturally to musical feeling, another part of you must remain objective and observe the whole process in a detached way. You should notice, for example, that your upper torso swings toward the keyboard as you approach a climax and that your sternum and forehead tend to rise as you progress to a soft note. It is extremely important that you observe all such natural movements during your practicing. When your feelings become blocked, whether because of nervousness or fatigue, you can induce your most expressive playing by consciously reproducing those movements that had accompanied your spontaneous feeling. Sir Clifford Curzon relates a striking incident that illustrates this point. Quite early in his career, he turned pages for Dame Myra Hess during a performance of a Bach *Concerto.* Suddenly, he noticed the words written above a certain passage, "Look up!" Thinking that this might be a sign of some sort for himself, he looked toward Dame Myra in time to see her *actually look up* "at a particularly exalted moment in the music, just as the saints in so many great paintings look up in ecstasy." It is probable that during a very successful performance of this work, Dame Myra noticed how well that particular passage went and ascribed it partly to the fact that she looked up. And once she became aware that this physical gesture seemed quite naturally to reflect her musical feeling, she was thereafter able to reproduce that very feeling simply by looking up consciously.

ACTIVATING YOUR VOCAL CORDS

When you listen inwardly to the sound of a musical idea *before* you play, what kind of sound do you actually imagine? For instance, do you hear the phrase being played on an instrument? And if so, who is doing the playing, you or another pianist? It is a curious question—one that has not received the attention it deserves. Yet, its answer will shed light on an important aspect of your practicing. In my own case, I experience all piano playing in my *vocal cords,* and, as I have discovered, so do many other pianists. Once reminded of this vocal response, they invariably say, "That's it! Of course! That is exactly what I experience." This may explain why so many performers grunt and moan when they play. After all, since musical expression began with the human voice, singing offers the most natural means for communicating musical feeling. When J. S. Bach wrote on the title page of his *Two- and Three-Part Inventions* the instruction: "To achieve a *cantabile* style of playing," he used the singing voice as a criterion for musical expression. Therefore, when you imagine a musical phrase before playing it, sing it to yourself and be aware of the sensation in your throat. You will want to exhale as though you were about to sing aloud. Your throat becomes alive with sensations and the sound that emanates from your instrument seems to have originated in your vocal cords. I am sure I came upon the "kuh-kuhing" (discussed in Chapter 5) through this vocal awareness. A word of caution, however: there is no need to resort to banshee wails and owl hoots! The only sound you should hear is that of your own breathing— and this should be barely audible.

LISTENING TO OTHERS

One day, I was giving a lesson to a pupil on the Schumann *Phantasie in C major.* At one point, I sat at the piano to demonstrate a musical idea. But long before I reached the measures in question, my pupil suddenly exclaimed, "I don't agree!" Such interruptions were habitual with her, but this time I lost my patience: "Obviously, you have no interest in listening to anyone but yourself. I am in no way criticizing your musical sensibilities or challenging your right to have an opinion; rather, I object to your denying *me* the right to an opinion. By your mindlessness, you cheated yourself out of a musical idea and robbed me of the pleasure of sharing it with you." Evidently, my outburst had an effect on her, for she never again behaved in that way. Indifference to the opinions of others is a fault that can also show itself in the way a musician interprets markings in his music. For example, he may play a chord forte when it is marked piano simply because he happens "to like it that way." Although a musician may have a strong conviction about a musical interpretation (in fact, the more gifted you are, the stronger your convictions tend to be), still, his first obligation is to the composer. He demonstrates this by adhering strictly to the printed score (unless, of course, it contains an obvious error). But if, as frequently happens, the composer's intentions are not sufficiently accounted for in the score, your obligation then is to explore alternative interpretations, especially when they are presented by the teacher whose ideas you presumably trust.

The disciplines and skills gained after years of processing musical information prepare you to assimilate stimuli of various sorts—especially those intimate feelings which a friend may wish to share with you. He would, in fact, have good cause for singling you out. If he reasons that the heightened sensitivity with which you listen to music eminently qualifies you to listen to him, he could conclude that a person who can lavish such attention on a single note of music can just as readily lavish attention on him. For your friend to recognize your sensitivity by daring to reveal his intimate self to you is to pay you a tribute of the highest kind. And you, in turn, could not but give back to your friend the same care you bring to your practicing and the same compassion wrought from your deepest musical feelings.

THE AUDIENCE LISTENS

A performer who wishes to communicate to an audience prepares himself by practicing in all the ways thus far discussed. He appears on stage and acknowledges the applause. As he sits at his instrument, he is aware of his audience waiting expectantly for the sound of the first note. But to whom does he project that sound? Does the performer imagine the audience to be a collective listener or does he in fact project his performance to one person? Artur Rubinstein, for example, chooses the latter approach. By his own admission, he singles out an attractive woman to whom he projects the entire recital. The audience, unaware of this, is struck only by the warmth and intimacy of his playing—an intimacy they interpret as being meant for them collectively. Another type of performer, however, inspires a different kind of listening. Far from consciously projecting to his audience, he actually continues the same soliloquy in which he was engaged at home. The audience serves merely to heighten his private experience, one in which he communes with the music and with himself. Thus, on the one hand, a performer uses his natural tendency for extraversion to project his playing either to a single individual or to the audience collectively; on the other, a performer's communion with himself, reflective of his natural tendency for introversion, draws the audience into the music. Interestingly, both types of performers succeed in establishing an intense rapport between themselves and their audiences, despite the striking differences in their approach. The fact that you, the listener, can respond to both not only testifies to your own potential for feeling, but also to the validity of either type of projection.

By training his responsive powers to music, a performer may shift from one emotion to another, either between pieces or even within the same piece. But, above all, his desire to communicate these emotions should derive from the music itself rather than from a need for an audience's response. As I see it, a performer who sets out to "wow" his audience is exhibiting a tendency that is demeaning to them and to the music. To use music as a means of arousing surface emotions is to admit that the performer and the audience alike are incapable of a deeper and more aesthetic reaction. Paradoxically, though, a performer whose sole intent is to share his comprehension of music with others ends up indeed "wowing" his audience. Then, too, even when a performance fluctuates, at one moment conveying the essence of musical thought and at another that of superficiality, the response of some listeners may nonetheless be the same. The extent to which you, a member of that audience, can discriminate between these subtle variations indicates the breadth of your own talent—a talent that can be nourished through your participation as both listener and performer. It is the interaction between the two that promotes the integration of all your artistic faculties, one which, as we have suggested, can influence your personal development as well.

ABSOLUTE PITCH

A boy of six stands with his back to the piano. You are asked to play clusters of notes for him anywhere you wish on the keyboard. Instantly, the boy names each note in whatever order you ask of him. Obviously, he has absolute pitch. Since he is born with it, he deserves no more credit for identifying pitches than you do for distinguishing green from red. The boy, of course, had to learn the names of notes just as you, at one point in your life, had to learn the names of colors. But his innate ability to correlate certain vibrational frequencies with particular pitches was already permanently fixed. If you have absolute pitch, or perfect pitch as it is sometimes called, you are approximately one in a thousand. It is an attribute that most people find hard to imagine, much less understand. Curiously enough, though, there are nonmusicians who have absolute pitch without being aware of it themselves. Thus, it is not uncommon for an individual who has never had musical training suddenly to whistle a theme in the exact key in which he originally heard it. There are musicians with absolute pitch who, though they are fully aware of their gift, fail to use it to best advantage. Yet, like all natural gifts, it can be harnessed to simplify a musician's task. For one thing, it adds to one's security when performing from memory. It also facilitates composing away from the piano. Nevertheless, many musicians function perfectly in these two areas even though they are without absolute pitch. In fact, many musicians possessing absolute pitch suffer as many memory slips as those without it simply because they rely on this natural ability to the exclusion of intellectual comprehension of the music. In short, a secure memory depends on much more than a highly developed sense of pitch in that it calls for a synthesis of the ear and the mind whereby the one reinforces the other. The ear, working in harmonious collaboration with the intellect, will not only support the memory but will also contribute to a convincing performance.

Whether or not absolute pitch is inherited or acquired through training is still an unresolved question. When a thousand musicians were tested, it was discovered that among those who began musical training before the age of four, as many as 95 percent possessed absolute pitch. Among those who were trained after the age of twelve, only 5 percent were found to possess it.²⁸ There is just as much evidence to suggest that it is inherited. The late dramatic soprano Kirsten Flagstad, who had absolute pitch, reported that it was in her family for three generations. Whether inherited or acquired, the type and accuracy of pitch identification varies widely. Some musicians have an acute sensitivity for all pitches, while others can respond *absolutely* to only a limited number of pitches. Some musicians seem to possess absolute pitch for only one instrument; others can name pitches singly or in combination only when they are played, but cannot sing a particular pitch upon request. This also works in reverse. A musician may be able to sing any pitch, but may not have the ability to name pitches when they are played by instruments.

Some performers who possess absolute pitch are able to learn a new composition en route to a concert and, with a few try-outs, perform it from memory. Such accomplishments, however, do not belong exclusively to musicians with absolute pitch. There are resources that trained musicians, like performing actors, know how to draw upon. Suppose that you have a gift for reciting poetry. You are engaged to do a recitation for a literary group in Washington, D.C. Just before boarding the train in Boston, a poet hands you one of his works which he feels would be suitable for the occasion. The train pulls away and you settle down to study the poem. Since you are a performer, you can imagine exactly how you would recite every word, every phrase. Using the various techniques of your profession, you convert each sentiment into articulations of the tongue, lips, and jaw. Every muscle in your body plays a part in expressing the sounds and pauses. Your eyes, too, take on the expression implicit in the poem. The words, the feeling, the technique of projection—all are practiced and memorized. You arrive in Washington, take a taxi to the meeting place, and recite the new poem perfectly. Such feats are not uncommon among musicians—even those without absolute pitch. A musician with trained ears knows the language of music as intimately as a poet or actor knows his native tongue. A phrase to a musician is thus a total experience; he not only hears it, but he can also feel it in his muscles. It is primarily a question of refining and developing the sense of pitch you do have and tapping your powers of concentration.

RELATIVE PITCH

But what if you are not able to learn a piece en route to a concert? And suppose that you are unable to name a cluster with your back turned to the piano? Should you regard yourself as less of a musician for this reason? Hardly. As a fact, solfege experts have proved that sensitivity to pitch can be developed to a surprising extent. All that is required is patience and a desire to improve. Moreover, any musician who has trained his relative pitch can learn scores just as quickly as the "absoluters." Despite this, some musicians continue to view the absence of absolute pitch as a serious detriment to their growth. The assets of absolute pitch are, of course, not to be denied, but the notion that it is essential has no basis in fact, as history has proved. Schumann and Wagner, for example, did not have absolute pitch, nor do many of our present-day composers and instrumentalists. This is not to suggest that a composer such as Schumann did not have good relative pitch; in fact, it is probable that his perception of pitch was refined to the point that it matched or even surpassed the absoluters. In any case, there can be no disputing the fact that Schumann managed to write some of the world's greatest music without having absolute pitch. Why, then, should musicians envy those with absolute pitch when so much has been accomplished and can be accomplished without it? Besides, who enjoys a bird call more—someone who knows that a meadowlark shifted from B♭ to E natural, or someone who feels the beauty of his song? While absolute pitch does not necessarily prevent an emotional response to the song of a bird—or any music, for that matter—it can, nevertheless, lead some individuals to neglect their capacity to feel by tempting them to exploit their gift for the sheer pleasure of it, just as some instrumentalists do with their natural technique.

A poorly trained ear, like a faulty technique, hampers your ability to express yourself. It is necessary, therefore, to acquire a good sense of *relative* pitch. This enables you to distinguish any tone from a given tone by relying on a sensitivity to intervallic relationships. In its most refined form, your perfected sense of relative pitch will permit you to write down whatever you hear in your mind's ear without relying on an instrument. Here are some ways to acquire it:

1. Take a course in solfege and dictation. Apply solfege to simple

instrumental compositions, concentrating on one voice at a time. To supplant solfege and dictation books, most of which are dull beyond description, sing together with a friend and take turns dictating to one another.

2. Choose some musical themes that appeal to you and try to play them by ear on the piano. If necessary, use the "hunt and peck" system. Now try to transpose these themes into other keys. Try to pick out the melody and harmonies of other tunes that occur to you and experiment playing them by ear.

3. Purchase a tuning fork pitched at A-440.[29] Carry it with you during the day and place it by your bed at night. When you awaken in the morning, strike it and sing "la" along with it. Do this throughout the day at least twenty times. Occasionally, try to sing A before striking the fork. As you will discover, a pitch, like notes and words, can be memorized. When you have learned to sing A without the tuning fork, you can then find all other pitches by using A as your reference point.

Let us now view all of this objectively. If you wish to feel secure when playing from memory, you must develop your relative pitch to the extent that you can pick out melodies divorced from the context of the piece in which they appear. For this purpose, the ability to remember the sound of A is a mere convenience, one that Handel himself did not enjoy, for he always carried around a pitch pipe in his pocket. The importance of knowing A is that it gives you a reference point from which you can judge other pitches. But a sensitive ear does not stop at the mere naming of pitches. Rather, a properly focused ear not only triggers musical sensitivity, it also initiates the correct physical responses to all that you hear and feel. In light of this, your sense of hearing is one of your most prized possessions.

7 You and the Piano

INTRODUCTION

There have been a great number of books written on the physical aspects of piano playing, all of them dealing with a host of familiar technical problems. It is unnecessary, therefore, to repeat what has already been stated so excellently by other musicians. Instead, this chapter will stress what I believe to be key issues—issues that, when properly understood, will assure your physical comfort at the keyboard. The subject matter and the experiments will, I am sure, have an immediate appeal, for they are both musically and biologically sound. Moreover, I am convinced that practicing them will lead you toward the ultimate achievement—that of making a physical connection to your musical feelings. Also, I will challenge the entire relaxation theory which I believe has hindered the progress of many practicers. After all, practicing is far too important an occupation to be endangered by the pursuit of futile goals.

What follows represents a lifetime of searching for that gesture, that sensation that would alleviate my own physical discomfort at the keyboard. For the most part, my labors have yielded rewards beyond my expectations. Far from feeling satisfied, however, I begin each day questioning and experimenting in a never ending search for what is comfortable in piano playing. Through all of this, I have arrived at some very important conclusions. Although I could demonstrate in a moment what it may take pages to explain, I trust, nevertheless, that the ideas set forth in this chapter will serve as companions during your practicing. Either they will stimulate you to find a fresh approach to whatever problems you may have or they will arouse your resistance, thereby causing you to clarify your own convictions. Be assured, though, that everything discussed in this chapter has been of inestimable help to me and to my pupils. It is natural, then, that I should want to share this information with you.

ARM WEIGHT

When I was sixteen, I heard a great deal about arm weight, but I was perplexed as to its meaning. Although I read several books dealing with it, its real significance continued to remain a mystery. Even my teachers seemed at a loss to explain it fully. Necessity being the mother of invention, I finally reasoned that the only way I could understand this principle was literally to simulate a sensation of arm weight. My father, who sold metal and used machinery, furnished me with the supplies necessary for my experiment—a mound of small, steel balls approximately 3/4 of an inch in diameter. I sewed two pieces of leather around a group of the steel balls and fastened wrist bands to their ends. I then tied them around each wrist and began to practice. The results were startling. I suddenly heard myself playing with a rich and resonant tone. Inducing a feeling of pressure, the weights forced me to rest in the key beds. I had no choice then but to transfer this pressure from finger to finger. Since the weights pulled my arm downward, I instinctively counterbalanced this pull, thus engaging muscles in my arms and fingers that I had never used before. This enabled me to lower each key a little more slowly—a technique necessary for controlling sound. All of this caused my fingers to grow stronger and my arms and wrists more flexible. Once having benefited from my arm weight invention, I was able to simulate the same sensation without it.

Then one day a few years later, Katya Delakova, my physical movement teacher, asked our class to purchase *Tone-O-Matic* weights (this being their brand name) and attach them alternately to our ankles and wrists for certain exercises prescribed by her. You can purchase these weights in athletic supply stores or in health food stores. Those weighing three pounds each are sufficient for an adult, while one-pound weights are suitable for a young student. They are conveniently designed to fasten around the wrists by means of magnetic grips. As I began to practice my exercises at home, I was reminded instantly of my old experiment at the piano. What had been an interesting experience years before now became a revelation. That same day, I eagerly fastened the weights to the wrists of my first pupil. Amazed at the depth of sound that emanated from the piano, he exclaimed, "I can hardly believe it! I sound like Rubinstein!" He then added, "Maybe I should sew some weights into the cuffs of my jacket!" Try them for yourself and you will agree that they unquestionably simulate the feeling of controlled arm weight. In the beginning, do not practice with them for more than five minutes at a time. As your muscles adjust to them, however, you can increase the time proportionately. Play slowly at first and do not try to play too loudly. Build up your endurance gradually.

One of the most pleasurable sensations afforded by the weights comes from hooking the first joint of each finger in turn on the tips of a white key. Hang there with the weights pulling you down, and feel the pressure on your finger pads. Roll your arm around luxuriously and feel your arm weight centered on these pads. Choose a passage from one of your pieces—one for the right hand and one for the left—and transfer this pressure from finger to finger. Removing the weights will then make you feel supple and light so that you will want to soar through the most difficult passages in your repertory.

THE RELAXATION MYTH

Tobias Matthay, one of England's foremost piano pedagogues, wrote extensively on relaxation and the natural weight of the arm from the shoulder to the fingertips ("dead" weight). Never admitting at all to the necessity for controlled tension in piano playing, his exaggerated views on relaxation (he even used the phrase "The Gospel of Relaxation") did, nevertheless, help many pianists whose training had been influenced by the rigid methods of the late nineteenth and early twentieth centuries. What he was not guilty of, however, was advocating the uncontrolled drop of the arm onto the keyboard. Still, many teachers absorbed this very approach into their teaching, dutifully ascribing the results to the "Matthay Method." Outraged at having his theories misrepresented by other teachers, Matthay finally issued the following statement: "The arm is never dropped onto the keyboard except by fools!" Evidently even this did not stop the "arm droppers," for I witnessed an example of this faulty approach only a few years ago during a master class held at a famous New York conservatory. To my dismay, a world-renowned teacher actually lifted her pupil's arm at least a foot in the air, waved it around loosely, and then dropped it onto the keys—"ka-plunk." (What would Matthay have said!) All of this was an attempt to relax the pupil's arm for the opening chords of the Tchaikowsky *Concerto in B flat minor.* Paradoxically, this teacher, an accomplished pianist herself, demonstrated the passage by staying close to the keys and swinging her arms forward and backward for each chord. Having mistakenly interpreted her own comfort at the keyboard as a state of total relaxation, she advocated for her pupil's benefit, therefore, a limp, "dead-weight" approach. Obviously, this teacher had no idea that she herself was playing with *controlled tension.*

NATURAL AND CONTROLLED TENSION

If you wish to learn to control tension at the piano, you must first recognize the sensation resulting from contracted muscles. A simple way to begin is to lie on the floor and attempt to release as much body tension as possible. This is more easily said than done, for you may not even be aware that certain muscles are contracting involuntarily. It would be better, then, to induce tension consciously and, in fact, to *fight tension with tension.* Start with your right leg; tighten your lower leg muscle and relax it. By tightening a muscle you become aware of your control over it. Once you induce contraction in a muscle, you will be able to relax it consciously. Now tighten and relax muscles in other parts of your body—your arms, neck, back, for example. This is a simple way to gain conscious control over numerous muscles in your body.

In observing an athlete's ease of execution in his particular field, it is often difficult to distinguish between tension and relaxation. Far from being relaxed, the athlete has worked out a sophisticated system of controlled tension—no less sophisticated than that used by someone who has mastered his instrument. Through practicing, an athlete learns to contract his muscles in proportion to effort expended—no more and no less. In other words, he knows that it is counterproductive to work harder than his task requires. Similarly, every activity in life demands a certain degree of muscular contraction. Obviously, some activities require more than others. Even the act of breathing while you sleep involves a sequence of tensions and relaxations. Needless to say, each act at the piano also requires contractions of innumerable muscles throughout your body. To know how much contraction is needed is to learn the most important lesson of all—*economy of motion.*

Without economy of motion (resulting from economy of effort) no activity in life can be performed efficiently. Let us suppose that you wish to lift a heavy suitcase. You say to yourself, "Go easy there. Better relax your muscles. Don't strain yourself." You bend down with a supple back and relaxed abdominal muscles. *Result:* The suitcase stays where it is and you have initiated your first bout with back trouble. *Analysis:* You did not contract your muscles sufficiently. Undaunted, you try again. You reason that the suitcase is heavier than you thought. You decide, therefore, to brace yourself in advance. You consciously increase your body tension in preparation for this herculean task. You bend down with effort and lift the suitcase with ease. *Result:* The following morning, you ache from head to toe. *Analysis:* You overcontracted your muscles.

Suppose that you wish to practice a piece filled with loud chords and octaves. You want to conserve your energy and make a full, resonant sound without banging. The very thought of loudness, however, causes your muscles to contract involuntarily and you feel the tension spreading through your body. You won't have it! Instead, you make a valiant effort to relax your body and fight tension. At this point, we come to the crux of the problem and, by so doing, closer to the secret of how to control energy. By the time you are compelled to fight tension, it is too late. Let us focus then on why all that excess tension was there to begin with. In playing a difficult passage on the piano, excess tension (involuntary tension) will accumulate as a compensation for a lack of muscular strength—a strength that ought to have been consciously organized in advance of the difficulty. Excess tension sabotages effort; *organized tension* facilitates effort. In other words, organization is a plus factor. By consciously *adding* the required degree of tension, ease of execution is assured.

The act of living is itself a process of addition. That is, every experience in life adds something to what you already know. This principle is manifested in nature, too, although it is often difficult to interpret its signs. When fall comes, for instance, the leaves on a tree wither and die, but the tree continues to live and to go forward in its own life process. When spring comes, you realize that what appeared to be death was only a transition toward a re-awakening. Such transitions, like rests in music, are periods of expectancy.

New concepts, new inspirations, and new revelations thus often appear after silences and periods of inactivity. Moving forward enables you to discover them and through this discovery you experience joy. Yet, joy in its turn may induce muscular spasms throughout your body. Does that mean you should then relax and inhibit your joy? I am sure you will agree that you should neither inhibit your joy nor be overly concerned with the natural muscular tension it induces. In fact, all such emotions—joy, passion, sadness, tenderness—are accompanied by specific tensions in various parts of your body. Since these very emotions are portrayed in music, it is necessary to become aware of the physical sensations that accompany them. When the proper degree of tension does *not* occur naturally during your playing, you must consciously induce the muscular contraction necessary to express the emotion portrayed in the music. Joy, as we mentioned, causes a natural contraction of muscles thoughout the body. Similarly, every emotion in music should automatically trigger a corresponding muscular response—one that is as natural as it is spontaneous. Through your awareness of this natural tension and your ability to control it consciously, you will have created a backup system which all performers need at one time or another.

Muscular tension must never be confused with emotional tension. The latter derives from psychological confusion. However, natural muscular tension is in itself a result of opposing forces— that of strength versus relaxation. In life, we learn to balance opposing forces in our nature just as an athlete and a musician learn to mobilize tension and make it work for them. Opposing forces of a certain kind create conflicts which, most psychologists agree, are necessary to the development of our personalities. Other types of conflict can be ruinous to our well-being, just as certain tensions are destructive to our playing. The wrong kind of emotion, for example, will cause the wrong kind of tension. It is necessary, then, to experiment and analyze—in short, to practice—until (1) you define the right kind of emotion you desire to express in each phrase that you play; and (2) you discover the corresponding physical sensation for that emotion. Eventually, your body will assume attitudes of natural tension, giving you the ability to control whatever sound you choose to produce. Nothing should escape your awareness as this entire process unfolds during your practicing. In time, you will learn to welcome natural tension and wholesome conflict as necessary functions in your development. Without them, you can neither develop your personality nor create works of art.

Above all, tension and firmness must not be confused with stiffness, the latter being an exaggerated contraction of your muscles over which you have no control. Rather, the kind of tension I am suggesting is fully controllable, for it is a biological response to a resistance. However, should this response (for our purposes, muscular contraction) not occur naturally, we must then consciously induce it or on occasion even minimize it. Consider, then, the amount of energy required to depress a piano key. If you try to do it with a limp string, nothing, of course, will happen. Since the key offers a resistance, your finger and arm must be strong enough to engage it. To overstep the demands of resistance, however, is to court stiffness.

EXPERIENCING NATURAL TENSION

In conditioning your body to function at an optimum level of efficiency, you must first discover how natural tension converts feeling into action. You may begin by trying the following experiment:

1. Set your metronome at 60, duplicating the second hand of your watch.
2. Sit in a chair, or at the piano, with four albums of music within reach.
3. With your left hand, grasp one album and place it on the palm of your right hand. Balance it for eight ticks.
4. On the ninth tick, place the second album over the first.
5. Continue adding one album at a time every eight ticks until you have used up all four.
6. Now reverse the process, *removing* one album every eight ticks until you are left with one.
7. Repeat the entire sequence once again, this time, however, paying attention to the increase and decrease in tension (muscular contraction) in your right hand and arm. The degree of tension will coincide with the weight of the albums.

This simple exercise demonstrates the muscular counterpart of dynamics at the piano. The natural tension needed to hold up one album is equivalent to playing piano; two albums are equal to mezzo-piano; three albums, mezzo-forte; and finally, four albums, forte. To apply this experiment to your playing, find various sections in your pieces that either remain on the same dynamic level or swell and diminish in intensity. In discovering a physical counterpart to these dynamics, you will recognize the same tensions and relaxations experienced in the experiment with the albums. The louder you play, the greater the tension; the softer you play, the less tension you need. Be aware, though, that even one album requires a degree of tension. Similarly, playing softly requires some degree of firmness and stability. Being aware of muscular sensations enables you to generate the exact amount of tension needed for each musical feeling. With practice, you can train your muscles to do this naturally. In other words, it is possible for your entire body to respond instantaneously to the ebb and flow of the music.

HOW MUCH TENSION

As you have seen, every activity in life, whether it is playing the piano or carrying a bag of groceries home from the store, requires a certain degree of tension. We have discussed the futility of attempting to relax when a task demands your exertion; by the time you do this, uncontrollable tension may exceed the optimum required for the task. This will be your indication that you are not estimating properly what it is you are about to do. In short, a heavy bag of groceries requires your strength. Relaxing will only confuse the issue; instead, flex your muscles for the task.

A supercharged emotional attitude may also trigger the wrong kind of tension. If, for example, you are going to play a loud, passionate piece, you may allow your emotions to overcome your objectivity and thereby lose control of your physical responses. In other words, in being carried away by the emotional intensity of the music, you may become stiff and end up banging. Conversely, playing tenderly may cause you to abandon all tension; your sound may become too soft or disappear entirely. In playing an instrument, you must make every sound audible. Thus, it is necessary to generate sufficient energy to lift the hammers toward the strings with adequate speed. All of this may be reduced to two simple guidelines: (1) loud, passionate playing tends to make you too tense;

therefore, minimize your muscular contraction; and (2) soft, tender playing tends to make you too relaxed; you must, therefore, increase your muscular tension. You must learn to make the necessary adjustments in accordance with your own natural tendencies.

It is as important to balance tension and relaxation as it is to balance thinking and feeling. Too much tension makes you nervous and aggressive; too little tension makes you ineffectual. Only natural tension enables you to function convincingly and economically. Quite apart from musical considerations, many people constantly seek remedies for the tensions of everyday life—tranquilizers, sleeping pills, drugs—all providing the means for escaping conflict rather than assistance for mastering and resolving it. But practicing actually teaches you to meet difficulties head-on and to convert them into assets. The delicate balance required for synthesizing your thoughts, feelings, and muscular responses sets a standard for overcoming difficulties in everyday life. Consider, for example, all that is required of you in beginning a loud, passionate piece. As we have seen, your tendency may be to flood yourself, and subsequently your instrument, with more energy than is needed. Tension controls you. To counteract this tendency, imagine that you are imposing sound upon silence. You will see that you do not have to play as loudly as you thought. Besides, loudness is not just an intensity of sound but rather a specific feeling—a feeling that grows out of silence and emerges from your instrument. The motions needed for expressing loudness show themselves in curves of energy rather than in abrupt and angular configurations. Loudness thus surges through you, reaching a peak of intensity at the moment the hammers strike the strings. To blow out a candle, for example, your breath must increase to the point of extinguishing the flame. Your eyes tell you whether or not your breath was strong enough. If the flame still flickers, you then increase the force of your breath. To make a musical sound of the desired loudness, you must gauge the intensity with your ears. It is important to have a clear idea of the loudness you want before you begin a piece, for this will prevent you from flooding your emotions and muscles with more energy than is needed.

Playing softly requires as much control as playing loudly. Analogous to whispering, it is a very intense activity. Just as a whisper is energized by the contractions of your abdominal muscles, so, too, playing softly involves a certain amount of tension, needed for firm support in the bridge of the hand. In neither of these activities are you ever at a zero level of energy. Even the act of holding up your arms to the piano requires energy for muscular contraction. In short, natural tension arising from the proper expenditure of energy affects everything you do—whether playing loud or soft or holding a cup or pencil. Nothing can be accomplished without it. Natural tensions result from necessary contractions of muscles and, as such, not only can enhance your playing, but also enable you to perform all activities with grace and efficiency.

MY ARM IS FALLING OFF!

I once played the *Wanderer Fantasy* by Schubert for the late Alexander Brailowsky with whom I studied for many years. Those who play it will agree that it has one of the most taxing finales in the entire repertory. History has it that even Schubert succumbed to its difficulties, for when he performed it for the first time, he suddenly threw up his hands in despair and exclaimed, "Only the devil should play this piece." For me, such historical evidence came after the fact, for a cautious tempo was my own admission that it is a hazardous piece. Brailowsky, however,.had his own notion of the tempo. After the opening measures, he cried, "Faster!" I went faster. But suddenly I felt my arm muscles contract. As the difficulties increased, so did the contractions in my arm. Just as my strength was waning, Brailowsky shouted over the fortissimos, "It's not fast enough!" That was too much. Forgetting my awe and respect for him, I raised my hands from the piano (not unlike Schubert, evidently) and shouted back at him, "I can't go any faster!" Having played this piece himself many times, he was all too familiar with its difficulties and burst into laughter at my distress. "You know," he said quite good-humoredly, "I am right, you are right, and Schubert is wrong!" We both had a good laugh over this virtually impossible piece (see Illustration X).

The expression, "My arm is falling off," refers to tightness and pain in the forearm that eventually make it difficult to move your fingers. The pain is caused by muscles that contract involuntarily, not unlike those leg cramps that seem to have a mind of their own. There are three precautionary steps to ward off arm cramps: (1) command your fingers—and not your arms—to assume the major

Illustration X.   Schubert, *Fantasia*, Op. 15 (*The Wanderer*)

share of responsibility; (2) allow natural tension to keep your fingers taut; and (3) acquire endurance.

TAUT FINGERS

In strenuous passages, a battle rages between your arms and your fingers. In other words, coping with a difficulty requires strength from some part of your body. Should your fingers not assume their share of responsibility, your forearm muscles will then contract involuntarily as a compensatory action for what your fingers ought to have been doing. Thus, you initiate an arm cramp. Keeping your fingers taut at all times will help you avoid this. The following exercise is designed to teach you the sensation of taut fingers:

1. Hold your right hand opposite your chin with your thumb nail facing you. Keep your fingers slightly curved.
2. Cover the nail of each finger (including your thumb) with the corresponding finger tips of your left hand.
3. As your left hand fingers gently bear down, press up against them with the fingers of your right hand. First, bend each finger of your right hand up and down elastically (your thumb will

move from left to right), and then bend all five fingers at once in a similar fashion.

4. Now reverse your hands and try this exercise for your left hand.

Taut fingers do not imply stiff fingers. Taut fingers are always flexible and flexibility is the antithesis of stiffness. Notice, for example, the condition of your legs when you are standing: though straight, they are potentially flexible and, therefore, not stiff. It is this flexibility that enables you to walk in a controlled fashion. Your fingers, too, step from note to note in a curved or straight position just as your legs bend and straighten when walking. In whatever position they are held, taut fingers, moving from your bridge knuckles, assure clear finger independence.

THE THREE KEY POSITIONS

Since piano tones disappear as soon as the hammers strike the strings, a pianist must create illusions of prolongation. He does this by controlling the dynamics of each tone both horizontally and vertically. This infinite spectrum of color is derived principally from the speed at which the hammers rise to the strings. Therefore, your chief concern must be the rate of speed with which you depress the keys. The following terms refer to three key positions, a knowledge of which is necessary for your control of sound: (1) on the key; (2) the key bed; and (3) the escapement level.

On the key means that your finger rests on the surface of the key *before* you lower it. When you depress the key as far as it will go, you reach the *key bed*. The *escapement level* is a virtually unknown factor to pianists; yet, a knowledge of it is indispensable for voicing chords and creating contrast between the hands. Here is how to find it:

1. Place the third finger of your right hand on middle C (on the key). Keep your finger taut.
2. Lower the key gradually until you feel a slight resistance.
3. Without producing a sound, gently penetrate this resistance and continue on to the key bed.

The slight resistance between the surface of the key and the key bed is known as the escapement level. Every key will have it if the action of your piano is properly regulated. Now that you have felt the escapement level, it is important for you to observe its effect on the hammers. If you have a grand piano, remove the music stand;

for spinets and uprights, lift the board in front of the strings. Once again, silently depress middle C to the escapement level and then to the key bed. As you do so, watch the hammer rise to the strings (it may be necessary for you to stand in order to get a better view). Notice that as soon as you pierce the escapement level, the hammer literally escapes your control and drops down slightly below the strings. No matter how much you squeeze or press your finger into the key bed, the hammer continues to lie there quietly, unaffected by anything you may do to the key. You have lost all contact with the hammer.

This experiment has important applications to the question of tone control, especially in voicing chords (a detailed analysis of which will follow). Meanwhile, the following will aid you considerably during your practicing:

1. In producing sound on the piano, fix your attention on *lifting the hammers toward the strings.* The image of "lifting" something assists you to lower the keys at a slower rate of speed, thus assuring greater control.
2. Depress the keys with sufficient speed; otherwise you cannot transfer enough momentum to the hammers.
3. Your only chance of controlling this momentum is between the key surface and the escapement level.
4. Nothing you do between the escapement level and the key bed can affect the sound. The hammer has at this point escaped your control.

Supporting your arms and stopping the keys at the escapement level (the keys will be partially depressed) is very useful for voicing chords and playing accompanying figures. However, it is generally more economical to transfer arm pressure from one key bed to another (more especially on long notes) via your finger pads—"bedding down," so to speak, the natural weight of your arms. (See p. 156.) Finding this sensation very compelling, many pianists want to roll their arms around and even vibrate their hands, luxuriating, as it were, in the key beds.

HOW TO VOICE CHORDS

Several times during my musical training, my teachers presented ideas to me that profoundly influenced my musical thinking. On one such occasion during a counterpoint class, our teacher, about to introduce three-part counterpoint, went to the blackboard to write out a *cantus firmus* in the alto voice. He then proceeded to fill in a bass and soprano voice, speaking all the while of the autonomous beauty of each voice. Suddenly, in the middle of the exercise, he stood back from the blackboard and stared at us in amazement. "Look at what we have here!" he cried. We could not imagine what he was referring to; none of us noticed anything unusual. Before we realized what had happened, he circled the last three vertical notes of the exercise, and with flashing eyes exclaimed, "Behold! We have a chord!" No sooner did he utter the word "chord" than it occurred to me that a chord is actually a meeting place of three or more independent voices, a fact that was a revelation to me. The dramatic way in which he explained this was as impressive as the information itself. His own enthusiasm, admirably intact after years of teaching the same subject, had a lasting effect on me. Many musicians would no doubt have discovered the properties of a chord before the age of nineteen; the fact that I hadn't served to intensify the meaning of my discovery. From that moment on, I ceased to think of chords in terms of verticality only, but began instead to hear the voices within them. Delineating through dynamics the autonomous properties of a chord is a technique called *voicing*.

Voicing a chord on the piano is one of the most pleasurable auditory and physical sensations. Knowledge of the escapement level prepares you for this experience. Voicing a chord means simply that when you play a chord, you treat each of its notes as a separate voice (or a separate instrument). In a series of chords, the independent voices which comprise them meet like the four voices of a string quartet—all forming a synthesis of sound. To be able to control the dynamics of each voice within a chord is a feat, as you will soon realize. Go to the piano and think of the following C major chord as a meeting place of a bass, tenor, alto, and soprano voice:

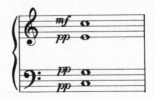

The following exercises will teach you to control each voice of this chord. Preliminary steps:

1. Cup the palms of both hands and make all ten fingers taut.
2. To play the above chord, use 1 and 5 in both hands; the middle fingers—2, 3, and 4—remain taut and extended straight out.
3. The fifth finger of your right hand is straight and pointing down at a right angle to your palm. Since it is desirable to play on the pad of your fifth finger, allow the first joint to collapse. Thus, in the profile view of your fifth finger, the area between the tip and the second joint (the mid-joint) will appear bowed.
4. During this entire exercise, concentrate exclusively on your forearm, thinking of your fifth finger merely as an extension of it.

You are now ready to try a silent run-through of the C major chord:

1. Silently depress the soprano C down to the key bed. Allow your arm to rest there supported by your perpendicular finger (the first joint of which may be collapsed or bowed).
2. Silently depress the other three voices to the escapement level.
3. Study the sensation: your right arm has released its weight onto the fifth finger; your right thumb is floating in the escapement level of the alto E; your left arm is holding itself up in an effort to keep the bass C and the tenor G only partially depressed (to the escapement level).

You are now ready to sound a voiced chord:

1. Depress the right pedal and be sure to keep it down for the duration of this exercise.
2. Before actually sounding the soprano C, place your taut fifth finger on the surface of the key. With your finger still taut, lift your right forearm approximately a few inches into the air and *lower* your fifth finger into the C. Generate enough energy to play *mezzo forte*. Do it over and over again, approximately once every two seconds. Be sure that the pedal is held down, thus catching the resonating sounds of the repeated C's. Rest in the key bed between repetitions. Listen to the rich *mezzo forte* sound and be aware of the sensation.
3. Keep swinging your arm for each repeated C. *Nothing you are about to do must interfere with the mezzo-forte sound of this soprano C.*

The following is perhaps the most important step in this exercise:

4. With the next repetition of C, allow your right-hand thumb to

fall on the surface of the alto E. Do not actually depress the E. Try this several times.

5. With your pedal still down and the soprano C still ringing, allow your right-hand thumb to penetrate the surface of E. Do not try to produce a sound with it at first. Keep swinging your arm.

6. As your arm continues to swing over and over again, allow your right hand thumb to fall to the escapement level of E. As each C continues to ring out, the alto E will be heard faintly in contrast to it. Do not be concerned if the C and E do not arrive together. In time they will.

7. Continue to swing your arm. Enjoy the beauty of the two distinct colors produced with one hand—the soprano, rich and resonant; the alto, soft and muted.

8. Filling out the chord will now be quite simple. Rest your left-hand thumb on the surface of the tenor G. Lower it to the escapement level with a gentle, rolling motion of your arm.

9. Now do the same with your fifth finger on the bass C.

Listening to all four sounds, hold the chord and enjoy its texture. Notice that you are positioned exactly as you were in the silent run-through—that is, your right-hand fifth finger is resting in the key bed while all the other voices are hovering in the escapement level. To view this position properly, remove your right hand without disturbing its mold and observe it with the thumbnail facing you. You will notice that your fifth finger is hanging slightly lower than your thumb. This is because your fifth finger has positioned itself to fall into the key bed while your thumb is positioned to remain at the escapement level. Your cupped palm allows your right hand to stay in a mold so that your fingers can asume the correct position *before* lowering the keys.

Having succeeded in making the soprano *mezzo forte* and the other voices *pianissimo*, you can now experiment bringing out each voice in turn. After you have mastered this, you can allow all your fingers to continue on to the key beds. Eventually, you will be able to voice chords by starting your swing stroke either on the keys or above them.

To have voiced a chord means that you have succeeded in accomplishing a feat of coordination as difficult as it is important to the art of piano playing. The sound, the feeling, and the muscular sensation of voiced chords will soon become a natural part of your musical expressiveness. Above all, to experience polyphony with your own two hands is one of the privileges of being a pianist. What can be more rewarding, for example, than reading through the *Chorale Preludes* of J. S. Bach, the master of polyphony, and experiencing the perfection of the independent voices? Like the converging rays of the sun, each voice fuses into a radiant whole.

PEDALING

The Right Pedal

It is impossible to achieve the full range of color associated with beautiful piano playing without the use of the right and left pedals. When Anton Rubinstein called the right pedal (or *damper* pedal) "the soul of the piano," he was expressing the veneration for it shared by all pianists. A skillful use of both pedals can spell the difference between a good and a truly artistic performance. The sostenuto or middle pedal is rarely used and only for the specific purpose of sustaining one or more notes usually in the bass. The mere mention of the sostenuto pedal reminds me of a former pupil, now a medical doctor, who was an excellent pianist at the age of twelve. When he was nine, I assigned him the *Prelude in C minor* by Chopin, instructing him to take a new pedal with each chord he played. At his next lesson, the chords sounded strangely disconnected; there was also a curious shuffling sound coming from the floor. I looked down in time to see him play one chord and then shift his foot to the middle pedal; he then played the second chord and shifted his foot to the left pedal. Having used up all three pedals, he proceeded to start all over again. He was, as it turned out, following my instructions literally—taking a new pedal with each chord!

Very often, piano students must discover for themselves how to use the right pedal since teachers all too frequently neglect to discuss its use. Pedaling, like musical feeling, is often added—and arbitrarily so—after the physical requirements of a piece are mastered. Considering the involvement of the whole body, including the feet, in expressing music on the piano, such neglect is inexcusable. Alas, a student may be left to fend for himself, trying his best to co-ordinate his feet with his fingers.

TO CONNECT OR NOT TO CONNECT. Using the pedal for legato is as natural as using a bow on a stringed instrument. As pianists, however, we may have certain scruples about connecting sounds with our feet instead of with our hands. Suppose, though, that you are playing a slow, lyrical melody in octaves that requires an intricate manipulation of slip-fingers. If your hand is small, you may feel uncomfortable or even strained in playing such a passage. In truth, you can create a legato effect on the piano only by a proper use of dynamics, provided, of course, that the sounds themselves are connected (this means of connection is to be discussed shortly). Should one note deviate from the proper dynamic scheme, the legato effect is destroyed. The contour of dynamics to express legato may be chosen from the following possibilities:

You may even decide to play a series of tones all on the same dynamic. When attempting physically to connect octaves and chords, strain or discomfort may prevent you from controlling these contours; if one tone deviates from your dynamic scheme, it will ruin the legato line in spite of your connecting the notes with your fingers. Freeing your hands from a finger legato, however, enables you to control the exact dynamic of each note—thus creating a true legato effect. In other words, for the sake of comfort, *disconnect with your hands and connect with your foot.* Most octave passages, whether they are slow or fast, will often sound better when they are fingered consistently with 1 and 5 and properly pedaled.

PAINTING WITH THE PEDAL. Try the following suggestion for pedaling the opening of the *Sonata Pathétique* by Beethoven:

Notice my suggestion to depress the pedal *with* the first chord. Such pedaling gives thrust to a chord. Now experiment with two other possibilities: (1) depress the pedal and then play the chord; and (2) play the chord and then depress the pedal. Each variation of pedaling gives the chord a different sound. I have already indicated my preference; choose the pedaling you like best. Keep in mind all three possibilities, however, and make them part of your pedaling technique.

Let us continue to study the opening measure of the *Sonata Pathétique* for other pedal effects. Focus your attention on the last two legato chords (marked with an arrow). Try to play them without the pedal, using a legato fingering, and make the second chord softer than the first. Most pianists find this difficult to control. Now you are going to be asked to be extremely daring: play the first chord marked with an arrow with a downward motion of your wrists and forearms (arch your bridge knuckles and swing your upper arms toward your body); depress the pedal and remove both hands from the keyboard. With your foot still down, prepare the second chord by placing your fingers toward the front of the keys. Concentrate on the first chord fading away. Now, play the second chord with a gentle, forward motion of your upper arms and wrists. As you do so, try to make the second chord match the dying timbre of the first chord. Change your pedal as you play the final chord.

I have been persuading you to indulge in a practice that some pianists view as sinful—namely, to rely on the pedal for legato instead of on your fingers. If you can achieve the same effect with your fingers, do so, of course. You should know, however, that some of our greatest pianists create persuasive legato effects in the way I have just described—by disconnecting with their fingers and connecting with their pedal. Before we leave this example, let us return once again to the last two chords specifically to examine the legato fingering—5 to 4, or 4 to 3. Connecting a black key (E$^\flat$) to a white key (D) traps whatever finger you use toward the back of D where the key is narrow and also offers its greatest resistance. Conversely, the front of the key offers your finger less resistance, thus making it easier for you to play softly. It is for this reason that I use 5 on D. I encourage you, however, to use whatever fingering is most comfortable for your particular hand.

THE SOLE AND THE HEEL.   Most pianists do not give enough consideration to the posture of the foot when using the right pedal. The pedal will work most efficiently when your entire foot is lined up with the pedal and the ball of your foot is resting on its tip. Positioning your heel to the left or to the right of the pedal diminishes your control of it. If your foot is very small, it will be necessary to pedal with your toe instead of the ball of your foot.

The right pedal has a spring that resists its downward motion. Should this spring be unusually firm, your heel will then tend to rise off of the floor when you depress the pedal. But no matter how great the resistance of the pedal, your heel must never leave the floor. Rooting your heel to the floor not only enables you to depress and lift the pedal with greater control, but it also serves as a fulcrum for "grounding" your body. I once taught a man who had a habit of lifting his heel each time he depressed the pedal. Subsequently, he developed a severe muscle spasm on the entire right side of his body which adversely affected his finger control. Once he corrected his pedaling technique, the muscle spasms disappeared and his playing showed marked improvement.

Correct pedaling involves the use of natural tension in that the resistance offered by the pedal must be met by contracting the muscles in your leg and foot. Opposing the pedal resistance by consciously contracting your muscles enables you to lift the pedal and depress it again with greater control. Recall, if you will, the exercise for making your fingers taut—the fingers of both hands pressed against each other exerting a force in opposing directions. This technique is applied to pedaling in the following way:

1. Position your right foot on the pedal with your heel firmly rooted to the floor.
2. Place your left toes over the right (for obvious reasons, don't wear your favorite shoes).
3. Press down with your left toes and up with your right. Now, slowly move the pedal up and down, paying close attention to *lifting your foot slowly.*
4. As your foot comes up, exercise a braking control by increasing the pressure with your left toes. This action prevents the dampers from slapping against the strings.

Try playing a series of chords with this slow pedal action. By lifting your foot slowly and then immediately depressing the pedal, the dampers will remain off the strings save for a brief instant of contact. Free from pedal noise, your sound will bear a striking resemblance to that of an organ. Try playing the chords once again, but this time simulate the same pedal control without the aid of your left toes. Allow natural tension to stabilize your foot.

Since most pedals have free play near the surface, it is unnecessary to lift the pedal all the way to the top in order to clear the sound. Your ear will tell you how high to lift the pedal. Because this distance varies with each piano, you will have to adjust accordingly.

Above all, always keep your foot in contact with the surface of the pedal and your heel rooted to the floor.

SOME HELPFUL HINTS

1. The speed at which the dampers rise and fall affects the sound of the piano. Experiment with slow and fast pedaling.
2. You may depress the pedal to different levels for different effects: there is a quarter pedal, a half pedal and even a vibrato pedal. The latter is used for brilliant scales and fast-changing chords and requires that your foot move up and down rapidly (see Illustration XI).

Vibrato pedaling—a rapid up–down movement of the right pedal —is very effective for brilliant scale passages:

Illustration XI. Beethoven, *Concerto No. 3 in C minor,* Op. 37

A *half pedal*—depressing the right pedal only partially down, thus barely raising the dampers from the strings—produces an effect similar to an echo chamber. The quarter or minimal depression of the pedal calls for the ultimate in control:

Debussy, *La Cathédrale engloutie* (*The Engulfed Cathedral*)

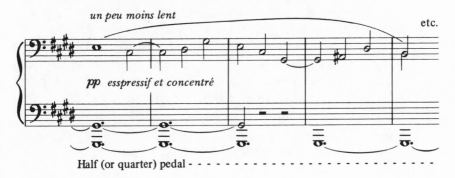

Few pedaling effects are as beautiful as that which results from lifting the right pedal slowly:

Beethoven, *Klavierstück (Für Elise)*, Klinsky-Halm WoO 59

lift pedal slowly

[the dynamics and slurs are mine]

3. No matter how quickly you lift your foot, you must exercise braking control. This diminishes damper noises.
4. You can make a sudden diminuendo on a long note by changing the pedal several times while you hold the key down with your fingers.
5. Legato playing requires that your foot go down *after* the note is played. You can achieve accents and stresses, however, by depressing the pedal together with a note.
6. When starting a piece, it is often helpful to depress the pedal *before* playing. Sir Clifford Curzon once advised me to depress the pedal before starting the *Emperor Concerto* by Beethoven; when the orchestra triumphantly announces the opening E♭ chord (without the B♭), the entire piano thus vibrates sympathetically which makes it easier to begin the piano cadenza with a full sound.
7. Long pedals can be used under the following conditions: (a) if you carefully gauge the dynamics from note to note and also between the hands; (b) if there is a sustained bass note or a bass note that repeats (a pedal point as in the *Rondo* of the *Waldstein Sonata* by Beethoven); (c) if you can maintain a *pianissimo* throughout the passage (notice Beethoven's long pedal indication in the recapitulation of the first movement of the *Sonata*, Op. 31, No. 2, in Illustration XII).[30]
8. Curiously, descending scales high up in the treble sound clearer with the pedal than without it.

ILLUSTRATION XII. Beethoven, *Sonata in D minor*, Op. 31, No. 2 (Excerpt from first movement, measures 142–148)

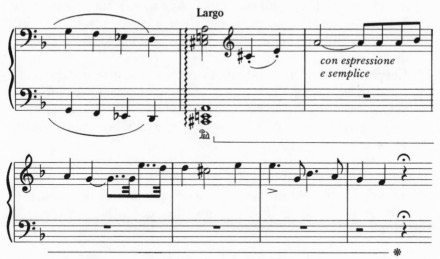

Note Beethoven's pedal indication through measure 148.

The next example, though similar to the one from Op. 31, No. 2, requires a far more subtle treatment of dynamics [the dynamics are mine]:

Beethoven, *Sonata in C major*, Op. 53 (*Waldstein*)

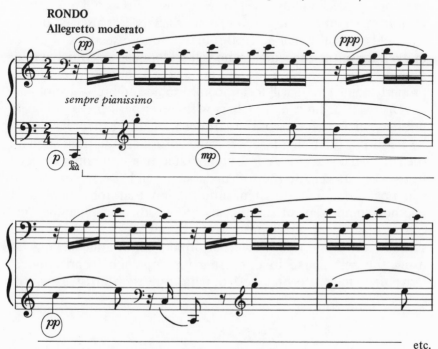

Note Beethoven's indication to hold the pedal for 8 measures.

9. Some composers, such as Beethoven, indicate pedalings only occasionally. They are usually intended for special effects or merely to set the trend for similar passages. When such pedal indications cease, however, or when a composer fails to indicate pedalings, you are expected to continue to pedal at your discretion.

10. Keep this image in mind whenever you use the pedal: when your finger lowers a key with braking control, you are *lifting a hammer* toward the strings; when your foot lifts the pedal with braking control, you are *lowering the dampers* toward the strings.

Alas, there is a pianist's disease know as "pedalitis." Its symptoms are a tendency to hold the right pedal down indefinitely or else not to change it clearly. There is only one cure for this: careful listening.

The Unmentionable Una Corda

There is a great aura of confusion surrounding the use of the soft pedal (also called left pedal or una corda). The extent to which it is maligned, misunderstood, and, finally, avoided merely proves what little attention is given to the elements that comprise beautiful piano playing. Yet, observing the pedaling of a great pianist on even one piece should silence forever those who would presume to keep from us one of the piano's greatest assets. For a skilled pianist will hold the soft pedal down throughout entire sections of pieces or even for entire movements; he will seldom play the final note of a tender phrase without it and, moreover, if the soft pedal is not properly adjusted, he will feel uncomfortable and probably not play as sensitively as he can. Teachers who never perform in public do not recognize such uses of the soft pedal, many of them having inherited from their own teachers some absurd assumptions such as: the soft pedal is a crutch; it is comparable to a mute on a stringed instrument; never use the soft pedal in a hall because your sound will not carry. This is all misinformation that robs pianists of another component of the piano's "soul," the incomparable una corda, that divine mechanism used by all great artists to mold sound. Even some well-known performers suffer guilt feelings for using the soft pedal. In discussing his approach to an ethereal movement in a late Schubert Sonata, one such artist explained almost apologetically, "Well, I know I shouldn't, but I keep the una corda down throughout the movement." It is time then for pianists to repudiate such guilt feelings and accept the soft pedal as an important mechanism of the piano that is meant to be used and enjoyed. Both Mozart and Beethoven used it extensively, the latter even indicating its use. On Mozart's piano, the engagement of the soft pedal caused the hammers to move over and actually hit one string—hence, una corda. On our present-day grand pianos, the soft pedal shifts the hammers over to play two strings (at least in the treble); literally speaking, it should therefore be called *due corde*. Interestingly, Beethoven's piano had five pedals, three of which functioned as soft pedals: one lowered a strip of parchment over the strings; another engaged a piece of felt between the hammers and the strings; a third was similar to our modern soft pedal but even more efficient, for a lever fastened to the right of the keyboard moved the action alternately from una corda to due corde. Moreover, some pianos in Beethoven's time had a pianissimo pedal which brought the hammers close to the strings, thereby lessening the striking distance. With the hammers no longer able to gain speed in their thrust toward the strings, the resulting sound was not only softer, but also rather diffused. Most upright pianos still employ this mechanism. Far from merely lessening sound, the soft pedal on grand pianos is, more importantly, a coloristic device that actually changes the quality of *piano* tone. This quality and the method of bringing it about bear no resemblance whatsoever to a muted sound on a stringed instrument. As the hammers move toward the right, aligning themselves with two of the three strings in the treble, one string is now left free to vibrate sympathetically with the other two, thus producing a ravishing sound, free from percussion, that no degree of muscular control could ever achieve. To eliminate, as far as possible, the element of percussion in sound is one of the aims of all serious pianists—sufficient reason why the soft pedal entices them and why they use it so frequently.

Because the soft pedal lessens percussion, it can be used very effectively in *forte* playing. When you have a piece that is consistently *forte*, as for example, a *Polonaise* by Chopin, you may create different intensities of *forte* in the following manner: (1) play the first section *forte* with the soft pedal; (2) play the next section *forte* without the soft pedal; and (3) play the third section *fortissimo*. In this way, you will be able to conserve your strength for the climax. You may use this pedaling technique in all pieces that require different intensities of *forte*.

Unfortunately, many soft pedals are not properly adjusted. Many of them move the action either too far to the right or not far enough, thus causing a thin, nasal sound. It would be better not to use it if it distorts your sound. If you are skillful, though, you will discover just how far down to depress the left pedal, thus engaging that section of the felts which produces the desired una corda sound. If out of alignment, soft pedals can be adjusted simply by the turn of a screw inside the piano on the extreme right of the action. This screw maintains the correct distance to which the hammers slide over toward the right. The first time I attempted to adjust this screw in my own piano, I removed the action and promptly snapped off the last two hammers in the treble. Be cautioned, therefore, and ask your tuner to instruct you in this procedure. Subsequently, I did learn to remove the action. In fact, one time, during a rehearsal, I surprised a well-known pianist by offering to adjust the soft pedal on his piano. Not having a screw-driver, I performed the delicate operation with a quarter. From that moment on, we both referred to the una corda as the *una quarter*.

Some pianists are as extreme in their overuse of the soft pedal as those who malign it and avoid it altogether. These pianists, on the contrary, are so enchanted with the soft pedal that they hold it down almost continuously, taking it up only for *forte* passages. This is yet another form of "pedalitis." Too much use of the soft pedal will limit the color of your playing. Used judiciously, however, it will enhance your playing, enabling you to create effects otherwise impossible to achieve with your two hands. Use it without guilt and know that musical heaven is peopled with scores of pianists who, like you, used their two feet and ten fingers to serve music.

FINGERS, FINGERS, FINGERS!

Although all impulses in piano playing originate in your torso and upper arms, your fingers, nevertheless, assume the major share of responsibility for all that you play—even chords and octaves. I often remind my pupils that *their fingers must do everything*. Our fingers are a kind of distributor for the exact amount of energy required for a particular sound. As extentions of your upper arms, your fingers are the primary source of control for selecting the exact amount of speed needed to activate the keys. This applies whether you are above the keys or on them. Your fingers can maintain their independence only as long as your arm muscles do not overcontract. The way to assure the proper balance between your fingers and arms is to arch your knuckles and to keep your fingers taut at all times. The following is a variation on the exercise for taut fingers:

1. Gently stretch your second fingers of both hands and move your wrists up and down.
2. While continuing to stretch your second fingers, stabilize your wrists and move your forearms up and down from your elbows.
3. With the palms facing the floor, move your upper arms forward and backward from your shoulders.
4. Now try these three steps for each finger in turn. Do not neglect your thumbs.

Energizing your fingers without overcontracting your arm muscles preserves your finger independence. You must not think, however, that you can stretch a finger even minimally without inducing a whole series of other contractions throughout your arm. But if those contractions develop into involuntary spasms, your fingers will be robbed of their independence. Remember that *your fingers must always be stronger than your arm.*

Exercise for Finger Independence

The best way to achieve finger independence is to practice with high fingers—that is, fingers that initiate their swing from above the keys. Since the left hand is often neglected, let us take for our example the opening measure of the *Prelude in G major* by Chopin:

(Chopin, *Prelude in G Major*)

Since your goal is to play the left hand of this piece *leggieramente,* practice *piano.* In the following method, each note of this *Prélude* is used as the basis of a repeated note exercise which is designed to build finger independence and clear articlation. It can be adopted for practicing all fast passages:

1. For each repetition, lift your *stretched* (taut) finger approximately two inches above the key. Articulate each finger from the bridge knuckle. Lower each key into the key bed. Do not allow your finger to collapse at the first and second joints.
2. Pay as much attention to retrieving each finger as you do to lowering it.
3. Do not allow the muscles in your lower arm to overcontract; this will rob your fingers of independence.
4. Ground your body on the note that is held. (See p. 156.)

The following is a variation of this method and is similar to the exercise for achieving taut fingers:

1. Hold down your fifth finger on G.
2. With your second finger still in the air above D, cover the nail of it with the third finger of your right hand.
3. With each repetition of D, stabilize your left-hand second finger by gently pressing against it with your right hand. There is no better way to achieve strong, flexible fingers.
4. With each repetition, feel the dynamics and study the muscular sensation throughout your body. Also, observe the profile of your hand to be sure that each finger articulates from the same distance above the keys. Always arch your palm by gently pulling up on your knuckles.

ENDURANCE

Thus far, we have discussed the importance of natural tension—taut fingers included—as a means of supporting physical demands at the piano. Often, though, it is difficult to maintain the proper degree of tension over a long period of time. In other words, you may be able to harness your energies for a section of a fast, loud piece, but then you may falter as you approach the end (this, obviously, was my problem when I studied the *Wanderer Fantasy*). It is necessary, therefore, to acquire endurance.

Frequently, a pianist may have plenty of endurance during his practicing but in performance suffer from "the arm falling off" syndrome. This predicament clearly illustrates the effects emotions can have on muscle tone. For a practice session devoid of emotion and a performance filled with it will produce two distinctly different muscular responses, the contrast between which will not only confuse the pianist but also affect his threshold of endurance. To avoid this pitfall you must develop the kind of endurance that enables your muscles to adapt successfully to emotional responses, thus allowing you to maintain a peak performance. This requires that you be as emotionally charged at various stages in your practicing as you are during a performance so that the intensity of the actual experience does not come as a total surprise to you.

Endurance, whether it is in playing the piano or in exercising, must be built up gradually. When I jog, I am reluctant to restrict myself exclusively to the scientific charts which compute distance and time according to age and sex. I prefer instead to "listen to my body" and to slow down my pace on those days when my breathing becomes more labored than usual. Although building endurance at the piano requires that you practice fast pieces fast and loud pieces loud, no one, alas, can accurately predict how long you should do so (although you can, no doubt, endure longer periods of such practicing than you realize). You must, therefore, consult your own body to learn when to shift to a less strenuous piece or when to take a break. The process is one in which your muscles must *gradually* adapt to stress. Practicing loud and fast for too long a period of time may strain your muscles, thereby making your playing worse instead of better. Since the number of repetitions and the time factor itself differ with each individual, you must discover your own optimum limits. Here, I am reminded of my mother, who, when asked how long to leave one of her recipes in the oven, replies, "Until it is done." In practicing for endurance, the sound and the sensation tell you when "it is done." Be forewarned, though, that a prolonged high decibel level of sound can adversely affect the nervous system. Without pampering yourself then, exercise moderation—if not for yourself, then in consideration of your family and neighbors.

GROUNDED

The technique of being grounded while playing the piano will be described here perhaps for the first time. In addition to being one of the most pleasurable of sensations, being grounded is a freeing agent, facilitating technique and affording you an amazing comfort at the keyboard. The previous exercise—that of holding one note down and repeating the next—was meant to prepare you for being grounded. Holding down a note or a group of notes and/or holding down a hand requires pressure; and pressure is the secret of being grounded. Think for a moment of how you pivot when you play basketball; should you wish to pivot to the right, you anchor the weight of your body on your right foot. This frees your left foot so that you can pivot toward the right. Similarly, when playing the piano, the weight of your arm is anchored by means of one finger which instantaneously frees the other fingers. This weight on one finger is, of course, induced by pressure. To understand how the principle of being grounded works for single notes, examine the following exercises:

Grounded within One Hand
The turn written below is a conventional interpretation of Mozart's indication, *tr*, in measures 1 and 5.

Mozart, *Sonata in G major*, K. 283 (third movement)

1. Although this example is from a *presto* movement, practice it slowly at first.

2. After depressing A–D (marked with an arrow), immediately increase your arm pressure on your thumb A.
3. While maintaining this pressure, proceed with the other notes of the soprano voice, C, B, C. As you play this voice, rotate your hand and arm from left to right.
4. Transfer your arm pressure to the final chord, B–D, with two and four. Do so by rolling forward with your upper arm.

Notice that grounding your thumb A induces a sensation of freedom in your other fingers—4, 3, 2, 3. The alto A has pressure; the soprano D, C, B, C is devoid of pressure. Now try this example faster and in its context:

Grounded Between the Hands

This principle of being grounded applies equally between the hands in that grounding one hand frees the other. Try the following example:

Beethoven, *Sonata,* Op. 27, No. 2

In Beethoven's incomparable *Sonata quasi una Fantasia*, the grounded left-hand octaves enable your right hand to play the murmuring triplet figures with infinite control. Simply maintain both arm and body pressure throughout the duration of each bass note. It is not necessary to "squeeze" your fingers into the key beds; rather, a gentle pressure will suffice for grounding one hand and freeing the other.

In the following examples, grounding between the hands is achieved by applying pressure where indicated:

Mozart, *Sonata in G major*, K. 283 (third movement, measure 25)

Mozart, *Sonata in G major*, K. 283 (third movement, development)

The technique of grounding is particularly useful in playing compositions that have long bass notes and swirling right hand passages such as appear in the *Etude in C major*, Op. 10, No. 1, by Chopin. Here, a grounded left hand will not only alleviate the difficulties of the right hand arpeggios but will also give each bass octave its full complement of sound. It is on the bass line that the musical structure of this piece ultimately depends. Because it thus allows for muscular freedom and economy of motion, grounding is one of the most important of techniques for promoting true musical expressivity.

Chopin, *Etude in C major*, Op. 10, No. 1,

SCALES AND ARPEGGIOS, YES OR NO

Let us state emphatically that a knowledge of scales and arpeggios and the ability to execute them are indispensable to fluent and convincing music making on the piano. First, arpeggios require an extended position of the hand, while scales require a contracted position; second, both make demands on the thumb, requiring that it *turn under* the hand for smooth transitions from one position to another on the keyboard. Some methods refute the turning under of the thumb and advocate instead the transference of the hand from position to position unassisted by the thumb. However, I believe that the more we refine the technique of turning under the thumb, the more effectively will we execute all passage work. Finally, a theoretical knowledge of keys (which scales and arpeggios teach) and the adaptation of the whole playing mechanism to various combinations of white and black keys facilitates sight-reading and, moreover, forms the basis for conscious memorization (see Chapter X).

Although most musicians would agree with the above, there is nonetheless a divergence of opinion regarding the method in which scales and arpeggios should be taught. Offensive and even harmful to their students are those dogmatic teachers who insist on the "right way," namely, *their* way. Without considering the emotional and physical differences between their pupils, they force-feed scales and arpeggios to the exclusion of music in much the same way that some parents enforce certain regimes upon their children in disregard for their individual tendencies. This is not to deny that there are benefits to be derived from various methods and regimes; rather, it is to challenge the manner in which they are imposed. When Liszt, for example, who himself practiced technical methods of all kinds (an impressive number of his own exercises have been published), strongly cautioned against giving scales and arpeggios to young students, he was in effect voicing his disapproval of those dogmatic methods of teaching (even more prevalent in his day) that advocated the practicing of scales and arpeggios to the exclusion of pieces. Certainly, adhering solely to this method would be as stultifying to musical growth as teaching the sciences to the exclusion of the liberal arts would be to personal growth. How then can we perfect the physical without forfeiting the musical?

Sound technical methods notwithstanding, the answer must surely lie in adapting those methods to the individual needs of the student. Whereas some students will happily practice scales and arpeggios, others, when forced to do so, may rebel even to the point of stopping their lessons entirely. With musicality as a priority, a teacher must make it clear to the student that an ability to play scales and arpeggios provides the means for expressing music. In order to do this effectively, a teacher must help the student to use the scales and arpeggios as vehicles for musical feeling. For this, a teacher needs patience; and he must wait for the moment when the pupil will be ready to act upon the principles set forth.

Confusing in all this is the amount of conflicting information written by famous instrumentalists concerning the pros and cons of practicing scales and arpeggios. Many of them, because their technical gifts were such that they were able to play scales and arpeggios from the earliest age seemingly without practicing or because they have long since forgotten the years of technical training which emancipated their fingers, advocate an exclusive reliance upon difficult technical passages in the repertory for all technical work. Critics who oppose this method insist that mechanical practicing of passages in pieces results in a mechanical performance, their assumption being that all such practicing would necessarily be divorced from musical content. But, as Schnabel pointed out, there need not be anything mechanical about repeating a passage even 200 times when each repetition is infused with musical meaning.

That all instrumentalists must at one time or another learn to play scales and arpeggios in all keys is a fact of musical life. To conclude that a beginning student cannot learn to play pieces unless he is first grounded in scales and arpeggios would be as false as saying one cannot speak a language until one learns the alphabet. However, scales and arpeggios are as essential for musical literacy as the alphabet is for a reading knowledge of one's language. Once having learned to play scales and arpeggios, each student must then learn to adapt his practicing of them to his own needs. Many of my students can play scales and arpeggios perfectly without practicing them; others, not so fortunate, must work on them every day or whenever they feel a need for their beneficial effects. Still others rely on their repertory for all technical work. All of them in choosing practice methods that suit their individual requirements achieve remarkable results though their choices may vary at different stages in their development. Most important, however, is to take whatever steps are necessary to ward off boredom during practicing. If scales begin to bore you, then practice them in a Mozart Sonata (if the scale is in the right hand, be sure to adapt it to the left hand). But should you practice scales one day and then neglect them for the next three days, do not expect results. In short, concentration and consistency are far more important considerations than which Sonata you choose to practice. Be sure that *what* you practice contains a diversity of technical demands. Vary your routine not only with fast and slow pieces, but also with technical challenges that require your hand to be extended as well as contracted; or, quite simply, practice scales and arpeggios as a supplement to your repertory. When one piece or exercise yields results, replace it with a more challenging one. By constantly learning new repertory (and new exercises) you can rekindle a spontaneity in your old pieces. Thus, most of us, after making a new friend, experience a similar feeling—what we call "a new lease on life." Familiar patterns of conversation established after years of exchange with people you know are suddenly replaced with unfamiliar ones. Under the right circumstances this can stimulate you to view your old friends in a new light. A similar situation obtains when you change your environment; an excursion, even for one day, often brings a new freshness to your day-to-day existence. On the other hand, some individuals are able to sustain as much interest and enthusiasm for one person or one environment as some practicers can for one composition. In other words, there are no absolutes regarding the necessity for change. The following suggestions for practicing scales and arpeggios are intended to stimulate you to a fresh approach. If they confirm what you already know to be functional for your hand, they will be no less valuable. First, let us discuss the position of the hand itself.

PREPARATION FOR SCALES

There has always been a diversity of opinion regarding the correct hand positon at the piano. Chopin, who did a great deal of teaching, would take his pupil's hand and place it over E, F♯, G♯, A♯, and B. Try this for yourself; you will see how naturally your hand fits over these keys. You will notice also that the shortest fingers, namely, 1 and 5, lie on the two white keys, while the longest fingers—2, 3, and 4—lie slightly extended, grasping the three black keys with the finger pads. Thus, the hand feels open and ready to be activated.

Curved or Flat

Focus once again on Chopin's suggested hand position and notice that 2, 3, and 4 are only slightly curved. Two factors determine the degree to which you should curve your fingers: (1) the amount of flesh between the top of your nail and the end of your finger (the finger pad), and (2) the position of your wrist. Your best control in activating a key occurs when the fleshier part of your finger comes in contact with it—especially on black keys. This finger pad should feel like a magnetic cushion, grasping the key and lowering it at a controlled rate of speed. The result is a predictable tone. If you have long, pointed fingers with small pads, you cannot play with extremely curved fingers; otherwise your nails will click along with your playing. As Chopin's suggested hand position proves, the geography of the keyboard determines the extent to which your fingers should be curved or flat. Try the following experiment:

1. Place your right hand once again over the five finger pattern and in the position suggested by Chopin.
2. Shift your position to the first five notes of C major. Curve your fingers only to the degree that your finger pads will grasp the keys.
3. Touch both groups of keys alternately without playing. Study the position of your wrist for each group. You will naturally accommodate the black keys by raising your wrist slightly; conversely, playing the white keys calls for a lower wrist position. Notice, too, that your fingers are slightly extended for the black keys and more curved for the white keys.
4. Depress the five white keys once again, but this time raise your wrist exaggeratedly. Your nails should be touching the keys. In order to play on the finger pads in this position, you must flatten your fingers. This, incidentally, is a very useful position for producing certain effects.
5. While still on the white keys, return to the former position—that is, with curved fingers and a low wrist. Notice how easily your finger pads come in contact with the keys as your fingers retain their curved position.

The following rules apply to those with small finger pads: (1) if your wrist is high, you must flatten your fingers; and (2) if your wrist is low, you must curve your fingers.

Pianists with large finger pads have no difficulty one way or the other since they can play with extremely curved fingers at all times. They never have to be concerned about clicking noises. The length of the fingers has little to do with the size of the finger pads; some tiny hands have lovely cushions, while large hands and long fingers often have small finger pads. You must therefore adjust your hand positon accordingly.

As we find in Mme. Auguste Boissier's diary of her daughter's lessons with Liszt, the master evidently played in a rather unorthodox fashion: "I would say that he (Liszt) has no touch at all, and, at the same time, that he has all possible touches. His fingers are very long, and his hands are small and pointed. He does not keep them in a rounded position. He maintains that this position lends a feeling of dryness to one's playing and this horrifies him [for Liszt's hand such a position evidently would lead to nail-clicking]. Neither are they altogether flat, but are so flexible as to possess no fixed position. They are able to approach a note in every way, but never with stiffness or dryness. Mr. Liszt detests these two faults."[31]

Turning Under and Over

Although five-finger exercises are extremely beneficial, they do not adequately prepare you for playing scales and arpeggios. Of foremost importance, you must train your thumb to turn under your hand and your hand to glide over your thumb. In Heinrich Neuhaus's book, *The Art of Piano Playing*, beginning on page 102, you will find some excellent suggestions, including exercises, which will prepare you for turning under and over.[32] Another helpful source is James Cooke's *Mastering Scales and Arpeggios*.[33] Also, a must for all practicers is *The Technique of Piano Playing* by József Gát.[34]

Let us return once again to the study of your hand. Notice that all your fingers have three visible joints with the exception of your thumb, the third joint of which is considered to be a part of the wrist. All vertical and lateral movements of your thumb, therefore, originate in this hidden joint. Exercises 1, 2, and 3 are designed to free this joint.

1. Sit at the piano—shoulders down, neck and jaw relaxed.
2. Arch your palms by drawing up on your second finger bridge knuckle.
3. Place your curved fingers—2, 3, and 4—on the three black keys, F#, G#, A#. Keep your wrists relatively low so that your finger pads are in contact with the keys.
4. Depress the black keys all the way down to the key beds; rest there with arm and hand pressure (grounded). All the pressure must center on the finger pads. *Keep this pressure constant throughout these exercises.*
5. Your thumbs must articulate each note with a vertical swing from the hidden joint at your wrists. As your thumbs move laterally toward the fifth finger for each successive note, your thumb tips should turn in slightly.

Exercise 1

6. For soft playing, keep your thumbs on the keys; for loud playing, articulate your thumbs from above the keys.
7. The correct angle for your elbows will be determined by the angle you reach at measure 5. Adjust your elbows outward to facilitate this difficult position, keeping them aligned in this way for the entire exercise.
8. Do not rotate your arms. Concern yourself instead with the vertical and lateral movements of your thumbs.
9. Large hands may extend these exercises to include C in the right hand and E in the left hand.
10. As the exercises become easier, move the metronome up to a faster tempo.
11. Feel the dynamics and make a physical association with them. Always play exercises expressively. Try inventing your own exercises.

Exercise 2

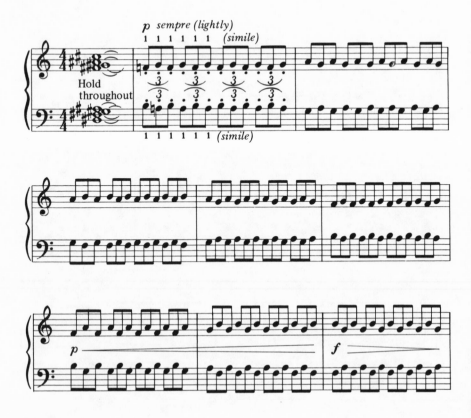

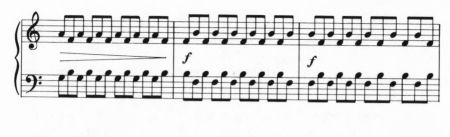

Exercise 3

In playing scales and arpeggios, the entire hand is stabilized by a point of gravity centered at the second finger bridge knuckle. Try to sense this when you depress the five-finger hand position suggested by Chopin. As you rest in the key beds, imagine a line of stabilizing energy starting at the second finger bridge knuckle, continuing across your wrist and forearm and ending at your elbow. This center of gravity has a twofold purpose: (1) it stabilizes your hand in turning your thumb under and/or turning your hand over for scales and arpeggios; and (2) pulling up gently at the second finger bridge knuckle helps you to maintain a hollow palm, a structural asset from which your fingers can articulate freely and flexibly.

Following are some additonal suggestions for practicing scales and arpeggios:

1. In swinging your thumb under or turning your hand over, the two large muscles on either side of your hand contract toward each other in a narrowing action of your palm. Do not force this action, but allow it to happen naturally.

2. In swinging your fourth finger over your thumb onto a B flat, such as in a descending scale of E flat major, the fifth finger side of your hand should be slightly higher and level with the second finger bridge knuckle. Some pianists like to slope the knuckles toward the second finger while descending a scale or arpeggio.

3. Slow arpeggios invite a physical connection; when you go fast, however, *jump* the positions. Small hands, especially, will appreciate a free hop between the third finger and the thumb or between the fourth finger and the thumb (ascending). After hopping, however, there will be a tendency to accent your thumb. Guard against this by giving added arm pressure to your third finger, G, on an ascending C major arpeggio (right hand). In other words, you will disguise the hop by playing the note directly before it a little louder. Try this on a left hand arpeggio.

4. In an ascending C major scale, your thumb will naturally glide toward the right, under your palm, on its way toward F. To discover an important rule, begin the C major scale, stopping on E and preparing your thumb on the surface of F. Study this position for a while. Somehow, your hand must swing over your thumb once you play F. To facilitate this recovery of your hand, play F with a swing stroke of the tip of your thumb from *right to left*. In a descending scale, your thumb will swing from *left to right*. The same applies to arpeggios. Therefore, apply the following rule when playing scales and arpeggios: *The swing stroke of your thumb in scales and arpeggios is always in the direction opposite to that in which your hand is moving.*

5. It is not enough to concentrate solely on lowering each finger in a scale or arpeggio; think also of retrieving each finger as you proceed toward the next note.

6. Most pianists agree that the second finger is the source of numerous problems. Therefore, consciously retrieve your second finger in all ascending scales. Observe it in C major, for ex-

ample, as it traces a half circle from D to G. Your thumb, swinging in the opposite direction, and a high arch between your thumb and second finger facilitate this action.

7. Do not move your elbows in and out each time you swing your thumb under or turn your hand over. Rather, glide with your torso and upper arms in the direction of the scale or arpeggio. In order to simulate the proper motion and sensation, play a glissando up and down over the entire keyboard. Notice how naturally your torso follows the path of the glissando; notice, too, how your upper arm steers your elbows as it glides over the keys. However, minimize these torso movements when playing scales. It helps considerably to start by slightly extending your elbows away from your body. Then, with your elbows as a point of reference, line up your forearm and fingers on a straight line with it. Also, in the right-hand descending scales and arpeggios, turn your elbow out slightly toward the right; in left-hand ascending scales and arpeggios, turn your elbow out slightly toward the left.

8. With your right hand, play a descending G major scale, stopping on your thumb (G). Simultaneously, prepare your fourth finger (F#). When you play the F#, do not be anxious about sending your thumb, G, ahead to C. Your thumb need not go on its way until you play your third finger, E. While playing your fourth finger (F#), simply retrieve your thumb (G) and allow it to lie at rest on the surface of the key. In this position, your fourth finger will draw strength from your thumb. Enjoy this feeling of *seating* your fourth finger on a black key without any extraneous motion from your thumb.

Most practicing methods and exercises aim specifically at two requirements—strength and flexibility. Practicing with high fingers is an excellent way to achieve the first, provided that you pay attention to the posture of each finger as you raise and lower it. In other words, collapsed first and second joints militate against finger strength. Most important, remember to keep your shoulders down, your bridge knuckles arched, and your upper arms free. The extent to which you build up strength and flexibility depends on the duration and frequency of your practicing. Flexibility will come more quickly, however, if you incorporate stretching or extension excercises in your daily routine. Doing them each day will ease your execution of legato skips, broken chords, arpeggios, and difficult chord positions. Once you achieve elasticity and a feeling of *letting go* in your bridge knuckles, you may discontinue them on a steady basis and return to them only when necessary.

Extension Exercises

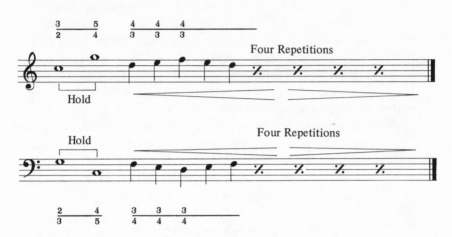

1. Shoulders down, neck relaxed, jaw easy.
2. Contemplate the dynamics and feel the mood.
3. Keep your fingers slightly curved, wrists level, thumbs, and fifth fingers hanging down in front of the keys and pointing toward the floor.

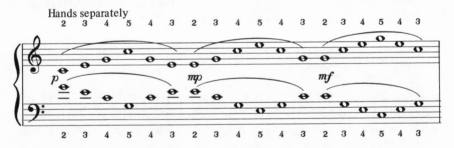

1. Play hands separately.
2. Adjust your tempo and take whatever time is necessary for stretching the difficult intervals.
3. Keep your palms level while stretching your fingers laterally.
4. Transpose to all keys. Should an interval strain your hand, do not attempt the impossible. Simply hold the first note as long as you can and then disconnect before going to the next note.

STABILIZE YOUR ARMS

When your fingers have achieved strength and independence they will function even more efficiently when you stabilize your arms and then line them up with your fingers. The following exercise will help you in this respect:

1. Choose any right-hand passage from one of your pieces or simply play an ascending and descending scale.
2. Before you begin to play, position your fingers on the surface of the keys. Now gently press the finger tips of your left hand against the left side of your right forearm—approximately five inches from your wrist.
3. Stabilize your right arm by gently pressing it against your left-hand finger tips. In this position, play the passage you have chosen.
4. Now remove your left hand and play the right-hand passage once again, trying to preserve the same sensation of stability.
5. Reverse hands and repeat this exercise to stabilize your left arm.

A stable arm assures strong, free fingers. Moving with economy of motion, your arms can then adapt to the needs of your fingers. Like tubes of concentrated energy, they enable your fingers to move unimpeded. Try now to stabilize the vertical movements of your arms:

1. This time, place the finger tips of your left hand *on top* of your right forearm, approximately five inches from your wrist.
2. Press down with your left-hand finger tips and up with your right forearm.
3. Play C, D, E with your right hand and make a diminuendo by gliding forward with your upper arm (your wrist will glide up).
4. Now remove your left hand and allow your right hand to function on its own.
5. Reverse hands and repeat this exercise for your left arm, playing C, B, A.

Stabilizing the vertical movements of your arms enables you to lower each key with infinite control. This is extremely helpful for diminuendos and legato passages. As a final experiment, stabilize both the lateral and vertical movements of your arms. While playing a passage with your right hand, gently press your left-hand finger tips over the top of your right arm. Your right forearm will then press upward and toward the left against the gentle pressure of your left-hand finger tips. It is unnecessary to overcontract your muscles when practicing these stabilizing exercises. Playing a glissando will be a good indication of just how much muscular contraction is needed.

8 Choreography

INTRODUCTION

Your fingers are, quite obviously, of paramount importance in playing the piano. Only seemingly independent, they are actually influenced by all the other movements of your body. Were I to single out the most important of these movements, I would unhesitatingly draw your attention to the forward-backward movements of your upper arms. When properly coordinated, these movements must be considered the primary source of your musical and technical control. They influence the shaping of your phrases as much as they do the ease of your execution. In short, your understanding of upper arm movements will unquestionably lend a sense of naturalness and predictability to your playing. Before we begin to apply these movements to your playing, I must ask you to agree to three conditions and, moreover, to adhere to them consistently:

Condition 1
From this moment on, you must relax your jaw and keep your lips slightly parted when you practice. Clenching your jaw and tightening your lips reflect a tension that will invariably spread to your neck and shoulders making it impossible for you to control sound at the keyboard.

Condition 2
From this moment on, you must never again lift or hunch your shoulders whether at the piano or away from it. For this action not only shrinks energy impulses in your arms, but it also diminishes the flexibility of your shoulders, elbows, and wrists. Tension due to anxiety naturally causes you to draw your shoulders up toward your ears. Therefore, your first step in preventing this contraction is to

pull your shoulders down and at the same time lift up your sternum. Once you experience the freedom of your upper arm movements that comes from this alignment of your torso, you will want to keep your shoulders down; in time, this position will become completely natural. As we have seen, a conscious effort, when practiced, is converted into a spontaneous reflex action. Eventually, your shoulders will "let go," abandoning their old habit of "holding on." Only then can they assume their important role in aiding upper arm movements.

Condition 3

You must learn to sit at a height compatible with the proportions of your body. The chief factor determining this height is the angle of your elbow in relation to the key beds. Experiment by depressing a C major chord with both hands and study the alignment of your forearms. If you have a short upper arm, your forearm will tend to slope toward the keyboard (your elbow will be above the key beds); if you have a long upper arm, your forearm will slope away from the keyboard (your elbow will fall below the key beds). The length of your torso will, of course, alter considerably the alignment of your forearm; that is, given the length of your upper arm, a short torso will bring your elbow lower. These determining factors—namely, the length of your upper arms and the length of your torso—indicate clearly that each pianist must find his own height. Therefore, any serious piano teacher must provide an adjustable seat for his pupils. Finding your best height often involves experimentation, pianists sometimes having to go through phases in which they sit at various heights. Eventually, though, you will discover that optimum height at which everything seems to flow naturally and comfortably.

Determining Your Height

Sit at the piano and depress a few keys with both hands. Keep your shoulders down and allow your arms to hang from the key beds. Adjust your chair so that your elbows are lined up with the key beds.

The height you have just reached can be considered a working norm which can be modified slightly in either direction. Most great pianists prefer to sit in a lower position so that their elbows are below the level of the key beds (Louis Kentner and Glenn Gould are two pianists whose coattails practically touch the stage). If you have any doubts about where to sit, try a low position. You will find that sitting low makes it far easier to transfer arm weight and/or pressure from one key bed to the other. Equally important, it will help you to keep your shoulders down. Sitting at the correct height—but aiming for a low position—is, therefore, essential. Rather than jeopardize your progress by sitting at the wrong height, buy an adjustable chair or have a carpenter saw down the legs of your present one if it is too high. (Better not try this yourself. I once went about stabilizing a wobbly table by sawing off a bit here and a bit there. In almost no time, I had a nearly legless table.) With your chair at the proper height, your jaw relaxed, your shoulders down, you can now proceed to the all-important movements of your upper arms.

THE MOVEMENTS OF YOUR UPPER ARM

Easing Your Shoulders

A precondition for the undulating movements of your upper arms (and subsequently your wrists) is a freedom and flexibility at your shoulder joints. Whereas many pianists faithfully practice finger independence exercises, very few understand the necessity of exercising the neck and shoulders. The following, therefore, should be a part of your daily practice routine:

1. Sit in a chair (or on the floor), close your eyes and relax your arms in your lap. You are going to roll your head around in a large circle—first clockwise and then counterclockwise. Begin by tucking in your chin; now roll your head all the way toward the left and up, tilting your head backward as you do so. Continue rolling toward the right and then down again. One helpful guide is to trace a circle with your chin.
2. Keep your head erect and hunch your shoulders toward your ears. Hold them there for four counts. Now drop your shoulders and allow your arms to hang down from them. Hold this position for four counts. Do this ten times slowly and ten times faster—one count up toward your ears and one count down toward the floor. Also, try this exercise while standing.
3. Drop your shoulders and move them forward with a gentle pressure. Hold them in this position for four counts. Now move them backward and hold them there for four slow counts. Do this ten times. Now try it quickly.

4. Stand up with your legs slightly apart. Swing each arm in turn ten times—first clockwise and then counterclockwise. Your shoulders will trace a small circle while your hand describes a large one.

To apply a shoulder consciousness to your playing, practice while sitting in a straight-backed chair with your shoulders resting against it. Try two positions: (1) place your chair far enough away from the keyboard at a distance proportionate to the length of your arms; with your arms held straight out, move them up and down from your shoulders; and (2) adjust your chair closer to the keyboard. With your shoulders still pressed against the back of the chair and your elbows lightly bent, play as expressively as you can—continuing, of course, to direct your playing from your shoulders.

Practicing with your back against a chair helps you to let go of unwanted tensions in your neck and jaw—tensions that invariably center in your shoulders. Notice that when your torso is stable and at rest, your upper arms by necessity will have to move. This produces a legato in your playing that appears to originate in your body, the sensation being what I call "body legato." Actually, such musical sensations begin deep within you, rising from your solar plexus upward through your torso and then radiating through your arms and into your fingers. The rich tone that thus emanates from your instrument compels you to direct your listening to the *sound-board* rather than to the keys. When you are no longer concerned solely with key manipulation, you will be able to listen objectively to what is really coming out of the piano. The result is a synthesis of thought, feeling, and action.

The suggestion to sit in a straight-backed chair without moving your torso was intended to induce the proper movements of your upper arms and also to enable you to produce a rich, resonant sound that is a direct result of those movements. But the normal procedure for expressing your musical feelings at the piano is to move the torso economically. Sit now in your normal position—that is, with your shoulders away from the back of the chair. As you play, make whatever adapting motions are necessary; but whatever motions you do make must originate in your upper arms, exactly as they did in the above exercise. If, however, you have benefited by experiencing the control gained from sitting quietly, you may decide (as have so many artists) never again to move about while you play, or at least to move minimally, regardless of what kind of chair you use. You may also decide to continue using a straight-backed chair. The incomparable Artur Schnabel sat in one for each performance.

Initiating Wrist Movements

Sit in a chair and place the third fingers of each hand on your legs a few inches from your knees. While resting on your finger pads, gently roll your upper arms forward (away from your body) and backward (toward your body). Do not allow your third fingers to slide.

Notice that as you roll forward, your wrist glides up; as you roll backward, your wrist glides down. This simple experiment proves that the undulating movements of your wrist are initiated by the forward-backward movements of your upper arms. You can, of course, move your wrist between two fixed points—your elbow and bridge knuckles. However, such a movement not only induces strain but also lacks efficiency. Play the following examples with a forward-backward movement of your upper arms (I refer to this movement as the *upper arm roll*):

Upper arm rolls toward you—wrist down = ⟋

Upper arm rolls away from you—wrist up = ⟋

Let us now use the upper arm roll to sculpt a melodic line by applying the following choreographic movements:

J. S. Bach, *Two-Part Invention in C minor*

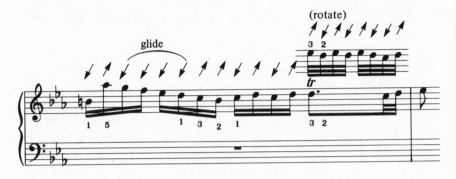

Alberti Basses

Domenico Alberti (c. 1710–1740) was the first composer to popularize a broken chord figure such as appears below:

Used chiefly as accompanying figures for the left hand, such groupings subsequently became known as *Alberti basses*. Musically and technically an Alberti bass poses a challenge to a pianist for it can easily sound dull and commonplace. However, synthesizing finger articulation with an upper arm roll will convert this simple figure into a musical experience. Let us go about this in two stages:

When you add your thumb, continue to connect 5 to 3 and then 5 to 2:

The following instructions will help you to control an Alberti bass as in the above example:

1. 5 and 3 may articulate on or above the key; your thumb,

however, must always lie on the key and on its side, generating movement from its hidden third joint at the wrist.

2. Ground your arm (inject pressure) on your fifth finger; then, gradually decrease this pressure as your arm rolls away from you and into E—third finger.

3. As your fingers articulate, rotate your forearm from left to right, but be careful not to use too much rotation in your playing. You can check this tendency by allowing your fingers to initiate the side-to-side motion of your hand and forearm—another example of the sovereign role played by your fingers in everything you do at the keyboard.

4. The faster your tempo, the less motion you require.

Octaves

The upper arm roll will greatly improve your ability to play rapid octaves. Hold your hand in a mold (arched bridge knuckles); extend your middle fingers, holding them together if you can; point your middle fingers in the direction of your fifth finger; experiment playing all octaves with 1 and 5 consistently. Now, with your torso held erect and supported by contracted muscles in your waistline and abdomen, steer your octaves in and out of the white and black keys with a forward-backward movement of your upper arms (try this on a chromatic scale). As your octaves become faster and more brilliant, draw upon your abdominal muscles for additional support and stability. Allow your torso to glide slowly and almost imperceptibly to the left or to the right following the direction of your playing.

We will use the following passage from the *Polonaise in A flat* by Chopin to emphasize some important principles in the performance of octaves:

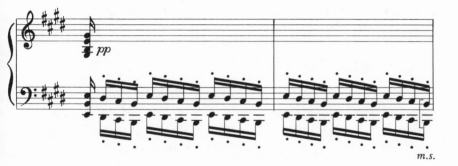

m.s.

1. A consistent use of 1 and 5 almost always facilitates the playing of octaves.
2. Play each octave with a separate hand stroke—down and up—from your wrist.
3. Roll your upper arm forward for the black keys (your wrist will be higher) and toward you for the white keys (your wrist will be lower).
4. Line up 1 and 5 on the *tips* of the keys. Remember that the keys offer less resistance toward the front.

By coordinating all of these motions, you will enable your thumb to trace a perfect circle starting on E and returning to E. The freedom resulting from an upper arm roll will then be immediately apparent to you. For each time your arm rolls forward for the black keys, your shoulder blades will open, easing your hand and wrist motions. Also, 1 and 5 will feel as extensions of your shoulder, enabling you to grasp the keys with a cushioned firmness.

CURVES OF ENERGY

A beautiful piano sound is produced by eliminating as far as possible extraneous noises—finger taps, key-bed thuds, hammer blows—and using both pedals judiciously. There is, alas, nothing you can do to change the quality of sound after a key has been struck beyond *preselecting* a carefully graded dynamic for it. But no sooner do you play two or more notes than you are challenged by the limitless possibilities for creating tonal effects. When playing a piece, your task, therefore, is to control the exact dynamic on each note of a chord (vertical) and from note to note (horizontal) and at the same time to balance the dynamic distance between your hands (vertical and horizontal). This requires that you have an image of the sound you wish to produce and that you lower each key at a rate of speed that will reproduce your sound image. The particular speed is then transferred to the hammers. In addition, piano sound is affected by the shape and duration of each movement made by your fingers, wrists, arms, and torso. Such movements are usually expressed in curves and only rarely in angles. Let us call these movements *curves of energy*. With this in mind, it is especially important for you to focus your attention on the various ways in which you can lower the keys:

1. You may direct your energy straight down.
2. You may direct your energy from right to left or from left to right.
3. You may begin *on* the key and trace a curve of energy *away* from you and down, landing in the key bed. Let us call this an *upstroke*.
4. Conversely, you may begin *on* the key and trace a curve of energy *toward* you, landing in the key bed. We will call this a *downstroke*.
5. Finally, there are various combinations of the above.

With the exception of the piano, virtually all instruments require a constant flow of energy to *prolong* sound or to *alter its quality*. String players direct this energy to the bow and left-hand vibrato; wind players and singers marshal it through breath control and changes of embouchure. Because pianists can do none of these things, they sometimes tend to relinquish all responsibility for a tone once it is sounded. Playing a single tone or chord defines clearly enough the inherent limitations of the piano. But once a second tone or chord is introduced in melodic or harmonic sequence, the distinctive capabilities of the piano are revealed by means of the skillful use of dynamics. How can we assure the exact dynamic coloration? By our physical attitudes *during and after* the first note or chord is played.

Let us suppose that you wish to play two slow chords at the end of a piece: you decide to use a downstroke for the first chord and an upstroke for the second. If the first chord happens to last for four slow beats, a problem arises: how can you keep your musical and physical impetus alive during what appears to be an interminable length of time? There are several ways in which to approach this problem. Detailing one of them will demonstrate to you how a musical feeling, when consciously conceived and executed, will yield predictable results. Let us take for our example the last two chords of the *Berceuse* by Chopin.

The steps for executing these chords are as follows:

1. With arms relaxed and wrists low, place your fingers on the surface of the first chord. To generate momentum, swing your arms away from you and then toward you into the first chord (a downstroke). Your sternum rises and your fingers are taut. Inhale. Maintain a gentle pressure in your finger pads (ground them) for the first four beats of the first chord. Your hands and arms remain still. Depress the right pedal.

2. As you swing into the chord, your torso should simultaneously describe a slow curve of energy by moving almost imperceptibly forward and toward the left. This motion of your torso will have traced a narrow elliptical path after the second chord has sounded. It has a dual function: (a) it reinforces your concentration throughout the length of the first chord; (b) it activates a *body legato* necessary for the controlled execution of the second chord.

3. On the fifth beat of the first chord, remove your fingers from the keys (you should remain in a low position) and prepare them on the surface of the second chord—well toward the *front of the keys*. Your torso will continue on its path, completing the first half of the elliptical path. Your right pedal remains down sustaining the first chord.

4. On the sixth beat of the first chord, part your lips and exhale. As

you do so, your upper arms will initiate an *upstroke*; at the same time, your torso continues its path toward the right and backward. Your sternum still rises for support. At this point, depress your left pedal.

5. As your wrists and arms rise in a curve of energy going forward, your fingers (still held taut) and your palms *tilt* the second chord in a curve of energy going both forward and downward. To gain the necessary traction on the key surfaces, your finger pads must grasp all the keys, not only pulling them toward you, but also toward each other—that is, 1 and 4 in your right hand gently pull toward each other; similarly, 1 and 3 in your left hand pull toward each other. Pull up on the bridge of both hands and simultaneously stabilize those fingers not engaged in playing the chord—especially your second fingers. This is done by keeping these fingers extended or curved.

6. Continue to concentrate on the disappearing sound of the first chord. At an exact time which you have predetermined, sound the second chord; simultaneously lift your right pedal slowly and depress it again. By the time the second chord has completed its required length, your torso will come to rest, having described an ellipse.

Your desire to play the second chord softly may cause you to delay it. Yet, it is most important that you play the second chord on time, allowing, of course, for a slight ritardando. Delaying the second chord too long promotes anxiety with the result that it may not sound at all. Two images can help you to find the courage to play the second chord on time and with the sound you desire. One is musical, the other, a vocal sound that will spark the second chord. The musical image was suggested to me by Sir Clifford Curzon when I was anguishing over a soft chord at the end of a piece: "The phrase," he said, "does not end with the sound of the final chord, but rather with its disappearance." This image instantly changed my musical and physical attitude from a vertical approach to a horizontal one. The notion of a vocal sound grew out of my solution for filling out rhythmic values with "kuh-kuhs." Thus, on the sixth beat of the first chord, I actually utter the sound "kuh" with the exhalation. The sound of "kuh" together with the sensation in my throat provides a welcome interruption to the disappearing chord. Psychologically, at least, it creates a fresh beginning on the weakest pulse of the chord, generating by the sheer surprise of its intrusion enough momentum (and courage) to make the second chord audible.

The following diagram represents all the movements discussed above together with their corresponding beats:

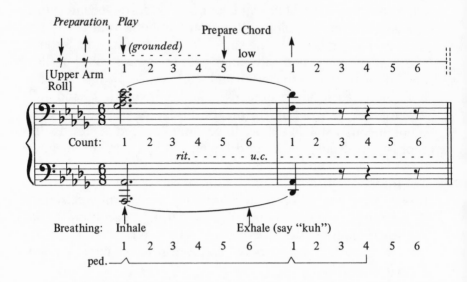

This detailed analysis is by no means complete, for I have concentrated only on what I believe to be the most conspicuous factors that constitute the execution of two chords. Each constituent in this process is subject to innumerable variations. Unlike an overprotective environment in which all decisions are made for you, the province of practicing leads you to make decisions for yourself, to follow, as it were, your own musical instincts and to arrive at those movements—your own movements—that will establish a connection between your musical expectations and their fulfillment through sound. In this sense, the above analysis is after the fact, for in recording it, I have merely objectified my own physical response to a musical feeling. It is hoped that you will do the same and that your physical choices will be governed fundamentally by your emotional response to music. In lieu of this, however, such an analysis can indeed serve as a guide during your practicing.

Exercises

In playing a five-finger pattern, your torso, arms, and fingers all form a coalition of movements:

1. Sit erect, shoulders down, sternum up, jaw relaxed.
2. Generate momentum for the first note by beginning with a low wrist, rolling forward with your upper arms, and making a downstroke into your thumbs.
3. As your undulating wrists glide up toward your fifth fingers and down toward your thumbs, your arms move laterally, transferring pressure from finger to finger. Remember to pull up your knuckles and keep your fingers taut.
4. The arrows marked in the exercise indicate the curves of energy. Trace their directions with your upper arms.

Now, let us reverse the left hand pattern and create curves of energy moving in opposite directions:

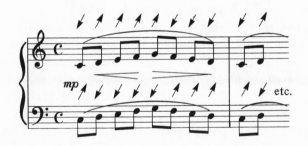

Once again, follow the arrows for the directional movements of your upper arms. When you begin this exercise, your torso should be twisted toward the right; when you reach G, your torso should be twisted toward the left. As the curves of energy flow up from your solar plexus and down through your arms, culminating in your finger pads, you will experience a pleasurable sensation unique to piano playing.

Having already discussed the various ways in which you can lower a key, it will be helpful, nevertheless, to review them with respect to the previous exercise:

1. Your right-hand thumb lowers the key in a curve of energy toward your body and down.
2. The other fingers of your right hand—2, 3, 4, and 5—lower the keys in a curve away from your body and up.
3. As the five-finger pattern descends, the curves of energy reverse themselves for 4, 3, and 2.
4. The curves of energy are applied in the opposite direction for your left hand.

Earlier in this section, we discussed the possibilities of lowering a key from left to right or from right to left. By injecting your energy into a key at an angle, you create traction, thereby enabling you to lower it at a controlled rate of speed. Returning to the previous example, study the right-hand pattern from D to G. Besides applying the curves of energy which we have discussed, you will also lower these keys at an angle from left to right. For the descending pattern—F, E, D, and C—lower the keys from right to left. Your left hand will proceed in a motion opposite to this.

To be able to coordinate so many diversified events is indeed an extraordinary achievement. In playing what appears to be a simple five-finger pattern, your fingers, arms, and torso must synthesize vertical and horizontal movements; your wrists will describe a circle by the time you have ascended and descended the pattern; your torso, a bulwark of stabilizing energy, acts as the major control center from which all other impulses originate—impulses which are contained in a body legato and radiate through your entire playing mechanism and into the keys, thus producing a rich, resonant sound by virtue of the exact speed of key descent. In applying these movements to various passages in your pieces, be willing to experiment indefinitely until you achieve the proper co-ordination. After all, something as demanding as a total organization of yourself—namely, the synthesis of feeling, thinking, and physical gestures—does not come without effort. Our love for music and our desire to share that love with others is, perhaps, the true sustaining element throughout the process of practicing. This love can, moreover, supply you with the patience necessary to wait for rewards. In other words, love, whether it is for a musical composition or for a person, can create a unique energy that enables you to find solutions to problems—problems which, formerly, you may have viewed as insoluble. Few know this truth as well as musicians, for they live it out in their practicing.

REVELATION NUMBER ONE: ADAPTING PHYSICAL MOVEMENTS TO ACCENTS

One day, I was practicing the following passage:

My intention was to play legato and to accent the first note of each triplet. A downstroke on C and F with my thumb felt very comfortable; but a downstroke on B with my fourth finger inhibited the flow of the scale. I wondered what I was doing wrong. Examining more closely the transference of my fourth finger (B) to my thumb (C), I suddenly deduced what perhaps ought to have been more obvious from the beginning: a downstroke on B quite naturally brought with it the bridge of my hand, thus inhibiting the passing under of my thumb. It was at that point that my revelation occurred: "Why," I asked myself, "must all accents be made with a downstroke? If the swing of my thumb were always prefaced by an upstroke, there would never be any difficulty in passing my thumb under the hand." As often occurs, one revelation leads to another, and soon I formulated the following maxim: *Choreographic movements at the keyboard are determined solely by the structure of the hand and the geography of the keyboard, but never by rhythmic accents.* Conversely, I arrived at the following: *Once you adapt choreographic movements to rhythmic accents, comfort is forfeited and technique itself is sabotaged.*

This simple C major scale was a turning point in my life. Recognizing physical comfort as the expression of a natural biological function, I set about to formulate the exact movements required in playing scales and arpeggios. My conclusions were almost embarrassingly simple; as I saw it, I needed only to choreograph two groupings applicable to all scales and arpeggios: 1, 2, 3 and 1, 2, 3, 4. These hold true even when a scale or an arpeggio does not begin on a thumb. This being the case, I arrived at the following choreographic movements for all scales and arpeggios.

The arrows signify downstrokes; all notes before and after the arrows are gliding upstrokes:

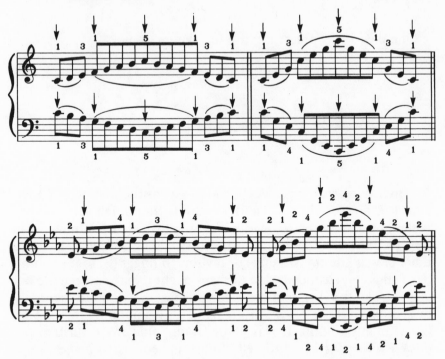

Whatever the rhythmic groupings may be—triplets or sixteenths—these choreographic movements never change (see Illustration XIII).

ILLUSTRATION XIII.   *Choreography in Scales*

Avoid this when you play a scale in sixteenth notes:

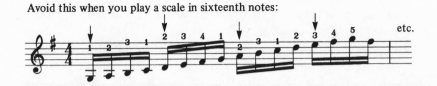

Maintain, instead, the following choreographic movements:

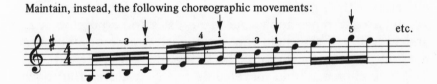

This is actually a comforting fact, for from now on, decisions regarding upstrokes and downstrokes need no longer be your responsibility—at least when playing scales and arpeggios. Remember, though, that in making their upstrokes, your wrists must never exceed a position higher than the back of your hand. Also, you must not treat all rhythmic accents explosively. Rhythmic accents are, for the most part, pulses that initiate the rhythmic groupings of a series of notes. As such, they should blend in with all the other notes of a passage, unless, of course, you wish purposely to accent them. In a previous discussion (see Chapter 6) you were forewarned against the tendency to play louder on a downstroke when hopping to your thumb in arpeggios and, conversely, to play too softly on the upstroke. The same tendency may show itself in playing scales. To prevent a "bumpy" thumb, decrease the pressure when your thumbs come into play and gently increase it as you glide up on 2, 3 or 2, 3, 4.

Some pianists view the weakness of their fourth fingers as a personal disability. The fact is that nature alone is to blame for this condition since the muscular structure of the hand is such that your fourth finger is bound to your third. Instead of worrying about it, or worse still, attempting by foolish means to rectify a biological flaw (as Schumann did with tragic results), simply take more rational measures by compensating for your "trapped" fourth finger—that is, *increase your hand and arm pressure* when your fourth finger comes into play. When you articulate your fourth finger, your third finger, as you know, will move along with it, and vice versa. Do not inhibit these movements. Because the muscle of your third finger overlaps that of the fourth, such compensatory movements are natural and therefore add strength and articulation to your playing. Moreover, these movements actually aid the third and fourth fingers on all upward choreographic swings. Mustering whatever strength you can to aid the fourth finger facilitates fast playing especially. In this case, as was explained in Chapter 5, all choreographic motions must be scaled down considerably. By compensating for this through increased hand and arm pressure, you will find yourself able to bring your fourth finger into comfortable focus especially within the short distances required in fast playing—that is to say, when your fourth finger must be *on the key.*

Finally, your choice of large and small choreographic arm movements or high versus low choreographic movements of your fingers should be guided by the style in which a composition is written. Baroque music, for example, generally requires high, articulate fingers without extravagant choreographic arm movements. Music in the Romantic idiom needs extensive legato for the most part, and for this, your fingers must remain close to the keys while your arms and wrists adopt the appropriate choreographic movements. The two extremes—finger versus wrist/arm movement—can both come into play for music of each of these periods, of course. Your own musical discretion will dictate how and when to select the one touch or the other. But no matter what touch you use, it is essential to remember that your fingers must always bear the greater share of responsibility. The choreographic movements for scales and arpeggios outlined above are not only based upon this principle but must also be more elaborately adapted to each note of the pieces you play. For the most part, you will make a downstroke on 1 and 5, coasting up, as it were, on the notes that follow. In other cases, your choice of a downstroke or upstroke will be optional. Those indicated in the following examples illustrate some instances in which necessity dictates one's choice:

J. S. Bach, *Partita in B flat (Minuet I)*

Chopin, *Etude,* Op. 10, No. 12

Schubert, *Sonata in B flat,* Op. Posth.

REVELATION NUMBER TWO:
THE THREE SPHERES

As a student at Fontainebleau, France, I had the honor of participating in the master classes conducted by Sir Clifford Curzon. Having to play before a master pianist and one whom I held in such high esteem understandably made me extremely nervous. I recall vividly the consequences of trying too hard to please him. No sooner did I begin the opening of the *Emperor Concerto* by Beethoven than my jaw, neck, and shoulders contracted into spasms of tension. With my fingers no longer the center of control, I weaved, pushed, and emoted to such an extent that I lost all objectivity in my musical approach; yet only an hour before, I had been soaring through the same passages with comfort and assurance. In my concern about what Sir Clifford was thinking, I concluded that this was just one of those "bad days" and yielded to the cruel reality of being a stranger to my own playing. At one point during a particularly exuberant passage in the *Concerto*, Sir Clifford walked up behind me, placed his fingers on my shoulders and gently pulled my torso away from the keyboard. Like a malfunctioning machine that needed merely a drop of oil, my entire body felt instantly liberated: the tension in my shoulder area subsided, my shoulders dropped at least four inches and my fingers suddenly became free. Within seconds I was enjoying the security and control that I had known during my practicing. But what had caused this miraculous shift in my playing? Unquestionably, the touch of Sir Clifford's fingers on my shoulders did much to distract me from my nervousness. But the experience held far more significance than mere distraction from nerves. In short, something in the gliding motion of my torso had brought me back full circle to my musical feelings.

There is a tendency in most of us to treat successful achievements simply as strokes of good fortune. This is understandable insofar as many rewarding experiences in life are unpredictable and therefore beyond our control. But such an attitude can have no place in your practicing. On the contrary. Not only must you be aware of musical and technical deficiencies, but more important, you must also pay close attention to your best playing and, in so doing, discover how you can reproduce it in an actual performance. And so it was that I brought a new direction to my practicing. With that liberating sensation induced by Sir Clifford always before me as a model, I waited patiently for those occasional flashes of excellent playing (which most practicers enjoy from time to time), ready to pinpoint the precise physical movements that accompanied my best playing. Twenty-two years later, the answer appeared in the form of Revelation Number Two. After a careful analysis, I was finally able to break down that harmonious state into three separate spheres:

Sphere 1: the fingers
Sphere 2: the palms, wrists, and arms
Sphere 3: the torso

Sphere 1: The Fingers

In light of the various movements of your fingers, the paths of curves and verticality that they trace in approaching the keys, it should be evident why they must bear the major share of responsibility in piano playing. But one more observation must be made—a rather obvious one—and that is that your fingers move faster than any other part of your body, a fact that leads us to liken their function to the second hand of a clock. For the second hand (just as your fingers) moves faster than either the minute or hour hand.

Sphere 2: The Palms, Wrists, and Arms

Study once again the instructions for choreographing a C major scale. You will observe that the three separate finger strokes, C, D, E, are bound together by one larger curve of your palm, wrist, and arm. In other words, the second sphere gathers together all the rapid and particularized movements of the first sphere. By moving forward, backward, and laterally, the second sphere creates a platform from which your fingers may work unimpeded. Since the movements of the second sphere are slower than those of the first, we may think of the second sphere as the minute hand of a clock.

Sphere 3: The Torso

Your torso is the overseer of your playing. Like the conductor of an orchestra, its movements reflect large musical ideas. The conductor (your body) retains a concept of an entire composition which the instrumentalists (your fingers) execute one note at a time. Moving more slowly than the other two spheres, your torso can be likened to the hour hand of a clock.

Thus, your aim in piano playing is economy of motion; that is, sphere 2 gathers together the rapid movements of sphere 1 and expresses them in slower movements. Finally, sphere 3 expresses larger ideas in what are by far the most economical movements of all three spheres.

Although these spheres operate independently, they also relate to each other. For example, your upper arm movements affect your finger articulation and vice versa. The simultaneous operation of the three spheres is demonstrated in the following example:

Mozart, *Sonata in G major*, K. 283

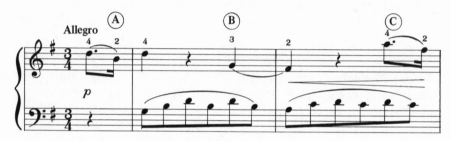

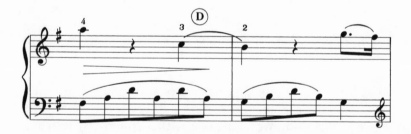

The choreographic movements suggested below make possible the uniform fingering indicated in this musical example (the dynamics are mine).

Analysis

The four fragments, Ⓐ, Ⓑ, Ⓒ, Ⓓ, are played with a down-up movement of your wrist and arm. The first notes of Ⓐ and Ⓒ are choreographed as follows:

1. Place your fourth finger on the surface of D (on the key).
2. Create momentum for the first note by starting with a low wrist,

then swinging up as though your arm were breathing. It is, in fact, helpful to inhale as you do this. As has been pointed out, all these movements must be initiated by your upper arm.

3. Now swing into the first note D with a downstroke. Allow the momentum of your hand, wrist, and arm to follow through in a rotary motion counterclockwise (toward the right) and upward. Your fourth finger stays grounded in the key bed.
4. Continue the rotary motion of your arm until it circles toward the left and swings down into the B.
5. After sounding B, your arm continues its rotary motion and circles back toward the right; during its path, play D on an upstroke.
6. Having held D for the length of a quarter note, your arm continues its follow-through and floats up into the air. Thus, in playing this fragment, your arm describes a circle.
7. The second fragment Ⓑ (G and F♯) is played with a down–up motion.

All of the above motions belong to Spheres 1 and 2. However, your torso (Sphere 3) gathers together the four fragments—Ⓐ,Ⓑ, Ⓒ,Ⓓ—into one large circular movement as follows:

1. As you start to play, stabilize your torso by dropping your shoulders and gently pulling up with your sternum. With your torso as your fulcrum, you may now swing your arms freely in any direction.
2. Once you sound the third note D, your torso begins to move slowly toward the left (clockwise). By the time you reach the fourth measure, your torso will have traced an ellipse.

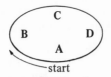

Moving your torso in an elliptical pattern is only one of many possible approaches: you may remain still for the first two measures and then move approximately one inch toward the left, the right, forward, or backward for the third measure; you may remain still for the entire theme but lift your sternum for the third measure. Whatever movements you may eventually arrive at should be reflective of your own musical feelings but moderate enough to be inconspicuous to your audience.

CONCLUSIONS

Interpreting a musical composition requires you to convert the symbols of musical notation into a synthesis of thought, feeling, and action, a process through which you glimpse into the feelings of the composer himself. The suggestions offered in this chapter are intended to guide all pianists, no matter what their range of talent, in this quest for musical expression. You are asked, therefore, to weigh carefully all this information and adapt it to your own emotional and physical needs. However, only by practicing every movement with concentration and consistency—the primary requisites for achieving artistic results—can you realize your ideal of making music.

Playing the piano with any degree of competence requires finger independence—the antithesis of the grasping instinct. In other words, you must transform each of your hands, programmed by nature to clutch, into ten autonomous fingers or, as one pianist put it, ten separate hands. To do this, you must compensate for the weak fingers of your hand as, for example, by exerting a little hand and arm pressure behind your fourth finger. Until such compensation becomes natural to you, the more *even* your playing may be, the more *uneven* it may temporarily feel.

Your immediate goal as a practicing musician is to balance your emotional and rational responses to music and articulate them through corresponding physical movements. Since you and your musical talent are inseparable, the balance you achieve in music ought to affect your personal life as well. Yet, many musicians, either consciously or unconsciously, perpetuate a schism between their musical and personal selves with the result that they may totally neglect their responsibility to others. This stems from an ignorance of or a disregard for the ultimate goal of practicing, a goal which is itself inseparable from the unifying effects of musical disciplines. When properly understood and directed, musical disciplines, because they are unifying agents, can infuse one's personality with the harmony and order inherent in music, thereby affecting one's relationships with others in a similarly harmonious way.

Yet, to express music on an instrument or by singing is an overwhelming challenge. Music, by its very nature, penetrates into our secret world, exposing our strengths as well as our weaknesses. On the one hand, we may lack the skills necessary to overcome technical deficiencies and thus fail to confront some of the issues discussed in this chapter. On the other hand, the feelings which music engenders in us stem from that core of sensitivity which, for various reasons, we may not wish to yield. But communicating music to others requires that we examine everything that pertains to music in all its organizational aspects. In the process, we must face the entire spectrum of our being. For this reason, performing is of inestimable value to our growth. Inasmuch as performing represents the culmination of all the disciplines of practicing, it is this that will occupy our attention in Chapter 9. Before we proceed, however, it may be helpful to sum up some important principles discussed thus far:

1. To become aware of your inner world through practicing, value the hours when you are alone by using them for honest reflection and constructive work.
2. Choose your friends with the same discrimination you bring to your practicing. A true friend must care whether or not you practice. This establishes a reciprocal bond between you that enables you to communicate to each other on all levels.
3. Always be aware of physical sensations during your practicing. Technical ease, for example, is a result of specific feelings, thoughts, and physical movements. Since each sound produced on your instrument has an accompanying physical sensation, learn to induce or even to turn off all such sensations and movements at will.
4. Devote some of your time to practicing performing. To do this, you must simulate all the attitudes you associate with performing and identify all the sensations they produce.
5. Maintain your musical spontaneity throughout all repetitious practicing and technical drills. Technical difficulties often arise simply because you have stopped feeling the music. Conversely, your musical feelings may be inhibited because of finger weakness and lack of flexibility. Thus, your practicing must be adapted to produce a balance between musical feeling and technical proficiency.
6. Yield to your creative impulses by improvising freely and spontaneously. This is a way of eavesdropping on your own musicality.

7. Sight-read every day not only to satisfy your musical curiosity but also to refine your skills and maintain your spontaneity.
8. Needless to say, we are all critical of our faults; but it is equally important to be aware of our best playing and to determine what factors brought it about.

Part III
Fulfillment through Performing

9 Performing

WHO PERFORMS AND WHY

A successful performance is the pinnacle of achievement in your musical development. In one sense, performing entails a synthesis of thought, feeling, and physical movements; but in a broader sense, it signifies a supreme act of artistic giving.

The act of performing is open to everyone—professionals and nonprofessionals alike. That is, anyone who practices diligently and plays or sings before others (teachers, family, or friends) earns the right to be called a performer. Those performers who maintain the highest artistic standards—and some nonprofessionals are included among them—are referred to as artists. Although the level of performance may vary from one musician to another, the rewards of performing should, nonetheless, be shared by everyone who performs. Thus, the amateur, through his sheer devotion to music, can benefit from performing in much the same way as does the artist:

The confidence he gains from meeting a challenge of such magnitude strengthens him to meet all other challenges.

His cohesive performance, even on the simplest piece, can arouse in others the desire to perform. He will then enjoy the glow of accomplishment for having served music in so exemplary a fashion.

His merest attempt at performing—whether or not it is successful—can be a humbling experience, making him more compassionate to the novice and more appreciative of the artist.

To mingle with the great minds of composers and to express the profundity of music with one's own two hands are privileges in their own right. Not only does the performer thereby perpetuate the noble art of music, but he also discovers within himself worlds of beauty that bind him to his art and to all other musicians.

For all of these reasons, we can say that a performer, at any level of advancement, is among the givers in society and is, as Balzac once said, as much a hero as a general in battle.

Anyone who has performed will understand why Balzac elevated the performer to a heroic status. For the concert stage is indeed like a battlefield where the artist wages a living battle between his strengths and weaknesses, the outcome of which is determined by how he practices. But such battles need not be waged in concert halls only; similar victories or defeats are frequently acted out in much less formal settings—living rooms and studios—where performers test their powers of concentration. Indeed, just as war games have their attraction for the professional soldier, performing can lure the musician to the stage. Some musicians in fact seem born to the stage and thrill to the demands of performing. A close friend of mine, who is a psychologist by profession, is in this respect a natural performer. He has for the last ten years spent the greater part of his free time studying voice, each year offering a full recital program. These have been memorable occasions not only for him but also for me, since they have given me the opportunity to make music with someone who dedicates himself to his art for the sheer love of it. We work together not as amateur and professional, but as two individuals committed to the same goals of artistic integrity. It is the anticipation of his yearly recital, though, that sparks the intensity of our collaboration.

To sustain themselves at peak performing levels, amateurs must often wage yet another kind of battle which consists in balancing their passion for expressing music with their responsibilities to their professions. Although my friend had successfully achieved this balance, even he did not fully appreciate the extent to which music had influenced his life—that is, not until a particular circumstance forced him to contemplate what his life would be without music. It happened that he contracted a respiratory infection shortly before one of his recitals. Feverish and anxious about not recovering in time for the performance, he fell into a troubled sleep and dreamed that he had inoperable nodes on his vocal cords. "When I awoke," he told me, "I was astonished to find myself crying. It was not only that I felt utterly bereft at the thought of never singing again, but more than that, the dream made me realize that I could not live without singing."

Like the life principle itself, music seems to have been wrought out of a higher order—an order that resounds in us when we perform music rather than when we merely listen to it. This dream, then, reminded my friend that being deprived of this order would actually rob his life of its meaning. Thus he came face to face with the realization that hidden within musical disciplines—and more especially in the techniques of performing—are all-encompassing resources which offered him rewards beyond the ability to express music. In other words, the process of practicing that ultimately led him to musical victories had helped my friend to achieve personal victories as well. Knowing this strengthened our musical collaboration and brought us even closer together as friends.

Not all musicians take to performing as naturally as my friend. After all, to emerge victorious in an activity as demanding as performing requires great courage and a superhuman organization of one's self. Small wonder, then, that many musicians shun performing even though they may be aware of its various benefits. Although most musically gifted people long to express those intimate feelings that only music can convey, they cannot—or dare not—because of fear, shyness, or an inability to practice properly and consistently. Rather than attacking the problem at its source, they invent rationalizations to justify their reluctance to perform. An amateur, especially, can convince himself all too easily that the demands of his other interests or profession are enough to frustrate his natural desire to perform. Such was the stand taken by a former pupil of mine who is now a writer and psychiatrist. How he eventually found the courage to perform inspires me to this day. Some years ago he and I heard Sir Clifford Curzon play the *Sonata in B flat*, Opus Posthumous, by Schubert—a performance that moved my pupil to put into poetry his love for Schubert and his admiration of Sir Clifford's playing. Knowing that Sir Clifford would be genuinely touched by a young person's devotion to a composer whom he himself held in such high esteem, I urged my pupil to send the poem to him. That Sir Clifford's response to the poem would help my pupil to deal with his fear of performing was something neither of us could have predicted. When he met my pupil the following week, Sir Clifford thanked him for the poem and added, "It is a grave responsibility to love a composer as much as you love Schubert. You have no other recourse then but to practice diligently so as to give back this love to others through performing." These words had an immediate and lasting effect on my pupil, for they gave him a reason to perform that made all other considerations seem of secondary importance. Responsibility to music, he realized for the first time, had to take precedence over all else—even fear. And by taking up this mantle of responsibility, my pupil was able to confront his own talent in such a way that his fear came to seem trivial to him when compared with his love for music. With this in mind, he was soon able to commit himself to a performance and prepare for it with the kind of motivation that led him to cope with his fear successfully.

As he gained more confidence in his ability to perform, he acquired a new insight that motivated him still further. "I don't mean to boast," he confided one day, "but I feel that my love for Schubert shows that I comprehend his music in some very special way. And I think it's this that gives me that grave responsibility Sir Clifford spoke about. You see, I used to think I had no right even to speak of my feelings for Schubert's music, let alone try to project what I feel to others in my playing. Now, I'm convinced that what I feel is valid. But only by practicing intelligently do I earn the right to communicate my feelings to others."

An unwillingness to accept the responsibility of which Sir Clifford spoke may also reveal itself in the professional musician. Because he, too, finds it hard to cope with his fears, he may eventually disqualify himself from performing with such rationalizations as, "I am talented in several directions and music is only one of them." "I am too nervous by temperament to perform; so, those who can, do—those who cannot, teach." Essentially, though, these expressions of insecurity stem from a lack of self-discipline that weaves its thread of irresponsibility through personal behavior and leads in the end to deep embitterment. Curiously enough, such musical self-indulgence is often matched by a lack of consideration for others: 'phone calls are not returned, appointments are not kept, and all the small courtesies we associate with responsible conduct are disregarded. In other words, responsibility to music, if it is to be served as Sir Clifford suggested, is not limited to the development of one's talent per se, but directly involves the people around us. It generates a vital energy that converts irresponsible behavior into a consideration for others, doubt into confidence, and weakness into strength. A commitment to a performance hinges, then, upon just how responsible you are to music, to others, and to yourself.

Some amateur musicians are discouraged from performing simply because it takes what seems to them an excessively long time to bring a new piece up to a performing level. They apparently do not realize that many professional musicians may also need to learn new material slowly. One artist may take a year or more before he attempts to perform a new work in public, whereas another may be able to memorize a new composition on a train and perform it in the next city. The fact that both artists end up performing with equal success proves that this variable time factor has no bearing whatsoever on the individual quality of their playing. Therefore, if your reasons for performing are clear, you will discover that preparation time (like fear) is, in the final analysis, of secondary importance. What matters most is that you practice as hard as you need to in order to serve music as responsibly as you can.

PERFORMING: AN INCENTIVE TO PRACTICE

Many years ago, I attended a social gathering made up almost exclusively of performing musicians. I remember that evening in particular because the discussion centered on practicing. Although I sensed even in those days that practicing was influencing my whole life, I was, nevertheless, still uncertain about what really motivated me to practice. As the discussion revealed, the other musicians in the room were as much in doubt on this point as I. Having studied music from early childhood, most of them practiced automatically and with an almost mindless obedience. Though they were now professional musicians, they seemed to be as unclear about their reasons for practicing as they were forgetful of their initial love of music. For some, music had become simply a "business." Others had even lost touch with their sensitivities to the feelings of their colleagues. In short, they were now blasé and, as became blatantly evident in the discussion, totally anesthetized to all issues pertaining to their musical development. Above all, not one among them so much as ventured to account for those great fluctuations in practice habits to which we all admitted. Suddenly, in the midst of the discussion, it struck me that my own motivation to practice was fed by something that no one had yet mentioned: "I love music and I express this love by playing the piano. But playing music and practicing it are two completely different activities. As for myself, I know for certain that I would not practice if there were no one to play for." My words surprised me as much as the others since I had never before made a conscious distinction between playing and practicing, much less articulated it. At first, several musicians present insisted that they did in fact always practice conscientiously whether they were to play for others or not. But interestingly enough, those who insisted the most on this point seemed to have more performing engagements than all the others; in the necessity to meet these professional obligations, they had apparently forgotten about those interims between engagements when they were not motivated to practice. Finally, all had to agree that a commitment to a performance provides more than any other single factor the chief incentive to practice.

Several years later, I had an opportunity to prove this point dramatically. After being discharged from the army, I, like so many other soldiers, found it very difficult to readjust to my former routine. I knew that only a severe challenge would dispel my lethargy. Therefore, I asked my manager to arrange for my New York debut, a commitment which soon motivated me to practice with more concentration than I had ever done in the past. It took me nine months of intense preparation before I began to feel musically and personally reconstituted. Finally, when the important day arrived, I was ready to meet the challenge.

Every musician must, of course, set challenges for himself that are realistic. Certainly, a nonprofessional or inexperienced musician will usually find more than enough stimulation in playing for family and friends or perhaps by participating in performing classes arranged by his teacher. In fact, for many students, the latter, if conducted seriously, actually reproduce the charged atmosphere of a professional performance and thereby inspire the most efficient practicing imaginable. Other students find that their music lessons alone supply the chief motivation for intense practicing. In any case, when one challenge is successfully met often enough, it must be replaced by another more demanding one. This holds above all for students who aspire to a career in music, for they must ultimately subject themselves to challenges of the most severe order—namely, public performances and competitions.

CONTESTS

"Winning a contest is proof that I am really a great talent. But if I should lose, that means I am not gifted enough to have a career in music." "If that is the kind of review my playing warrants, then I ought not to play in public ever again." We are all familiar enough with these sentiments; perhaps we have even had occasion to express them ourselves. They mean, of course, that the opinions of judges and critics are being accepted as the only criteria of excellence to the exclusion of one's own objective standards and taste. The young musician who endorses these criteria—and, alas, there are many who do—eventually loses all ability to judge his own individual gifts. Thus, in his estimation, his playing is good only if the judges and critics say it is. More often than not, directors or judges of competitions foster this kind of thinking in young aspirants by their sometimes cruel exercise of power. I recall auditioning for three judges during the preliminary rounds of a major competition. While the contestants were waiting backstage for the judges' decisions, the head of the auditions committee approached us with these words: "If all three judges vote for you, you will go into the finals; if two judges vote for you, you may or may not go into the finals; but if none of the judges vote for you, you had better open a candy store!" I can only conclude, as I reflect on this incident, that she was drawing a false sense of power from the contestants' vulnerable position. Certainly, her caustic remark was well calculated not only to undermine our confidence, but also to endow the judges with omniscience. We were being taught that our destinies were in their hands and that their decisions represented an absolute standard of excellence.

Many teachers believe that contests are by their nature unfair and for that reason forbid their students to enter them. This position gains acceptance from the fact that many contestants who are possessed of a truly formidable talent are sometimes eliminated from the early rounds. But in all fairness to the judges, such decisions are not always arrived at without good reason: the contestant may not have been adequately prepared; despite his talent, his skills may have been insufficiently developed at this particular time; he may have given a poor account of himself simply from having a "bad day" or from not yet having learned how to master his nerves. If, for all or any of these reasons, he played too many wrong notes or had too many memory slips, the judges would be entitled to view his work as unacceptable, particularly in a major competition. Sometimes, decisions of judges are based on less firm grounds: they simply may not have liked the repertory offered (in cases where it was not prescribed) or may have found the contestant's style and approach unappealing. A contestant who is rejected for these reasons should not feel totally defeated or unworthy of having a career. Rather, he should view this experience as an instructive guide to another attempt at competing. It is true that winning a contest can launch a career. But it is equally true that many an artist has achieved success without ever having won a major competition. Somehow, then, contests must be put into the proper perspective: winning may not necessarily guarantee a successful career and losing may not signify a mediocre talent. Considered objectively, the outcome of a competition attests to only one phase in a performer's total development and should not be regarded as an ultimate or irreversible decision. André Gide, at age twenty, protested against the critics' harsh appraisal of his writing: "Why can't they see what I will be just by the look in my eye?"

Besides the contestants' nervousness, there are other factors that may contribute to the tense atmosphere surrounding a competition: one is the unpredictability of its outcome; another can often be attributed to the offensive attitude adopted by some judges. Certainly, a judge must be dispassionate in rendering his decisions, but, equally important, he must never lose sight of the person involved in the performance. Barking commands and unreasonable requests ("... please start at the coda of the *F minor Ballade....*") succeed only in diminishing what may be a contestant's best efforts. Unfortunately, however, sitting in judgment over young hopefuls can easily induce in some people an exaggerated sense of their own importance. How else can one account for a decision delivered some years ago to the four brilliant pianists who survived the finals of an international competition? Acting as spokesman for the panel of twelve judges on this occasion, a renowned conductor handed down the verdict: "Some of you are talented but not gifted; others are gifted but not talented. Therefore, there will be no winner this year," whereupon he turned his imperious back on the stunned contestants and strode away. The assumption of a distinction where others could find no difference produced the desired effect—it was the judgment of an oracle. Presumably he meant that some of the contestants had technique but no personality and vice versa. Whatever the case, one would suppose that the four contestants who had reached the finals of such an important competition had already displayed sufficient technique and temperament to qualify as talented according to the accepted meaning of the word. The decision, compounded as it was by a semantic quibble, created a scandal in musical circles and did much to perpetuate a distrust of everything connected with competitions.

Expertise, impartiality, disinterested objectivity—all these are needed for the reliable judging of contestants. High-handedness, sarcasm, disdain, arrogance, or anything else that works toward other ends, have no place in competitions. Even if we could allow for the subjective response of the conductor in question here, we would have to find his manner completely out of keeping with the purpose and intent of competitions. As a matter of fact, his manner had already earned him a reputation for undue harshness in musical circles, quite apart from his behavior at competitions. A close friend of his dared to chide him for this on one occasion when his railing at the members of his orchestra seemed out of all proportion to the question at issue—an apparently insignificant musical detail. "For heaven's sake," his friend remonstrated, "you act like this is a matter of life and death!" "It is exactly that," the conductor replied. "To me, everything in music, no matter how minor it seems to you, is a matter of life and death." Certainly, we cannot question the right of a conductor or any musician, for that matter, to treat a musical detail with all the seriousness at his command. But to what extra-musical lengths should this attitude be carried? That is, can it be a sufficient basis for treating human beings as mere accessories to a musical idea? Does it give anyone the license to subject contestants, not to mention orchestral members, to what may be lasting psychological damage? In reality, all this amounts to using music as it was never meant to be—as a weapon for power—and, what is worse, as a divider of the person from his own humanity. For nothing—and least of all, music—entitles anyone to behave cruelly to others. If the behavior of some musicians seems not to bear this out, it is simply because they have apparently learned nothing from the music they have practiced—nothing of its harmonious workings and nothing of its unutterable humanity. Yet, if any good can result from the cruelty that is all too often dealt out to contestants or students by tyrannical judges or teachers, it would consist in providing aspiring musicians with examples to be avoided.

Apart from the difficulties posed by tyrannical judges, unfair decisions, and a general climate of tension, contests can be detrimental to a student's growth and even ruinous to his career for several other reasons. First, if the repertory requirements are unsuited to his temperament or needs at a particular time in his development, they may seriously hamper his progress. In some cases, the year or more spent preparing this material might have been devoted more advantageously to works of a completely different sort. Second, winning a contest does not necessarily guarantee a successful career. For one thing, the glamor and fame it can bring are often short-lived. And since the music business—like any other business—thrives on novelites, "there is no one more difficult to sell than last year's winner," as one manager told me. But even more serious problems than this can arise if a contest winner is not ready emotionally, physically, or temperamentally to assume the responsibilities of his new role. The many career casualties among contest winners testify all too well to this unhappy fact of musical life.

As for contests themselves, they can be a force for good only insofar as they are regarded as stages in a performer's total development rather than final goals. By providing the standards against which contestants can measure their present attainments, they are musically instructive; by setting the conditions wherein behavior—of contestants as well as judges—weighs heavily on each event, they test personal weaknesses and strengths. Therefore, even if a contestant loses the actual prize in music, he can be a personal winner in his own estimation by treating a particular contest for what it is—an exercise in learning.

REVIEWS

When the desire to get a rave review becomes an end in itself, it is an open invitation to trouble. A performer may play his best; he may even be acclaimed by the audience; yet the next day brings a bad review in the leading newspaper. His hopes are shattered and he shudders to think of the vast audience of readers who can never know how well he really played. The review has done its worst quite simply because he has allowed it to. By placing the critic's appraisal above his own standards of judgment, he undermines his ability to view himself objectively. The result is loss of self-belief. But the fact is that every well-practiced performer who is totally committed to maintaining the highest standards of his art knows better than anyone exactly how he played. His artistic integrity demands that he be his own best judge. If he allows a critic's assessment to supplant this special knowledge, he loses what every artist needs the most—trust in his own artistic vision.

Paradoxically, a rave review can be damaging for the same

reasons, as I learned from experience. My New York debut happened to have elicited excellent reviews from all of the five critics who heard it. "This," I thought, "is the best of any reward I could get for all my years of practicing." But the question was, did the reward consist in the critics' response or in my own knowledge of what I had achieved? The disillusionment that followed this experience gave me the answer all too well. I began to prepare for my second recital, this time concentrating on fulfilling the promise projected by the critics rather than on the artistic issues that had previously been my uppermost concern. With my attention divided and my mind diverted into the wrong area, my preparation had to be adversely affected. Alas, the reviews reflected this: the critics confirmed what I knew to be true. Although it was hard having to face the contrast between the two sets of reviews, I learned two things from the experience: performing for the right reasons guarantees adequate preparation; reviews, like contests, can be of value if they are placed in proper perspective. My debut was a critical success not because I played for rave reviews but because I gave all my efforts, my thoughts, and my concerns to the music. To be equal to its demands entailed endless hours of concentrated practicing. From this I derived strength and self-confidence and, above all, an unshakable belief in my musical judgment. If the reviews bore out my objective evaluation of my accomplishment, it was a bonus; but a greater benefit, as I learned in retrospect, came from the work I had done. During the period of arduous preparation, I had so totally united myself with the music I was practicing that nothing, it seemed, could impede the expression of my musical feelings. The result was that the mental image I had of the music was reproduced in my playing. This fusion of musical intuition and instrumental technique comes from one source only—practicing that probes music to its core. It was this factor that my second recital lacked.

Obviously, entering contests and performing in concerts are incentives to practicing. But even within this framework, your practicing must focus on one objective only—to do justice to the music. Playing to judges or to critics—playing if only to win a prize or to receive a rave notice—are essentially futile tactics. They may produce temporary results, but in the end they divert you from your responsibility to music and, worse, they impair your most valuable asset: the ability to be your own best judge. Although this ability is rooted in your musical intuition, it must be informed by a genuine musical knowledge if it is to stand up under the weight of others' criticism. But as your self-judgment deepens and solidifies, you will come to recognize the value of the various kinds of criticism you receive. You will learn to treat subjective responses for what they are and objective appraisals for what they can teach you. If the judgment of those you hold in highest esteem coincides on occasion with your own, you will know how to appreciate the worth of this also. "In time," as Sir Clifford Curzon once advised me, "your own inner voice will tell you all you need to know."

A MEASURE OF YOUR OWN WORTH

Every performer welcomes comments from members of the audience after a concert, whether backstage or at a reception following. He wants to know that his playing produced a reaction in his listeners and did not simply vanish into the ether. But sometimes post-concert conversations touch upon almost everything except one's performance. I used to think this signified an indifference to my playing and, naturally enough, it would perplex and unsettle me, especially if my "inner voice" told me my performance had been good. However, experience has taught me that many people quite simply do not know what to say to a performer after a concert or else do not know how to express what they feel. Shyness or the possibility of revealing their ignorance about the music inhibits them or makes them awkward in the presence of the performer. Others, who have been conditioned to repress their enthusiasm regardless of the intensity of their feelings, remain silent on general principles or, what is worse, resort to irrelevant small talk. Since the performer can deal only with the fact of their silence, awkwardness, or lukewarm attitude, he may assume responsibility for their behavior by underrating his performance. But this is as unfair as it is unjustified. If a performer is as good a judge of his playing as he ought to be, he will have armed himself against the apparent indifference of some listeners.

Being objective about your playing demands, of course, that you be your own best critic. Paradoxically, the most responsible of performers are more often than not their own worst detractors. Because they strive constantly to be equal to the highest standards of their art, they can rarely be totally satisfied with a given performance—there is always, they feel, something that could have been better. If, however, they project their own critical values onto the listeners, as they often do, they see only their own judgment reflected in the audience's response—praise is then interpreted as politeness and silence as indifference or even censure. And should they be suffering guilt for not having prepared properly, or otherwise hold themselves in low esteem as a matter of course, the mere hint of a compliment may actually rouse them to anger or to hostility. No doubt it was just such a case of self-denigration that prompted a pianist I know to dismiss entirely my enthusiastic response to her playing with, "You must be crazy!" In any case, it would do well for some performers simply to exercise common courtesy in the face of a compliment—no matter what their private hell—and learn to say, "Thank you."

Misconstruing an audience's response is a failing peculiar to performers, and it can sometimes produce startling consequences, as I once learned. I had given a concert in Seoul, Korea, which, I felt, was not one of my best efforts. I was understandably dejected afterward and did not particularly look forward to the private banquet that was to follow. Before the dinner was served, my interpreter ceremoniously introduced me to the distinguished assemblage of musicians and writers invited for the occasion. Each of them acknowledged the introduction with all due formality but said nothing about the concert. Then, as one delectable course followed another, the silence in the room seemed to grow more and more pervasive. I became more and more uncomfortable. A woman of striking appearance—one of Korea's foremost poets, I was told— caught my eye, but she, like all the others, averted her glance. For me, all of this had one meaning only—my performance must have been even worse than I thought. I had just about resigned myself to this gloomy conclusion when the poet, sitting to my right, murmured something to my interpreter. He leaned toward me and said for all the guests to hear, "Mr. Bernstein, the distinguished poet has just told me that she is so moved by your playing that she wishes to die." Whereupon everyone resumed eating, their faces as expressionless as his voice. I must have mumbled something in response, but all I can remember is the feeling of embarrassment that came over me. The extravagance of the compliment notwithstanding, I was astonished to realize how thoroughly I had misinterpreted the innate reserve and modesty of these generous people. That their behavior could mean anything but an implicit criticism of my playing had never dawned on me. In all, it was deeply unsettling to learn how far from the truth a performer's own frame of reference can lead him. My years of performing experience have since taught me that a true inner security, if constantly nourished by a well-trained self-objectivity, cannot be shaken, regardless of the external circumstances.

I value the opinions and judgments of my audience—especially those of my former teachers, friends, and pupils—but I have learned to be understanding of an occasional silence or apparent lack of enthusiasm on their part. The cause, as I have discovered, can be totally unrelated to the fact of my having just performed. There is, however, a post-concert situation of quite a different order that I am sometimes at a loss to explain and always find hard to tolerate. If it is rarely discussed, it is nonetheless familiar to all performing musicians because it is a characteristic feature of professionalism. It is, in short, a behavioral convention that prevents one's colleagues in the field from saying anything positive, supportive, or generous after a performance. To compliment a colleague for his efforts is felt somehow to be beneath the dignity of everyone concerned in the performance. But when competitiveness, jealousy, or insensitivity are injected into this atmosphere of artificiality, the effects can be downright chilling. All of this has, of course, nothing to do with the spirit and nature of music. It contradicts everything we try to express in our art and everything we strive to become as human beings. It is, in short, a mode of behavior that runs counter to the humanity of music itself. To deal with it, one has two choices: become immune to it by accepting it as one of the less pleasant facts of professional musical life, or reject it and adopt instead an attitude that conforms more nearly to the natural dignity within yourself that is enshrined in the music you play. Needless to say, it is the latter course that I have always recommended to my students.

THE FOUR STAGES OF LEARNING

An initial spontaneous attraction for a piece of music is the best of all possible encouragements to learning. But it is not enough to guarantee the total mastery that makes for a sustained artistic experience. It must be transformed from what it is—an indefinable stirring of the imagination—to a deeply complemented love. This is usually accomplished in four stages: spontaneity, awareness, commitment, synthesis.

Spontaneity

Who has not felt the impact of love at first sight? Who can say what stimulated it? It may awaken to a single theme, a subtle modulation, or an inner harmonic voice. Like some intangible quality in a human being that stirs the senses of another, a single chord of music can reach the heart. In this first stage of encounter, feelings are all spontaneous and charged with currents of passionate longing. Thought and reason are overwhelmed by exultation. Exhilarating and reckless freedom drives us into the music with abandon. Nothing daunts us as we discover more allurements and charms. Phrasings, dynamics, bewitching motifs all seem as comprehensible to us as daylight. It is a moment of love; and love, you may say, needs no definition. To retain this initial spontaneity of feeling over the long course of mastering a piece is one of the most difficult tasks a musician faces. Spontaneity, left untended a moment too long, disintegrates rapidly through its own uncontrolled force. Like blind infatuation, it engenders feelings that tend to fluctuate and, in some cases, vanish altogether, as a Spanish ballade reminds us:

Amores que tan fácilmente nacen,
Es lógico que pronto morirán.

Loves that are born too easily,
Are destined soon to die.

Paradoxically, spontaneity can be held in reserve only through discipline. This is because first love, however heady and rapturous, tends to grow less dependable the more easily it is gratified. Boredom then replaces ardor and all is lost in disenchantment. Thus what appears to be the cruel hand of destiny may more accurately be charged to lack of discipline or an unwillingness to sacrifice one's freedom to the requirements of one's love.

Awareness

There are two ways to maintain spontaneity of feeling. One is through observation; the other, through analysis. Together, observation and analysis lead you to a state of awareness that illuminates your love and encourages it to endure. It is a state in which feeling is tempered by thought.

Without observation, we experience only a fraction of what our senses report; without analysis, we understand even less of what we feel. In other words, to keep your ardor alive, you must observe your every response even as you are analyzing the music that inspired it. This means having to face yourself even at the risk of discovering something you would rather not know. Some musicians are wary of this sort of observation and analysis. Like lovers afraid to be awakened from a dream, they distrust it. "Examining the inner workings of music may actually divide me from my spontaneity," they say, "and then everything I feel will vanish into a maze of details." For them, self-expression is everything and must be defended at all costs. Any activity of the mind, any expenditure of energy that is not sensually gratifying, in short, any amount of concentration that places limits on their freedom is to be avoided. The problem is that a musical composition by its very nature sets limits on our mode of expression. Its markings, phrasings, dynamics are not ours to alter at will, but rather to honor with our deepest attention. Curiously enough, the analysis of such musical details required of us is what ultimately feeds the springs of our spontaneity. It is in these myriad details of form and content that the spirit of the composer is finally reincarnated. Our task then is to harmonize our feelings with that spirit and thereby permit it to speak through us.

To achieve awareness without analyzing spontaneity out of existence you need to learn to think—as well as feel—musically or, to put it another way, to take all that you love into your mind—as you have into your heart—and thus make it an integral part of yourself. This means treating music as a beloved and living thing whose special requirements and nature you must closely observe. Only then will you discover what there is within yourself that can best serve it. This kind of observation and analysis brings you at last to a point of contact between yourself and your art that is the purest form of awareness. It is a state in which nothing is left unexamined, least of all that indefinable quality of feeling—spontaneity. At this level of awareness you can give yourself over to your spontaneous feelings at the most important moment of all—during a performance.

Two things deserve your consideration. One is that if observation and analysis cause your spontaneous feelings to pale rapidly, your initial love was probably mere infatuation and was, therefore, indeed destined "soon to die." Second, it is possible to analyze a genuine love out of existence and thus lose all contact with its original stimulus. To prevent this, you must periodically suspend all analysis and play through your entire composition with abandon, reliving, as it were, your first encounter with it. Each time you repeat this experience, your awareness of your own control over feeling and thinking enlarges upon it until your original response to the music is finally rekindled and even intensified.

Commitment

There are times when trying to fathom what a composer intends is like pondering the meaning of a friend's behavior. Some vital connection seems to elude us so that what ought to make perfect sense becomes suddenly incomprehensible. The more we search for answers, the less confident we feel. Trapped in a labyrinth of confusion and misunderstanding, we seek solace in rationalizations. At a moment like this even the most ardent student is tempted to abandon his work on one composition and look for refuge in another. We have all experienced such moments and on occasion have perhaps even succumbed to disenchantment: "I was never meant to play Beethoven anyway; I lack some special understanding. Best to shift to that Schubert Sonata. At least I can trust my instincts there." But the moment you turn from one half-completed task to begin another for the sake of expediency, you set a dangerous precedent for yourself. Even though a residue of nagging guilt may linger, you will find it easier to justify a second abandonment and a third, until you drift almost imperceptibly into the ways of a musical philanderer, enjoying momentary pleasures without ever having to come to terms with your own inherent limitations. Only one thing can prevent this: commitment to a genuine purpose. If you are humbled by the genius of a Beethoven or a Schubert or a Brahms, your purpose must be to grow large enough in spirit and accomplishment to meet them on their terms. A commitment to this purpose is what replenishes your strength and lends constancy to your efforts. It is at its best when it is the natural consequence of spontaneity: "I love that piece and I am going to master it if it takes the rest of my life."

A commitment of this kind is often generated, if not demanded, by that state of awareness in which you reach a complete accord with your music. From this moment on, the piece is yours because you have earned it. Your commitment to grow with it, renewing and refining your understanding of it, whenever and for as long as you wish, is your passport to yet greater accomplishments.

In the absence of a spontaneous reaction to a particular piece and without the cumulative effects of awareness through analysis, such a commitment is more often than not virtually impossible. There is one factor, however, that can supply the missing ingredients, if need be—the enthusiasm of a genuinely interested teacher. Indeed, one of the few but great rewards of teaching is to see how a student will respond to the well-considered direction of the teacher. If a teacher is alert to a student's needs, he will not fail to notice two things: whether the student seems to be laboring under or is uninspired by his repertory, and whether he should be assigned repertory rather than be given free rein in selecting pieces to study. Since even the most advanced students can sometimes seriously misdirect themselves with respect to repertory, a teacher must be able to judge if and when he should interfere in the matter of selection. Above all, he must know to what pieces he should direct the student. And frequently, this requires no small amount of thought and discussion. It can happen that an assigned piece will at the outset make little impact upon the student. "It leaves me cold; I have no affinity for it," he may complain. If it was the right piece, six months later he will be utterly captivated by it and will scarcely be able to remember his initial reaction. Such a metamorphosis is usually brought about by the inspired and thoughtful direction of a teacher from whom even a single well-placed remark can supply a spark of excitement in a sensitive student. Commitment is the inevitable result and the beginning of serious growth.

Synthesis

This is the stage of enlightenment at which all your resources of feeling, thought, and physical co-ordination meet in a mutually supportive balance. At this point, everything you felt, dreamed of, and understood intuitively in your first moment of love is realized and fulfilled, but with this important difference: it is all informed now by awareness and knowledge. Your love is no longer a mystery nor are your responses vague and ill-defined. You have given your love space and dimension; you have fortified it with understanding. Armed with this new meta-knowledge or supra-consciousness, you are now in a position to gratify others with the beauty you have absorbed into yourself. You are ready to perform.

10 Memory

Until the latter part of the nineteenth century, it was considered bad taste and ostentatious for performers to play in public without their scores. Even Mozart, whose memory was prodigious, always placed the music before him whenever he performed, in deference to the conventions of his day. On one such occasion, the emperor himself was to discover inadvertently just how extraordinary Mozart's memory could be. He had been especially pleased by the premier performance of the *Sonata in B flat* for Violin and Piano, K. 454, and asked to see the score from which Mozart had just played. To his astonishment, he was handed a single sheet of manuscript paper—completely blank. When he asked the meaning of this, he was told that Mozart had completed the work only the night before at the request of Signora Strinasacchi, the violinist who performed it with him. With scarcely enough time to copy out the violin part for the Signora to practice the following morning, Mozart had to memorize his own part for the performance. It was in reality a multiple feat of musicianship, for not only did the Signora learn the work in a matter of hours and Mozart himself play it from memory, but they also carried off the performance without a rehearsal.

To judge from various accounts of their performing practices, other great artists before the twentieth century apparently played from memory even though they always appeared on stage with their scores. Small wonder then that audiences, long inured to established traditions, were shocked when Clara Schumann dared to go on stage without a score (she never performed concerti from memory, however—not even the one composed by her husband). It was now 1828 and a new precedent had been set. Clara Schumann demonstrated what was already an accepted fact to all performing artists before her—that a score was quite superfluous

219

since serious performers always memorized their performing repertory as a matter of course. It was not long, though, before Liszt, with his well-known predilection for showmanship, seized the opportunity to turn this new development into a dramatic ritual. He had always thrilled his audiences when he peeled off his white gloves and tossed them lightly into the first few rows. But at one performance he caused a veritable uproar by tossing his score after his gloves. If the average concert-goer was dazzled, certainly the opponents of memory-playing were positively scandalized by Liszt's theatrics. But it would take even more than a Liszt, however much he was given to flaunting his remarkable memory in the faces of his critics, to camouflage a truth that has been known to musicians for centuries—namely, that all performing artists, including Liszt, Clara Schumann, and Mozart before them, are able to listen more intensely and play more fluently when freed from the score. Even those musicians who agree that a fear of memory slips is the chief cause of nervousness would still defend the virtues of playing from memory. In any case, it would be many more years before audiences and critics would consider performances from memory as anything more than exercises in showmanship.

In 1861, Sir Charles Hallé, the British virtuoso, began the first in a series of concerts devoted to all the Sonatas of Beethoven. He played from memory. By the third concert, he capitulated to the conservative London critics and appeared on stage with the music. But, like Mozart, he continued to play from memory nonetheless. As late as 1870, Dr. Hans von Bülow, whose feats of memory were legendary, found the London critics to be as resistant as ever to performances from memory. In this case, however, the audience came in for a greater share of censure from the Daily Telegraph than von Bülow: it was his memory and not his musicality that seemed to make the greatest impression, the critics complained. It was not until the end of the nineteenth century that playing from memory came to be regarded as a serious practice and not mere sensationalism. Certainly today it is far more unusual for a soloist to play with a score than without it.

WHY MEMORIZE?

There is something very important to be gained from memorization that many musicians themselves may not be aware of. Apart from freeing a performer in musical and technical ways, memorization per se, despite current opinion to the contrary, actually sharpens the mind. In ancient Greece, students of rhetoric were required to memorize all of their texts and recitations not only to master public speaking, but also to hone their minds. Music, which occupied a status equal to that of arithmetic, geometry, and astronomy in the ancient curriculum or Quadrivium, was performed without exception from memory. In fact, it is quite probable that compositions—both vocal and instrumental—were handed down directly from master to pupil without scores, a practice that would explain why so little ancient Greek music has survived. They had a notation, but they relied primarily on memory. Thus, when Athenaeus said, "The study of music contributes to the exercise and acumen of the mind," he no doubt was referring to memorization as one of the many educative features associated with the disciplines of music.

There are, of course, as many variations in the ability to memorize as there are degrees of talent. Certainly, it would be difficult to imagine any feats of memory more awesome than those performed by Mozart. Once, while still a boy, he was more or less smuggled into Saint Peter's in Rome to hear Gregorio Allegri's *Miserere*—a work that had been the exclusive property of the papal choir for more than a century—and subsequently wrote down all nine voices from memory. Mendelssohn, at a comparable age, was said to have performed the identical feat. Very few musicians can boast of such extraordinary powers. Whatever your faculties, though, there can be no disputing the value of memorizing your music. A work cannot be thoroughly known unless it is committed to memory. For details which would otherwise go unnoticed are consciously absorbed only through memorization. Once you have memorized your music, you have the option to use it or not in performance. Some performers are in fact distracted by any visual contact with notation and therefore prefer to play without a score. Better to risk forgetting, they feel, than do anything that might interfere with their involvement in the music. Other musicians have a sense of complete freedom only when the score is before them.

Despite personal preferences, there are times when the decision is not yours to make. The problem then is one of adapting to circumstances, as I had occasion to learn. I had been invited to record a recital for the BBC and was somewhat surprised to find in my contract the stipulation that a page-turner be present in the studio. The reason, of course, was that the BBC quite simply did not want to waste more time than was necessary with retakes owing to memory slips. An occasional wrong note is one thing, but a serious memory lapse can ruin a taping session. As I knew, looking at the score during a performance requires a highly developed keyboard sense, an ability that is conditioned by sight-reading more than by any other single factor. This is because reading forces your eyes away from the keyboard and places the burden of judging distances wholly within your hands. Consequently, those musicians who rely solely on their memory are often quite deficient in this crucial ability to estimate large and small distances on the keyboard. Playing chamber music or accompanying other musicians, both of which entail reading, are aids to developing this sense of distance. In this case, the knowledge that the music would be before me during a recording session forced me to refashion my performing technique. First, I planned very carefully exactly when to look at the keyboard so that I would know which leaps and which fast passages needed watching. Second, I trained my eyes to find the right place in the score afterwards. These two simple steps, practiced diligently, made the recording session far less strenuous than I had anticipated—perhaps even less so than if I had played from memory.

THE KEYBOARD MEMORY

There are various methods of memorizing for a performance that can be used to good effect. Some involve conscious procedures that account for every detail down to the most subtle movements of the body and hands; others are devised to free the automatic pilot through the most efficient conditioning of the reflexes.

Where to Look

Playing from memory invites you to look at the keyboard. But where you should look and what you should look at, especially when your hands are negotiating fast passages, are covering great distances, are widely separated from one another or are executing leaps, are questions that have received comparatively little notice even from experienced pianists. In the following outline, various options for focusing your eyes are suggested as well as those physical movements that will best assist them. For eye focus alone cannot always insure accuracy in performance.

I. For fast passages that extend across or weave up and down the keyboard, choose one of the following:

A. Focus your eyes midway between the lowest and highest notes of the passage, relying upon your peripheral vision and tactile sense of the keyboard.
B. Hold your head stationary, keep your spine erect, and follow the rise and fall of the passage with your eyes.
C. Focus on the first note of the passage, hold your head stationary and let your torso glide gradually along with the rise and fall of the passage.

II. Leaps.
    A. Leaps of every kind.
        1. Strive for economy of motion. Since the closest distance between two points is a straight line, executing leaps will be greatly facilitated if you stay as close to the keys as possible. Because you cannot move your hands on the keyboard in a literally straight line—if you did, you would collide with the black keys—trace, instead, a slight curve from the beginning to the end of the leap.
        2 . To achieve the greatest accuracy in leaps, begin by moving your hand very quickly and then, as you approach the target key, slow down and come in for a "soft landing." Movements such as this are always initiated by your upper arm.
    B. Leaps in one hand.
        1. Hold your spine erect.
        2. Turn your shoulders and head in the direction of the leap.
        3. Your eyes will then focus naturally upon the note to which you must leap, while the other hand—if it is playing—remains grounded.
    C. Leaps occurring simultaneously in both hands.
        1. When the intervals are not too large, both hands may negotiate their leaps simultaneously.
        2. Should one interval be larger than the other, the hands must move sequentially; that is, the hand required to leap the greatest distance moves first, while the other hand momentarily remains grounded before negotiating its leap.
        3. Where to look: three options.
            a. Fix your glance midway between your hands, relying upon your peripheral vision.
            b. Shift your eyes from one hand to the other while keeping your head stationary.

c. Look at the leaps before playing:
  i Shift your eyes quickly to the first leap.
  ii Shift your eyes quickly to the second leap.
  iii With your eyes focused upon the second leap, the image of the first leap being retained in your mind's eye, hold your head stationary, your torso erect, and negotiate both leaps sequentially.

D. Leaping to the fifth finger.
  1. Your hand position is as important as the path which your hands trace. When leaping to the fifth finger (up in the right hand, down in the left), open your hand to an octave position. This forces your fifth finger to draw upon its own strength and also activates your thumb, making it a stabilizing fulcrum that fills in the distance between the leap.
  2. To negotiate the following leap,

Mozart, *Concerto in C minor*, K. 491 (excerpt)

prepare your thumb as follows:

Thus, the interval of a twelfth:

now feels and looks like a fifth:

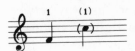

Practice all leaps to the fifth finger as follows:

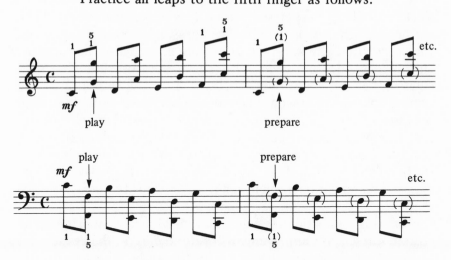

III. For distributions in which the hands are widely separated:
   A. Focus your eyes on the hand that has the most complex figures to play. Ground the other hand.
   B. If the difficulties are roughly equal for both hands, focus your eyes at a point midway between your hands, thus allowing your tactile memory to be assisted by your peripheral vision.
IV. For all three cases—leaps, extended passages, wide distributions—try practicing with your eyes closed. This takes bravery, but it helps to develop an accurate mental image of the keyboard that is retained through repetition.

Playing Slow Movements

Experience has taught me that focusing the eyes on some predetermined spot or area of the keyboard is essential for accuracy in certain situations, such as those discussed above. But if you have no technical reason for looking at one place more than another on the keyboard, there may be a tendency for your eyes to wander arbitrarily. This practice, if it becomes habitual, can lead to dangerous consequences. Slow movements in particular invite such tendencies. Long before I ever considered this problem, I recall having almost sabotaged my concentration during a performance of the *Arietta* from the *Sonata,* Op. 111, by Beethoven through a shift of focus. The sublimity of the *Arietta* had induced me always to play it with my eyes closed and my head tilted upward. For some reason, though, I happened on this occasion to open my eyes and glance down at the keyboard. This minor change in my now accustomed mode of playing the passage almost brought on a catastrophe. For one thing, I became distracted instantly at the sight of my hands moving slowly from chord to chord. This led in turn to confusion. "What is the next note?" I asked myself. And, as everyone who has ever performed knows all too well, such a question can trigger a memory lapse more often than we would like to contemplate. Sensing the impending danger, I quickly shut my eyes and dared not open them again until I came to the faster variations.

From this traumatic experience I learned how essential it is to accustom oneself to the movements of the hands on the keyboard. I realized further that eye contact with the keyboard, even if unaccustomed, ought not to disturb one's concentraton or conflict with a deep emotional involvement if the reflexes have been properly conditioned. What I had to face, then, was the fact of my deficiency in memorizing the *Arietta*. Because I had allowed my euphoric state to dictate how I practiced, my feelings were not sufficiently supported by reasoned analysis and my playing therefore lacked security. On the other hand, had I relied so heavily on analysis in my practicing that I lost contact with the sublimity of the passage, my playing would have ended up being tedious and boring. As I saw it, then, my task was to confront the keyboard in all its shiftings of pattern without ever losing touch with my emotional involvement in the music. Only then would I have earned the right and the confidence to look up or away if I wished—and even to close my eyes if I was moved to do so. Musical spontaneity, as we have seen, can be sustained only by that synthesis of thought and feeling that makes eye contact with the keyboard, or even the lack of it, wholly immaterial.

REPETITION AND THE CONDITIONED REFLEX (THE AUTOMATIC PILOT)

As we have seen, a movement, a gesture, even a glance, will become automatic if it is repeated often enough. For this reason, it is essential to feed the *right information* into your reflexes, as I mentioned earlier (Chapter 3). This means that the right fingerings, the right technical facts, the right physical movements, and, above all, natural musical feeling, must all be absorbed into that mental, muscular, and sensory axis—the automatic pilot—that governs your reflex system. Fed the right information, the automatic pilot does two things: it safeguards your memory, supporting it with a backup system, as it were, of well-organized reflexes, and it frees you to concentrate on musical issues only. The transference of all this information to your automatic pilot is accomplished through repetition of a series of acts in proper sequence. The process is not unlike that by which you learn to tie a shoelace automatically in so far as this depends also on learning through repetition a particular sequence of steps. In other words, if you radically alter the sequence, you will end up with a knot instead of a bow. The sooner the correct sequence is ascertained, the faster the transference of a conscious act to an automatic one will take place. The concluding pages of this chapter are devoted to a detailed analysis of this process.

Tying a shoelace calls, of course, for a fraction of the skill required to play a phrase of music. Yet, it illustrates the degree to which the reflexes must be conditioned if a musical act is to be performed automatically. Preparing for a performance requires the kind of repetition that brings this about—repetition not only of a series of consciously determined steps but also of the musical feeling that is an integral part of each step. Karl Ulrich Schnabel, the son of the late Artur Schnabel, tells a delightful story about this kind of practicing. One day, as he listened outside his father's studio, he counted two hundred repetitions of a single passage. Knowing how much his father disapproved of mechanical practicing, he questioned him about all these repetitions. "But I wasn't practicing mechanically," his father protested. "I was making music!" For Schnabel, repetition had nothing to do with mechanistic or rote practicing. On the contrary, it provided him with the means to make music through constant experimentation. Subtle variations in dynamics or changes of fingering may have occurred to him with each repetition—perhaps even two hundred of them. Hence, two hundred repetitions were needed. Ultimately, the purpose of repetition is to arrive at a convincing interpretation and to repeat that interpretation until your musical intentions become synthesized with the most efficient corresponding physical movements. Searching for those dynamic nuances that will adequately express your feelings means that you must always be *making music*—especially when you practice. Only then can you refine your sense of discrimination, thereby narrowing down your interpretive choices until you arrive at a course of action that favors your convictions. These convictions will then be projected to your audiences, arousing in them the fire, the passion, and the poetry that you experience from your own playing.

"My convictions are, like my tastes, my own," you may say. Even though personal tastes are proverbially indisputable, there is much to be said for the stimuli that activate these preferences. In other words, music itself is the higher authority to which we must ultimately offer tribute in the form of discrimination based on knowledge. It is the order and disciplined energy in music that teach us truths we could never discover otherwise. In the process, our convictions are not imposed on but, rather, are shaped by these truths. We can best serve music, therefore, by being its eternal student, always ready to discipline our natures to its greater efficacy. If music is thereby to ennoble us and if we are, in turn, to become its most faithful interpreters, we can do no less than absorb a work of musical art so thoroughly into our minds that it becomes a part of our life's experience. Memorization is the most direct route to this critical juncture where thinking, feeling, and physical coordination become synthesized. It is at this point that we are able to transcend all technical details and deliver in our playing the meaning music was meant to convey.

CONSCIOUS MEMORY

In memorizing music, there is no substitute for repetition. With each repetition of any part or parts of a piece, your tactile memory becomes more secure. And if each repetition is impregnated with musical feeling, this too is incorporated into your tactile memory. Thus, by having literally *touched* musical patterns repeatedly with the same fingering and with the same expression, you condition those reflexes that form the mainstay of your memory. All this notwithstanding, it is not enough to rely on tactile memory, however well you may have developed it. Another backup system is needed to fortify your tactile memory if you hope to perform with comfort. This system is based on *conscious memory*. It demands a conscious awareness of everything your mind can grasp from the music.

Without it, even the intrusion of a simple question, such as, "What is the next bass note?" or, "What interval do I leap to?" can subvert your tactile memory and invite disaster.

You can best begin by memorizing the hands separately, there being no more efficient way to develop a conscious awareness of musical particulars. Many pianists balk at this approach quite simply because it calls for more mental effort than they are willing to expend. It is not an easy method, but the results it brings more than justify the effort it requires. If you are trying it for the first time, start with moderate goals: memorize a few measures or perhaps only one line a day. By the end of a week, you will be gratified as much by the quality of your understanding as by the quantity of music you have memorized.

To gain a firm grasp of one of the more difficult memory problems in the literature—the first fugue in the *Sonata in A flat*, Op. 110, by Beethoven—a pupil of mine once elaborated on this method of memorization in the following way:

1. She memorized the hands separately.
2. She played one hand on the piano and fingered the other hand in her lap.
3. She reversed this procedure.
4. She fingered both hands in her lap.
5. As a final test, she closed her eyes and envisioned each note in her mind's eye.

With this indestructible backup system added to her tactile memory, her security was total. She could now perform without fear of memory slips. "I felt as though I had reached a transcendental state," she told me, "as though *I* were being played by the fugue."

DEADLINES

There are no short-cuts to memorization. Yet, occasions do arise in the life of a performer that call for rapid memorization of scores—a request to play a newly composed work, for example, or an unexpected invitation to participate on short notice in a summer festival program. Young musicians, anxious for an opportunity to perform, are loath to turn down such invitations and thus find themselves having to memorize new scores in record time. Facing a deadline, what would you do? It was probably her consciousness of this fact of musical life that induced the late Nadia Boulanger to announce one day toward the end of a summer session in Fontainebleau that a competition for instrumentalists would be held three weeks hence. The repertory for each category of performers was selected by her personally, the pianists being assigned: the first movement of the *Capriccio for Piano and Orchestra* by Stravinsky, the *Prelude and Fugue in D minor*, Book II, by Bach, and a work of our own choice (I selected three contrasting *Preludes* by Debussy). Having to master these works in only three weeks gave us no time even for despair. The tension mounting with each passing moment, I embarked on a rigid schedule that included ten hours of practicing each day. No more trips to Paris, no more forays abroad until all hours of the night. Everything had to yield to the single most challenging task—memorization. I began by memorizing each hand separately, and in the case of the *Fugue* by Bach, each voice, singing now one, now another, while playing the other two from memory. Sometimes, another student and I would work at two pianos, one playing one voice, the other playing the remaining voices from memory.

From this point on, I proceeded to employ every technique of conscious memorization that I could devise. I analyzed every structural feature of the music, taking special note of every modulation, an especially difficult task in the Stravinsky work. My analysis of chords and progressions focused particularly on all cadences since these served as structural points of reference or landmarks. I marked each section of the works with a letter and trained myself to start from any one of them at random. I carefully observed all variations of similar material and tabulated them in my mind (many musicians actually write down observations of this sort). Next, I accumulated an enormous storehouse of mnemonic devices, these consisting for the most part of the simplest or most elementary associations, such as: the melody moves stepwise for three notes and then jumps down a sixth; the bass plays two black keys followed by three white ones; the A♭ in the right hand coincides with the A♭ in the left hand; the third finger in both hands come together simultaneously. At no point did I fail to practice and, therefore, memorize dynamics, for these invariably fortify the memory through specific associations, as, for example: the *forte* always occurs with the C minor cadence or the subito *piano* marks the entrance of the second theme.

With one week remaining before the competition, I began to try out my pieces for others, at the same time attempting to reduce my conscious awareness of details to fewer and fewer associations. When the day of competition arrived, I felt prepared in all respects but one: the automatic pilot. In other words, my reflexes had not been sufficiently conditioned to withstand the onslaught of nerves that accompanied every note of my performance. But I did play every note; and even if I felt that my playing was not at its best, I had nonetheless to attribute whatever competence I achieved to the preparation I had exacted from myself. That the judges saw fit to award me the Premier Prix de Piano and the Prix Jacques Durand was a not unpleasant consequence of my efforts. More important, though, it encouraged me to know that I had faced my limitations and matched them with my strengths. Yet, to this day, I cannot establish dependable reflexes in just a few weeks of preparation—at least not sufficiently to stem the tide of nervousness that inevitably results from too little time. Many musicians are blessed with the ability to learn rapidly, but others quite simply require a certain span of time which no amount of labor can safely supplant. But this is something we all must learn about ourselves. Above all, my experience in Fontainebleau taught me that the methods of memorization I had developed to meet a deadline had their value for more normal situations by being sound, efficient, and trustworthy. They had only to be made as systematic as they appear at the conclusion of this chapter.

CONSCIOUSLY FREEING
THE AUTOMATIC PILOT

An automatic skill will operate efficiently so long as you do not interfere with it. One evening shortly before a concert, I stood before a mirror and began to tie my bow tie. For some reason, I became aware of the process and completely forgot one of the steps in the sequence. Thinking that this was just some momentary lapse, I tried again. Failure. With the concert only moments away, I began to panic. "This is ridiculous," I thought. "I have been tying bow ties for twenty years. Why can't I do it now?" I cannot remember now how many times I tried and failed, but suddenly I found the key to my problem. I started once again, but this time I tried not to think about the steps involved and simply allowed my hands to do their work without any conscious interference on my part. It was a great relief when I finally succeeded (the stage manager thought so, too) and I walked out on stage where, paradoxically, I felt far more in control of events.

This sort of lapse in continuity is common among music students. You may think that you know a piece perfectly from memory—that is, until someone walks into the room. Then, suddenly, your memory fails you. To attribute this to some inherent weakness in your talent would be just as foolish as to blame it on the person who entered the room. The cause quite simply is that you did not learn the piece as thoroughly as you thought. That the mere presence of one person was enough to interrupt your soliloquy and force you to listen to yourself—perhaps for the first time—shows that your grasp of the piece was in fact tenuous. But suppose you are convinced that you have taken all the necessary precautions against memory lapses and yet continue to suffer them under pressure of performance. There are two possible explanations. First, playing for an audience can make you uncomfortably aware of certain areas that were neglected in your practicing— those you always considered too easy to merit repetition and analysis. In performance, these are the very places that have a way of disintegrating beyond repair. Second, your consciousness of all the details you did in fact repeat and analyze may, during a performance, overwhelm and therefore defeat the workings of your automatic pilot. Assuming that your preparation has been sound in all respects, your task then is to use the full resources of your automatic pilot. The question is, of course, how this can be done.

Ideally, everything that contributes to a convincing performance ought to be automatic. You acquire any number of refined backup systems to lessen your concern about memory slips; you practice technical passages repeatedly to free your hands of impediments; you carefully plan the shape of phrases, repeating them until their musical content is programmed into your muscles. With your mind relieved of memory-related worries, your hands disciplined to their task, and your body conditioned to respond to every musical nuance, you can now address yourself to musical values exclusively. It is at this point that all your powers of concentration must be directed away from the details of your preparation and brought to bear instead on the functioning of your automatic pilot. For therein lies the key to a successful performance. Just as my ability to tie my bow tie came from the conditioned reflexes of my hands, the ease and security of performing music from memory depend upon the full development of the automatic pilot. However, to trust in your automatic pilot, you must first condition it by dealing consciously with each and every facet of the music before you. Once your skills have been brought to the deepest level of automatic activity through repetition, it is time to allow your automatic pilot to function unimpeded. I am suggesting that it is now in your power to *free your automatic pilot consciously*. Memorizing consciously is what enables you to do this. Supported then by your conscious memory and conditioned reflexes, you can actually switch back and forth at will—even during a performance—from a state of mental awareness to one of emotional release.

AURAL MEMORIZATION

Some musicians possess an innate hearing sensitivity that enables them to reproduce on the piano every pitch or group of pitches that are heard, sung, or imagined. Inborn (absolute pitch) or acquired (relative pitch), this highly developed sense makes the absorption of musical details possible. As was discussed in the section on sight-reading, it can be trained to guide the mind in all musical matters. Curiously enough, some musicians who are endowed with the extraordinary aural sense that is absolute pitch regularly suffer memory slips. In some cases, this is because they rely as little on their powers of hearing as do others on their automatic pilot. More often than not, the possession of absolute pitch is not adequate security against the danger of memory slips. Most musicians, however well endowed, must go through a process of conscious memorization.

In Chapter 6, I discussed various methods of training your ear for greater efficiency. If, despite such training, your sense of relative pitch is still not altogether trustworthy, you must compensate for this lack by accumulating through conscious memorization a large storehouse of landmarks (as I did at Fontainebleau). Still, no amount of analytical work can totally supplant the function of the ear, for performing from memory does make demands of the ear insofar as it requires you to hear in your mind's ear sounds composed of various pitches, durations, and intensities, and provokes you to sing them inwardly—a kind of listening with your vocal cords. To this extent, performing from memory is an aural and vocal experience that is prompted by and a direct result of conscious memorization.

MEMORIZING AWAY FROM YOUR INSTRUMENT

It would be wonderful indeed if we all could memorize complicated scores away from the piano. Think of the use to which we could put our time spent on trains, buses, and planes. One famous pianist is in fact reported to have memorized Beethoven's *Fourth Concerto* en route by train to a concert engagement. But such an ability is given to very few. And these rare individuals doubtless possess the added advantage of absolute pitch. For most of us, however, studying a score away from the piano can be useful provided that the music has already been thoroughly memorized. First of all, by being disengaged from a physical involvement with the keyboard, you can examine your landmarks and structural divisions with a special objectivity that vision alone provides. Second, mnemonic devices based on the appearance of the score can be added to your backup systems of memory as, for example, the deceptive cadence comes at the top of the second page; the recapitulation begins at the bottom of the fifth page. Of course, some students become so adept at this kind of mental photography that they tend to overlook the more organic content of the music itself. But used judiciously, this imaging of the score, because it allows you to bring into sharper focus all your emotional responses to the music together with their accompanying physical sensations, has its place in the total learning program.

MEMORIZING BACKWARDS

Let us suppose that you have memorized the first two measures of a piece by employing the various techniques we have discussed thus far. Now, you commit to memory the third measure. In order to test yourself, you start from the beginning of the piece and play through the first three measures. But at this point all those as yet unmemorized measures awaiting your attention may intrude upon your concentration and even frustrate your desire to continue memorizing the rest of the piece. In other words, because you are moving forward to something unknown, you may feel defeated even before you begin the work of memorizing. Suppose, instead, that you begin your memorization at the end of the piece, committing to memory the last two bars. You then absorb the third measure from the end. Having done this, you are now ready to test your memory by playing through the last three measures. This time, you are relieved to know that nothing awaits you beyond the final measure. The feeling is one of moving forward to something that is known. Many musicians employ this method of memorizing for the simple reason that it provides them with a psychological comfort. Some prefer to begin memorizing on the last page; others like to begin at the last section and work toward the end. Memorizing backwards is also an excellent remedy against a common ill—the tendency to become unfocused or distracted as the end of the piece approaches. If you find yourself feeling and sounding less secure the nearer you come to the conclusion of a piece, experiment with this reverse system of memorization. Needless to say, at the completion of all memorization, whether undertaken from the end or the beginning of a piece, all sections must be under your control. With your attention equally distributed, you can then expect each part of the piece to amalgamate into a unified whole. In any case, by knowing the end as well as you do the beginning, you will have reduced to a large degree whatever anxiety you may experience as you approach the end of a piece.

MEMORY SLIPS

It is rare for a concert artist to sustain his concentration throughout an entire recital program without having an occasional memory slip. Considering the range of complexity entailed in any recital program as well as the nervousness that plagues almost all performers, a momentary lapse is an ever present possibility. It is forgivable. However, not all members of an audience are forgiving. Minor slips, like wrong notes, no matter how inconsequential they may be, are added up like errors on a score board and the performer is graded accordingly. Many inexperienced performers— and a good number of them are teachers—deeply admire those who can perform but at the same time envy them, especially for their ability to memorize. Thus, those who cannot memorize music, whether because of poor training or lack of discipline, look upon memorization as the chief deterrent to their own performing ability. "If I had the score in front of me, I could play as well as anyone up there on the stage," is the sometimes unexpressed attitude of these pitiless concert-goers. Underlying this lack of sympathy for the performer is a characteristic weakness that displays itself given a certain circumstance. That is, if one musician measures his limitations—in this case, an inability to memorize—against the acknowledged strengths of another, forgiveness, especially of memory slips, is the very last courtesy to be extended.

Something in us hates memory slips. To a performer they can be mortifying; to a listener who is laboring under some bias of his own, they are unforgivable. And indeed, those who are given to capitalizing on the transient mishaps of others are usually suffering their own private torment. Such are the teachers consumed with envy of their more gifted pupils; and the parents, friends, or spouses threatened by the possible consequences of their loved ones' talent. Whatever the underlying cause, memory is all too often made the target of unfair criticism. No matter that you played beautifully on a given occasion despite a minor lapse. There is usually someone close enough to you who will invariably whisper in your ear: "You were great, but how come you lost a whole measure in the Mozart when you practiced that thing a thousand hours?" For the performer, all this conspires to make fear of memory lapses the single, most powerful cause of nervousness. One remedy against its devastating effects is the knowledge that memory slips, if they are minimal, easily recoverable, and unobtrusive, count for nothing in the total rendition of a piece. Major blackouts are, of course, another matter. From these there is no returning. They can be prevented in only one way—a faultless preparation.

The ability to discriminate between major blackouts and minor lapses depends upon how objective a judge you are of your own playing. Often, such objectivity is the only weapon you have against arbitrary criticism or destructive teachers. When I was around twenty years of age, I suffered what I knew to be a minor lapse in an otherwise well-structured performance of the *Mephisto Waltz* by Liszt. Far from chastising myself for a momentary slip in a chromatic harmony, I was thankful to have prepared well enough to be able to recover as rapidly as I did. In fact, it raised my self-esteem to know that I not only survived the lapse, but was also able to dispel its possible after–effects in my playing of the next difficult section. "This is what the professionals are so good at doing," I thought. My teacher unfortunately did not share my views. On the contrary, she leveled at me the sharpest criticism she could call upon from her arsenal of complaints. "Professional performers," she asserted, "do not have memory slips. Think twice before you undertake a career in music." At age twenty, it was difficult to counter the supposedly well-informed judgment of a respected teacher with a mere intuition. But that I was able to say, "My memory slip in the Liszt seems to be a bigger problem for you than for me," came from my belief in a fundamental truth: if you are deeply involved in communicating a musical idea, an occasional deviation from technical perfection does not diminish in the slightest the effectiveness of your performance nor should it be of- fered as sufficient reason for deterring you from a career in music.

Still, there is no denying that playing from memory is a difficult, if not heroic, task; that memorizing is tedious; that a fear of memory slips is the performer's greatest enemy; that anticipation is its most hazardous corollary. Consider, therefore, the following possibilities and their remedies:

1. You may not know the next note. This can happen especially at a *fermata* or at the end of a section. Therefore, spend some time *deliberately anticipating* the notes following such strategic pauses as well as each and every note of all thematic material. Always know what is coming next (conscious memorization). This will prevent you from anticipating during a performance, the dangers of which were discussed earlier (see Chapter 3).
2. You may not be concentrating on musical values. To repeat a previous suggestion, learn during your practicing to shift your at- tention away from technical details and toward the music itself—that is, command yourself to become totally immersed in the feeling of the music. Having arrived at this point, observe your mental, emotional, and physical state. Ideally, it is this that ought to be carried over to a performance. But it can be achieved only when you know exactly what is coming next.
3. If memory slips continue to plague you, examine each trouble spot. You may have overlooked a critical detail, as, for example, a fingering on an inside voice; or perhaps you sabotaged your automatic pilot by concentrating on the wrong items.

4. There may be nonmusical factors of a destructive nature at work. This will be discussed in Chapter 11, pp. 262–67.

OUTLINE FOR MEMORIZING MUSIC

Introduction

As was suggested earlier, the automatic performance of a simple skill such as the tying of a shoelace involves mastering a certain series of steps in sequence. Playing music on an instrument—as complex as any skill can be—comprises a seemingly infinite number of separate but interrelated acts, all of which must be executed simultaneously. Superimposed on this audio-visual-manual network of complex functions is yet another highly specialized skill—the memorization of music. It is, of course, repetition that renders these skills automatic—repetition not of haphazard acts, but repetition of consciously determined musical functions. It is the latter that is the key to a dependable memory. If the mind is to retain all the details of a musical score, it needs a well-organized program of repetition.

There is, of course, no one program that will be totally effective for everyone, considering the enormous range of differences in individual talent, experience, and mental acuity. Yet, everyone can be helped by being made aware of one thing: the importance of a systematic approach to memorization. Nothing contributes to security and continuity in the performance of music more than this. The system I have found most effective for the retention of music is one that is built on a series of steps in sequence. In the succeeding pages they are found implemented in an actual musical situation—Schumann's *Erster Verlust (First Sorrow)*. Throughout, you will no doubt notice the specific and diverse ways in which repetition is featured, whether repetition of the entire composition or that of separate sections; whether for one purpose or another. In other words, repetition should not be a mindless, rote activity. Rather, it must be purposeful and with specific intent. Advanced musicians may use this outline as a checklist against their own methods of memorization.

In the following pages I have used the words *melodic invention* to denote a complete musical idea in order to avoid the ambiguity that so often arises from the more usual term *phrase. Phrase*, as it is commonly used, can signify anything from a slur mark to a complete musical idea or even the subsidiary motifs of which it consists (Schumann slurred seven such motifs—or phrases—within the first eight measures of *First Sorrow*).[35]

I. General
  A. Read through the entire composition and analyze its general structure.
  B. Read through the entire composition and mark all key changes (modulations).
  C. Read through the entire composition and mark the end of each melodic invention with a check. Memorize the number of measures comprising each invention—is it an eight-measure invention, a four-measure invention? Observe the variations that occur between similar inventions. Memorize the dynamics simultaneously.
  D. Read through the entire composition and observe all cadences—that is, the harmonic progressions that occur at the ends of each melodic invention. Analyze them to the best of your ability. By-pass temporarily whatever you cannot analyze. These cadences will be your structural landmarks when you perform from memory.
  E. Observe all entrances of new voices.
  F. Memorize the simple vertical relationships, occurring between the hands, by-passing, temporarily, the more complicated ones.
II. Specific
  A. Study the first melodic invention without its accompaniment. Sing or hum it while you are playing. Analyze its structure (as the detailed analysis in Example 21, p. 251, shows, such structural motifs will not necessarily coincide with the slur marks).
  B. Without playing, scan the composition and try to find any repetition or repetitions of the melodic invention or any structural part of it. Mark them in your music (with letters or numbers or whatever system you wish). Play them, singing or humming them at the same time. Memorize each occurrence out of context, omitting at this stage their accompanying voices.

   C. Observe and memorize all imitative sections, such as canons and fugatos.

   D. Memorize the entire composition hands separately—first the left hand, then the right. While doing so, take note of the following:

     1. Memorize intervallic relationships, especially melody tones that outline chords. Sing them.

     2. Observe and memorize common tones, including unisons and octaves as they appear consecutively and non-consecutively—between chords, between the right and left hands, and in melodies.

     3. Reduce all polyphonic structures and decorative figures to simpler melodic patterns that move stepwise or outline chords.

     4. When rests or long notes occur, relate the last note of one section to the first note of the next section.

     5. Since most memory slips occur when the fingers or hands shift to large intervals, make it a point to memorize all intervals that span a fifth or more.

     6. Without playing, scan the entire composition for tones that do not belong to the key of a particular section. Mark them in your music. Sound them on the piano. Memorize them, first out of context and then in combination with all other voices.

   E. Finally, confront all details that were temporarily by-passed. At this point it may be necessary to expand your knowledge of theory.

IMPLEMENTATION OF THE OUTLINE FOR MEMORIZATION

Preliminary Steps

1. Memorizing takes energy. Build up your endurance by making economical use of your practice time. If you are not accustomed to memorizing, be grateful to absorb only a few steps a day.

2. Always feel the music you are memorizing. In other words, memorize your feeling.

3. You should know all scales and arpeggios thoroughly, including all the forms of the minor scales. Students in the early grades

should know the scales in which their pieces are written. Without such knowledge, it is impossible to recognize and, therefore, harder to memorize modulations from the established key.

4. A basic knowledge of chords and their inversions is essential in memorizing.

5. You must be able to recognize and name intervals. Students in the early grades need only identify intervals by their number name—third, fourth, fifth, etcetera. Ultimately, though, you should be able to distinguish between major, perfect, minor, augmented, and diminished intervals.

6. In the course of your memorization work, stop occasionally and read through the entire composition. This will help you to keep in mind the overall structure during each step of memorization. Reading through the entire piece from time to time after you have memorized it will reinforce your visual memory.

7. Once you have settled on an optimum fingering, memorize it with the utmost care. For nothing can sabotage the memory more easily than inconsistent or ad hoc fingering.

8. The point at which you begin the sequence of steps for memorizing music depends upon your sight-reading ability. If you are a good reader, you can begin to memorize immediately. Otherwise, do not begin memorizing until you can read a new composition with comparative fluency. Poor readers, it should be emphasized, will never improve their reading skills if they make it a habit to begin memorizing their pieces prematurely. To implement, therefore, the very first step in the Outline for Memorization requires that you gain through sight-reading an overall conception of the composition. Obviously, technically difficult pieces, such as études or fast Scarlatti Sonatas, require a longer period of sight-reading, at least for most instrumentalists, before a modicum of fluency can be achieved. In fact, such pieces are usually absorbed kinetically through sheer repetition. Accept this gratefully, but proceed to fortify it with a conscious application of the sequential steps of the Outline.

9. As a final preliminary step, number the measures of the composition for easy reference (notice the circled numbers in *First Sorrow* by Schumann).

10. Having stated all these preliminaries, we are now ready to apply the sequential steps of memorization to the following intermediate composition: *First Sorrow* by Robert Schumann, from *Album for the Young,* Op. 68.

Schumann, *Erster Verlust*, Op. 68

I. General
  A. Read through the entire composition and analyze its general structure.

EXAMPLE 1.   Measures 1–16 = Ⓐ; measures 17–24 = Ⓑ; measures 25–28 = Ⓐ¹ (recapitulation); measures 29–32 = closing section. Retain a mental image of these larger or smaller sections.

B. Read through the entire composition and mark all key changes. Memorize them. Try not to be overly analytical at this stage even if it means by-passing, temporarily, those measures where you have difficulty identifying the key.

EXAMPLE 2. Measures 1–16: E minor. The A♯ in measures 7 and 14 is the leading tone of B major. Here, the B in the left hand and the D♯ in the right hand are obviously the first and the third of the dominant of E minor.

EXAMPLE 3.   Measures 17–18: C major

EXAMPLE 4.   Measures 19–28: E minor

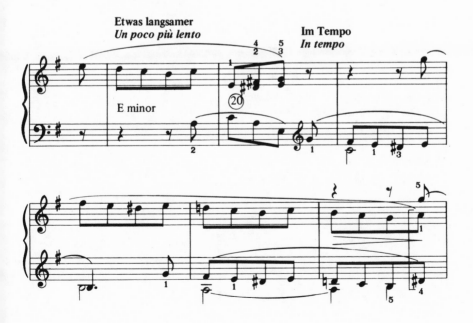

EXAMPLE 5. Measure 29: V⁷ — I of A minor. The chord of A minor however, is also the subdominant of the original key, E minor.

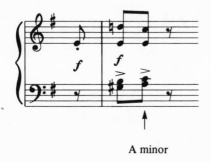

A minor

EXAMPLE 6. Measure 30: These chromatic harmonies may be by-passed
at this stage.

EXAMPLE 7. Measures 31-32: E minor.

C. Read through the entire composition and mark the end of
each melodic invention with a check. Memorize the number
of measures comprising each invention. Observe the variations that occur between similar inventions. Memorize the
dynamics simultaneously.

EXAMPLE 8

1. Measure 1–8: an eight-measure invention ending in a half cadence (this may also be interpreted as two four-measure inventions). Dynamics: *forte piano*; sing or hum the melody.
2. Measures 9–16: an eight-measure invention ending in a perfect cadence. Dynamics: forte piano; sing or hum the melody. Measures 1–8 form an antecedent or a question; measures 9–16 are a consequent or an answer. You may also interpret 1–4 as an antecedent and measures 5–8 as a consequent.
3. Measures 17–18: a two-measure fragment of the first invention; dynamics: crescendo; sing or hum the melody.
4. Measures 19–20: a similar fragment with a different ending; dynamics: crescendo–diminuendo; sing or hum it.
5. Measures 21–24: a four-measure invention consisting of fragments of the first melodic invention. No dynamic indication appears in the Clara Schumann edition. I would suggest the following:

EXAMPLE 9

6. Measures 25–28: a four-measure invention consisting of the first half of the first melodic invention; dynamics: *piano*; sing or hum it.
7. Measures 29–32: a four-measure invention—closing section comprised of a one-measure fragment (measure 29) plus three measures leading to the final cadence; dynamics: *forte*; diminuendo; sing or hum it.

D. Read through the entire composition and observe all cadences—that is, the harmonic progressions that occur at the end of each melodic invention. Analyze them to the best of your ability. By-pass temporarily whatever you cannot analyze. Memorize each cadence out of context. If, for example, you do not recognize the soprano G in measure 24 as the highest note in a V^{13} chord (see Example 14), it will suffice to construe B, D#, and A as a B^7 chord.

EXAMPLE 10.   Measures 7–8

EXAMPLE 11.   Measures 15–16

EXAMPLE 12.   Measure 18

EXAMPLE 13.   Measure 20

EXAMPLE 14.   Measures 24–25

EXAMPLE 15.   Measures 31–32

i_4^6 V^7 i

E. Observe all entrances of new voices as in the following three examples.

EXAMPLE 16.   Memorize the entrance of the alto, D♯—measure 8.

EXAMPLE 17.   Memorize the entrance of the alto, F to E—measure 18.

EXAMPLE 18.   Memorize each voice separately in the left hand—measures 21–25.

(Learn, separately, all other new entrances of voices.)

F. Memorize the simple vertical relationships occurring between the hands, by-passing, temporarily, the more complicated ones, as in measures 29–30.

EXAMPLE 19.   Measures 1–4

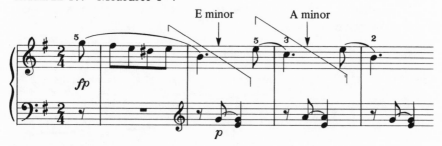

EXAMPLE 20.   Measures 5–6

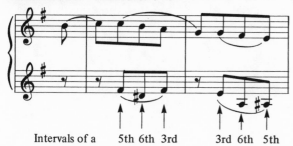

Intervals of a   5th 6th 3rd   3rd 6th 5th

II. Specific
A. Study the first melodic invention without its accompaniment. Sing or hum it while you are playing. Analyze its structure.

EXAMPLE 21

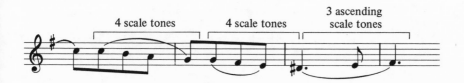

B. Without playing, scan the composition and try to find any repetition or repetitions of the melodic invention or any structural part of it. Mark them in your music with letters or numbers or whatever system you wish. Play them, singing or humming them at the same time. Memorize each occurrence out of context, omitting at this stage their accompanying voices.

EXAMPLE 22.   Four descending scale tones.

Measures 31–32 (soprano): Augmentation of the first three notes of the piece.

EXAMPLE 23.   Descending intervals of a third and fourth.

EXAMPLE 24.   Three ascending scale tones.

C. Observe and memorize all imitative sections, such as canons and fugatos.

EXAMPLE 25. Measures 2–4: Imitative thirds; imitative fourths.

EXAMPLE 26. Measures 21–24: Canons to the octave moving sequentially.

D. Memorize the hands separately—first the left hand, then the right. While doing so, take note of the following:
1. Memorize intervallic relationships, especially melody tones that outline chords (sing them).

EXAMPLE 27. Measures 2–3

L.H.

Think: 3rd   4th   3rd

Measure 20. L.H. outlines A minor chord—2nd inversion.

EXAMPLE 28.   Measures 29–30: Note constant repetitions of ascending
half steps in L.H. and R.H.

2. Observe and memorize common tones.

EXAMPLE 29.   Measures 1–3 (Compare above, Ex. 27: L.H., Measures
2–3): Note the repetitions of E's.

Measure 29–32. Note the repetitions of E's in the alto voice.

3. Reduce all polyphonic or decorative figures to more simple structures that outline melodies, scales or chords.

EXAMPLE 30.   Measures 2–6, L.H.

reduces to:

EXAMPLE 30a. In a different context, a figure such as this (In each group of four sixteenth notes, the first and third are, respectively, upper and lower appoggiaturas.):

reduces to this:

EXAMPLE 30b. Measure 1–4, R.H. Decorative figures may also be reduced to simpler melodies.

reduces to this:

J. S. Bach occasionally indicated polyphonic melodies as in the following:

EXAMPLE 30c. Excerpt (Measure 32) from the *Prelude in D major*, Bk. I of the *Well-Tempered Clavier*

EXAMPLE 30d.

Therefore, when you see this excerpt from the *Prelude in C minor,* Bk. I of the *Well-Tempered Clavier,*

you may follow Bach's example and hold the upper voice:

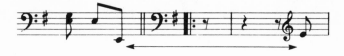

4. When rests or long notes occur, relate the last note of one section to the first note of the next section; find a mnemonic device for remembering the pitch name of thematic entrances.

EXAMPLE 31.   Measures 16–17: L.H. enters two octaves above previous E.

EXAMPLE 32.   Measure 2: L.H. enters an octave below R.H. entrance; or, L.H. enters a third below last note of R.H.

Measure 19. L.H. A enters a third below the previous middle C.

5. Memorize all skips that span the interval of a fifth or more.

EXAMPLE 33. Measure 8: F♯ to G is a ninth.

6. Without playing, scan the entire composition for tones that do not belong to the key, as for example, measure 6: L.H. A♯; measure 30; R.H. C♯. Mark all such notes in your music. Sound them on the piano. Memorize them, first out of context and then in combination with all other voices.

F. Finally, confront all details that were temporarily by-passed. At this point it may be necessary to expand your knowledge of theory. If you cannot analyze certain harmonic progressions, create landmarks based on simple associations, as, for example, in measure 30: the bass and alto voices ascend by half-steps. You should be able to construe individual chords, however, apart from their relation to the harmonic context, as for example:

EXAMPLE 34. Measure 30

1. D♯ diminished 7th, first inversion ($^6_5$)
2. E minor, first inversion (6)
3. F♯ diminished, first inversion (6)
4. A♯ diminished 7th

SOME AFTERTHOUGHTS AND CONCLUSIONS

Contrapuntal music, such as two- and three-part inventions and fugues, demands an exceedingly detailed analysis of motifs. You can best begin by marking with an arrow, a letter, or a symbol of your own choosing all the entrances of the subject or subjects. After learning each of these in turn without the other voices, you should be able to play from memory any one of them at random. Countersubjects and episodes must be analyzed and memorized in similar fashion. Indeed, as Nadia Boulanger often reminded us at Fontainebleau, a thorough memorization of a contrapuntal work depends upon knowing from memory each voice independently. Short of this, a pianist should be able to play from memory each hand separately.

With the exception of certain compositions or sections of pieces in which the hands follow each other sequentially—as, for example, in the *Prelude in C major,* Bk. I of the *Well-Tempered Clavier,* by Bach or in the first four measures of Schumann's *First Sorrow*—everything should be learned hands separately. It is the best way to safeguard the memory. In fact, as you may have discovered, freedom of expression when playing certain repertory—a *Nocturne* or a *Waltz* by Chopin, for example—depends to a large extent on knowing the left hand independently from the right.

Contemporary music—especially serial music—is, for most musicians, extremely difficult to memorize and, for some, impossible. Unless the composer incorporates into his writing logical motivic developments, a performer is forced to invent his own melodic associations, or, indeed, to rely exclusively on his automatic pilot. But music, if it is worthy of the name, cannot deceive the mind, the senses, and the central nervous system—they invariably register the difference between order and chaos, logical flow and arbitrariness. There is, therefore, a correlation between a composer's creative process and a performer's ability to memorize his works. It is not without reason, then, that some works are never performed from memory.

Phenomenally gifted musicians—those endowed with absolute pitch, a photographic memory, total recall, or extraordinarily well-developed reflexes—can dispense with all conscious steps of memorization without adversely affecting their performances. Quite obviously, they have no need to make conscious that which is functioning perfectly in the unconscious. If, for whatever reasons, such musicians do not trust their gifts, they, as well as their less favored colleagues, can benefit from a well-organized program of memorization such as I have attempted to formulate here. In any case, this outline is intended to motivate pupils and teachers alike to view the memorization of music as an achievable goal. It is never too late to begin. I have witnessed among some of my older pupils an amazing and at times totally unpredictable revitalization of memory skills that had lain dormant for twenty years and more. But what is even more astonishing, through the often laborious recovery of this mental power, these older pupils become for all intents and purposes young in their passion to learn, young in their perseverance, and young in the quickening of their minds. "Remembering music," as one of my oldest pupils once put it, "is not an escape from my age. It is a recovery of my youth."

11 Nervousness

BEING RESPONSIBLE

One summer toward the end of his career, the late cellist Gregor Piatigorsky was scheduled to give a solo recital at the Tanglewood Festival in Massachusetts. Several of his students, unable to find seats in the sold-out auditorium, were given permission to listen to the concert backstage. There, they witnessed their master, a lifetime of brilliant performances behind him, pace nervously back and forth. Finally, the moment arrived: the auditorium was darkened, the stage lights were slowly raised to full intensity, and all was expectancy. Suddenly, as though unable to contain his anguish one second longer, the great artist stopped his pacing, turned toward his students and exclaimed, "There are no heroes a moment before a recital," whereupon he set his jaw, lifted his cello into the air like a scepter and charged onto the stage amidst thunderous applause. In his playing he was the hero he could not be backstage.

Sarah Bernhardt, the legendary French actress, was also no stranger to nervousness. One evening, as she was about to enter her dressing room before a performance, a young actress rushed up to her and shyly asked for her autograph. Momentarily annoyed, Bernhardt quickly took the situation in stride and hastily signed her name. But even she whose acting technique was equal to any demand could not hide the slight tremor of hand and pallor of complexion that tell of preperformance nerves nor was this lost on her young admirer. "Excuse me for saying so, Madame, but I see that you are nervous. Why is it that I never get nervous before a performance?" As though responding to a cue that had been rehearsed a thousand times, Bernhardt replied, "Oh, but you will, my dear, you will—when you have learned to act."

During the Korean war, a group of talent scouts was touring service camps in the United States in search of servicemen to appear on the Kate Smith TV series. One of the great popular singers of the day, Kate Smith was by then as much an American institution as a celebrated TV personality. Needless to say, I was delighted to be picked to inaugurate the series, but at the same time I immediately fell prey to a fine case of nerves. There was not only the fact of my inexperience to contemplate but also my physical exhaustion to contend with, the rigors of basic training having had their effect on me. I looked at my now unpracticed hands and thought, "How on earth am I going to see this thing through?" Before long, I found myself in the theater where the show was to be telecast, a bundle of nerves in a sea of cameramen, make-up artists, directors, and orchestral musicians. Radiating the self-assurance of stardom, Kate Smith came to me directly and, taking my icy hands into hers, asked how I was feeling. "Terribly nervous," I answered truthfully. "My dear," she said with a look born of the deepest suffering, "you will never know what nervousness really is until you are in the public eye."

Thus did Piatigorsky, Bernhardt, and Kate Smith testify in their distinctive ways to the bane of the performer's existence—nerves. Nervousness belongs to performing. It plagues virtually everyone who performs and it can in some cases reach appalling dimensions. "No one suffers as much as I," is therefore a familiar lament among performing artists. Its primary cause is an overwhelming sense of responsibility to one's art, to oneself, and to others. For the famous, this responsibility involves not only upholding standards previously met, but also living up to the world's expectations. For all others—professional aspirants and amateurs alike—it is a testament to their seriousness of purpose and an acknowledgment of their will to succeed at something monumentally difficult. To be nervous at the thought of failure is therefore all too understandable.

Our task then is to enlist nervousness in the service of responsibility and thereby do everything humanly possible to prevent failure. In other words, let us convert nervousness into a deep motivation for working against failure. This is, in fact, what every true artist does. First, he accepts the fact of his nervousness as an indication of the seriousness of his pursuit. Second, instead of trying to minimize the meaning of his nervousness, he disciplines it to work in his best interests. To this end, he will probe music to its core, he will leave no stone unturned, he will ferret out obvious or potential difficulties long before they work themselves into his reflex system. Two things are thus accomplished: musical difficulties are solved through sound practicing techniques, such as those recommended in the Outline for Memorization, and a backlog of successful performing experiences is built up. If, therefore, a difficult piece or passage yields to hours of consistent and concentrated work so as to survive before an audience, it is a triumph of will that deserves to remain in the memory. And if a backlog of such triumphs is accumulated, it signifies a conquest of fear. Though remembering these past achievements does not eradicate nervousness, it does tend to lessen its sometimes devastating effects. As every artist knows in his heart of hearts, past triumphs carry the promise of future successes.

BEING IRRESPONSIBLE

Because he lacks knowledge and experience, a novice may be forgiven for not preparing adequately for a peformance. But an experienced musician has no excuse for ignoring the requirements of his art by being unprepared. Trusting to luck, cramming for a performance, or not practicing at all are not just signs of audaciousness—they are acts of extreme irresponsibility. To be sure, some supremely gifted musicians can maintain relatively high standards in performance with a minimum of practicing. But most of us must sustain our hard-earned skills through consistent and well-disciplined practicing. Without this, a performance will be unpredictable. As one of my students put it, "If I don't keep in shape, one thing *is* predictable: whatever can go wrong is sure to go wrong."

Just as virtue has its own rewards, irresponsibility fulfills itself at the moment of truth—in a performance. Paralyzing fear now takes command, causing involuntary muscular contractions throughout the body. The result: technical control is impaired, musical feeling is thwarted, and the memory function is sabotaged. Anyone who has ever had to agonize through a performance in such a condition understands the final meaning of the word punishment. What is beyond understanding is that any musician would dare to inflict this upon himself voluntarily. In short, irresponsibility and music do not live well together. Invariably, the product is nervousness—destructive, demoralizing, and self-denigrating nervousness.

SELF-DESTRUCTIVENESS

Suppose you are responsible to your art, productive in your practicing, and, as far as you can determine, always well-prepared for your performances; yet you continue to suffer memory lapses or other technical failures for no reason known to you. If you can honestly say you have prepared in every respect, certainly you have a right to expect your performances to stand up under the most rigorous kind of pressure. Without being fully aware of it, however, you may in fact have practiced improperly or, in some way, inadequately. Had you devoted your full concentration to the problems at hand, your practicing should have yielded predictable results. If the unforeseen occurs repeatedly—especially major memory lapses—it is time to ask, "Am I doing something to myself or is something outside of me disabling my practicing and my performances?" In other words, if you notice a significant deviation in your performances from the standard of playing you maintain in your practicing, you must be alert to some possible causes if you are to find a workable solution to your difficulties.

These causes may be self-induced, in which case you alone are responsible for ruining your own best efforts, whether by hating beyond reason what you are or by aggrandizing to excess what you do. On the other hand, you may be a victim of circumstances without realizing it. That is, if you so much as intuit that someone near to you resents your involvement in music and wishes you to stop practicing, this can affect your sensibilities in the most subtle ways imagineable. If a member of your family, a friend, or even your teacher is made uncomfortable by your success, you may unconsciously sacrifice yourself by failing in performance. The extra-musical causes of failure mentioned here—self-loathing, delusions of grandeur, and self-sacrifice—do not, of course, exhaust the possibilities to which we are all susceptible. But they do bear closer examination.

Self-Loathing

The more responsible a musician is, the less tolerable to him are the slightest departures from perfection. Carried to an irrational extreme, this drive for perfection can be so self-defeating that it may contribute to, if not guarantee, failure almost before a note is struck. It stems from a lack of self-belief so deep and pervasive as to develop in some cases into an unconscious need to fail. Failure can then be offered as proof of a subjectively perceived lack of true worth. At its worst, this form of self-denigration can lead a musician into situations in which failure is predictable, not so much because of the inadequacy of his preparation or skills, but because of his talent for minimizing the positive evidence of his attainments. Seeing to it that his failure is a foregone conclusion, he then proceeds to act out in performance his underlying opinion of himself. Such a person can be helped by the guidance of those he truly respects—colleagues and teachers whose recognition of his worth can effectively counterbalance his own destructive tendencies.

Delusions of Grandeur

Some people cope with character flaws such as insecurity and self-loathing by masking them under a veneer of confidence thick enough at times even to be self-deceptive. By so doing, such people make it possible for themselves to assume qualities they do not really possess. At its severest level, this form of self-deception can lead a person into endeavors that far exceed his abilities. These may involve repertory—in which case he undertakes to perform works that lie beyond his musical and technical capacities. Equally dangerous, he may beguile himself into situations that are wholly disproportionate to his performing experience. Certainly, you have every right to study what you wish—compositions of profound philosophical import or technical tour de forces—and even try them out in informal settings. But you must know exactly what you are about before you attempt to perform such works in formal or professional surroundings. If you decide to give a recital, clear objectivity should tell you what kind of environment is most suitable to the occasion. It is foolhardly to perform works of monumental difficulty or to present yourself in a professional recital hall before you have built up a backlog of successful performing experiences. To do less is to invite a disaster that only the cold appraisal of self-awareness can forestall.

Self-Sacrifice

If someone dear to you is working against your progress out of jealousy, resentment, or feelings of insecurity, your instinctive reaction can be a loss of all motivation to practice. Indeed, to maintain your best working level is almost impossible when you hear words to this effect: "Can't you play something decent for a change? I'm getting sick to death of hearing all this Bach." Or worse: "I've heard you play better," after you have poured your heart out in performance. If you yourself are laboring under any self-doubts or are unclear about your goals, the attitude expressed in such words as these can be enough to defeat you. The ruination of a performance may in effect be a peace offering, a way of insuring the love and respect of someone more important to you than music or anything else, for that matter. To the extent that you are the designer of your own priorities, only you can judge whether a choice must be made between music and all it entails and a person and all he or she requires. Ideally, of course, no such choice should have to be made.

If, however, you are unequal to the demands of practicing, you can all too easily blame your short-coming on the needs of someone else and ennoble it with the name of self-sacrifice. Using another person's requirements to excuse your own deficiencies is neither noble nor sacrificial in the highest sense of the word. Rather, it is a form of self-deception that inevitably results in blighted performances for which you and you alone are responsible.

Perhaps it is not too much to suggest that we all have a tendency to gravitate to those who answer our fundamental nature; that there is something in us that seeks its fulfillment in compatible surroundings. If we are given to irresponsibility and laziness, if we are undemanding of ourselves, we find solace in the company of those who distract us from what we know we ought to be doing. By sympathizing with our laziness, they sanction it. If, on the other hand, we are energetic, curious, and excited by challenge, we seek invigoration in the attitudes of stimulating and active colleagues and loved ones. To put it simply, we instinctively choose a society that will further our inmost desires. Therefore, the statement, "My boyfriend hates my practicing. He's jealous of the attention I give my music. No wonder I can't make any real progress!" might have been replaced to better effect by the more probing questions: "Why do I love someone who resents what I do? Is it because I need a watertight reason for not wanting to practice?"

Assuming that we tend to seek our own kind, we are to this extent in command of our own destinies, the guardians of our sensibilities, so finely conditioned through the disciplines of practicing. But we must be alert to all that influences us, whether for good or bad, and quick to recognize the enemy, whether it be ourselves or someone else. Whatever steps you take to protect your right to practice depends ultimately on how seriously you view your study of music. This means that everything you do will, as a matter of course, bear out that view.

Victimized by Others

An adult is a comparatively free agent insofar as he can make choices and act on them. If, by choosing unwisely, he creates a destructive or hostile environment for himself, it is open to him to take whatever action he must to preserve his own integrity. A child has no such option. He is a passive receiver of any and all favorable or destructive influences surrounding him. He acts on instinct only; he can feel it in his bones if he is being victimized even though he cannot give a name to his suffering. He can tell through some ageless human wisdom when he is being deprived of love, though he cannot know the cause.

To do well by a child, then, parents and teachers must work together by being alert to signs of trouble—a sudden lack of motivation, depression, excessive anxiety—and search for the possible cause in their own behavior patterns. Left untended, children who are subjected to the undue pressures of overambitious parents or overbearing teachers bear the scars of victimization into adulthood (see, for example, Chapter 1, p. 8). Not that a parent has actually to become a "stage mother" in order to initiate self-destructive tendencies in her child. Depending upon his psyche, a child may see himself as being victimized by too much adulation. Or, to put it another way, a parent who revels in her child's musical talent may unknowingly cause that child to feel incapable of fulfilling what is expected of him. "For whom am I practicing," the child may wonder? "For myself, or for them!" Rebellion, however unjust to a parent it may be, is the child's only defense against what he sees as an infringement upon his private world. It may take various forms: hostile behavior toward his admirers, quitting school in mid-term, or, in extreme cases, leaving music altogether. If, for reasons of their own warped development, parents or teachers happen to be laboring under jealousy of a gifted child, the results can be devastating. In such cases, a child, because he is still innocent of the darker side of human nature, sees only the obvious—a withholding of love. As he views it, "Everytime I play for people, my mother gets all upset. She hates me, so what's the use of practicing." Or, "The better I play, the crabbier my teacher gets. So what's the use of trying." In short, there is no better way to frustrate a child's musical drive than to withhold love, encouragement, and understanding of his nature.

To be a parent or teacher takes more wisdom, therefore, than we are often willing to admit, but together, parents and teachers can offset whatever deficiencies may exist in one another by being aware of changes in a child's moods and behavior with respect to the study of music. For a parent, this may require seeking a new teacher; for a teacher, this may mean becoming a surrogate parent.

Priorities

Illness or other emergencies can befall anyone in any walk of life. They take precedence over all else. Indeed, every musician at one time or another has to deal with circumstances or events that require him to put his practicing aside and bow to necessity. There are two things, however, that can help balance the demands of music with those over which you have no control—the clarity of your priorities and the consistency of your practicing. The one will tell you how to evaluate and react to events; the other will prevent you from suffering musically as a result of your actions. If you are forced by events to stop practicing for a time—even shortly before a performance—the consistent and powerfully motivated practicing to which you have devoted your daily efforts will enable you to survive under pressure. Your automatic pilot will not let you down. And what makes this consistency of effort possible? The clarity of your priorities.

Anyone who is dominated by a passionate interest in music is fortunate indeed, for he needs no instruction in charting his life's priorities. Like that single moment in a musical composition toward which all its energies gravitate, there is in his life a focal center. It exercises a powerful magnetic pull on all his vitality—mental, physical, and emotional. Nothing and no one can keep him very long from his course of action because he knows that to be a musician, he must always be anchored to music. No matter what his profession may be, there is a point to the life he lives and music gives it its meaning. Thus, just as Rachmaninoff was said to rush offstage on occasion muttering to himself, "I missed the point," so, a musician who fails to come to terms with his musical talent commits no less a violation against his own life.

TRY-OUTS

Importance of Try-Outs in Insuring a Successful Performance

Try-outs are indispensable in the preparation for a performance because they test your ability to concentrate in the presence of an audience. Nothing is more crucial to a dependable performance than the laser-beam concentration that binds you to your music, regardless of where you are playing or who happens to be listening to you (see Chapter 3). Just as the calling up of a fantasy audience when you practice encourages concentration, try-outs, by approximating the conditions of an actual performance, demand it of you. It is with this in mind that I always provide performing experiences for my pupils through regularly scheduled classes (see Chapter 2).

To produce the best results, then, try-outs should be conducted as seriously and formally as possible. Guests should be invited at a specified time and place—preferably at someone else's home where the surroundings and the piano are less familiar to you. The optimum time for scheduling try-outs varies considerably among musicians, some preferring to begin them months in advance, others confining them to a week or two before their performances. Some people like to schedule them every few days; others feel more secure when they try out their programs on consecutive days. Energy and how best to conserve it is what lies behind these individual preferences. As all performers know, the level of concentration that must be maintained during a recital program of normal length exerts a tremendous drain on the body's energy. The split-second timing, control, and coordination of the mind and body, the senses and emotions, not to mention the sheer physical strength required to play the piano, draw additionally on all the body's resources.

Small wonder, then, that some musicians elect to by-pass try-outs altogether. One such performer, a brilliant young artist whom I have taught for many years, thus proceeds directly from his practice studio to the stage, projecting his energy at peak intensity at the actual peformance. Although this method works wonderfully for him, it is risky for most others, including experienced performers, especially when new repertory is being introduced. Indeed, not too long ago, a colleague of mine spoke to me about this soon after he performed some new works in Boston without having left room in his schedule for a try-out. "Never again," he said. "Imagine me, a seasoned performer, feeling like a novice on stage. It wouldn't have been so unsettling seeing the audience out there if I had performed these works before. This time, it really jolted me!" Try-outs should, therefore, be incorporated into your preparation for a performance if only to condition you for facing an audience and easing your passage to the stage. Once there, you should show by your poise and bearing that you feel you belong there—a performer in spirit as you are in fact.

Transcendental Preparation

We should approach a performance in three stages: practicing to learn the scores, practicing performing, and trying out our program in the presence of others. At the second stage, we practice performing to test our powers of concentration while completely alone. Indeed, the level of concentration required for the synthesis of thought, feeling, and physical co-ordination that belongs to performing, parallels in intensity that demanded by yoga and other transcendental arts. It must be powerful enough to allow the performer to overcome—to transcend, if you will—all obstacles to his musical projection, such as nervousness, poor pianos, bad acoustics, and even noisy audiences. I *will* myself to reach this level of concentration when alone, first by calling upon my fantasy audience—all those respected and admired figures who have contributed so much to my musical life. Their imagined presence can in itself induce nervousness in me, my desire to please them being that great. Instantly, my studio becomes a concert hall. I then repair "offstage," to the kitchen, my "artists' room" for the occasion, where I wait for a signal to walk "on stage." I bow to the "audience" and sit quietly at the piano listening for a hush to descend on the "house." The moment has come, I tell myself—*one chance only* to play through works that have taken months to master. That thought is enough to make my breathing difficult. Sit erect, I command myself; rest your hands easily in your lap. Now, place your feet on the pedals and ground your heels to the floor. Breathe deeply and, for goodness' sake, stop clenching your jaw! Move your shoulders and head just a little to get rid of tension. Concentrate now on the first note—let it sound in your mind. With this flash of familiarity, the transition from silence to sound is eased. My fingers reach for the keys and as my mind focuses on each passing phrase, I hear in retrospect exactly what I would if I were myself a member of my fantasy audience.

At this point, I am *performing* in the fullest sense of the word—concentrating as I would before an actual audience. My automatic pilot is working with amazing efficiency. Every phrase I am playing is taking the shape predicted by my long hours of practicing, the emotional content of each being actualized through the corresponding physical sensations and movements I had trained into my muscles. I am accumulating the self-confidence and comfort I need to make my first try-out a truly productive experience.

Making Your Try-outs Productive

Try-outs are effective only insofar as they simulate the conditions of an actual performance, their usefulness being completely nullified if they are not treated seriously. Therefore, playing your pieces in a cocktail party atmosphere or under comparably casual circumstances is not only a waste of valuable time but can also be harmful. This is because you simply cannot give a fair account of yourself if your audience is not listening earnestly. It is essential that the try-out be well-arranged as much for your audience's sake as for yours. With this in mind, some musicians even have their programs xeroxed for the guests, while others enlist the aid of a friend to stand up, make a formal introduction of the artist for the evening and announce the pieces to be performed.

Serious consideration should also be given to the clothes you wear at your try-out. This may seem somewhat beside the point, but in reality it is a far more important issue than you may realize, especially if you are unaccustomed to playing in formal attire. Indeed, I have seen many a musician appear at his try-out in street clothes, to put on his tuxedo jacket only at the last minute to get used to the feel of it when playing. One of my pupils is so used to practicing in stocking feet—she claims she can feel the nuances of the pedal action better that way—that two weeks before her recitals, she must train her feet to the shoes she plans to wear with her formal gown. In fact, I myself have found it reassuring on occasion to perform for my fantasy audience in full concert regalia, as much to accustom myself to the feel of the clothes as to add seriousness to the event.

Finally, I recommend tape recording your try-outs. Certainly, using a tape recorder at your practice sessions, especially during the final stages of learning (see Chapter 9), provides you with an instant, objective view of your work. Taping a try-out does this and more: it tells you how you have performed under pressure; it allows you to contemplate the totality of your performance in the context of a participating audience. Allowing for the fact that most machines tend to level out dynamics and fine nuances, you will learn from the tape how closely you approximated the standard of your best playing. Our aim, of course, is always to reproduce or perhaps even transcend the quality of playing we are capable of in the privacy of our studios. The tape will give us a reasonably accurate indication of our success or failure in this regard.

Overpreparation

Some people would call this heading a misnomer on the grounds that there is no such thing as being overprepared for a performance. In reality, I use the term to cover two situations: the feeling of staleness that all performers experience at various stages of preparation and the tendency to "worry" a passage to the point of diminishing returns. As I mentioned earlier with respect to the first point (see Chapter 9), maintaning spontaneity over the long course of mastering a composition is one of the most difficult aspects of the complex art of playing the piano or any instrument for that matter. I offered various measures for dealing with this problem. I would add here that since your physical condition has a great deal to do with your frame of mind and general attitude, it is a good idea to rescue yourself from feelings of staleness and overwork by exercising, breathing fresh air (if you can find it), and interrupting your routine on occasion with a completely different kind of activity. You will return refreshed, your spontaneity rekindled by a change of pace, however minimal. For me, a short walk to the local pet shop to visit my favorite Myna bird often provides a whole new perspective on my work. Then, too, there are available to us such diversions as only music itself can offer. Nothing can restore your equanimity more readily than setting your work aside and looking into the pure light of Bach, Mozart, or Schubert. It is balm to the spirit and encouragement to the mind. Whatever your preference, read through something different in mood from what you are currently practicing. Improvising, inventing new exercises, or playing chamber music with a friend can be equally restorative.

I have referred more than once to the deep analytic process required to learn a musical score and commit it to memory—a process that leaves nothing unexamined. The problem for us all is knowing when to leave well enough alone. To put it more exactly, our task is to know when such deep probing should best be undertaken. Certainly, not directly before a performance. The observation, analysis, and sequential processing of musical information—everything, in fact, that leads to the full absorption of a score—should have been completed far enough in advance of a performance to free you for that final synthesis in which you and your music become one. Yet, we all have a tendency to stare so long at something that it turns into gibberish. Look long enough at a word on a page and it will become almost unrecognizable. One of my pupils did something tantamount to this on the day of her class performance. "I suddenly got alarmed about a left-hand passage in the slow movement of my Beethoven *Sonata* (Op. 90) and took it all apart just to be sure it was solidly in my memory." That night, when she reached the passage in question, she "froze," as she put it. The left-hand figuration became uncontrollable quite simply because she had disturbed the workings of her automatic pilot by doing what should have been done well in advance. In other words, timing is no less an important factor in the processing of musical information than the sequential stages of learning.

THE DAY OF A PERFORMANCE

Some musicians greet the day of their performance with joyous anticipation. "I am about to become the central figure in a musical rite," a clarinetist once told me, "one that allows me to share my artistic comprehensions with an audience." For most people, however, the day of a performance is fraught with nightmarish anxieties, and with good reason. However thoroughly a musician practices to secure predictable results—to remove all possibility of surprise, as one pupil expressed it—he cannot completely eradicate that fear of the unknown in which self-doubt is rooted. "Will everything go as I planned? Will I stand up to the demands of the music? Will my memory hold up under tension? Will I embarrass myself in front of my teacher, family, and friends? Will I live up to their expectations of me?" Questions such as these humble the best and most experienced, even the most heroic of performers, as Piatigorsky testified.

Musicians are not the only ones who have occasion to ask themselves such questions. A well-known attorney, for example, who is as responsible to the principles of law and to his clients as a musician must be to music and to his audience, becomes violently ill from nerves before entering the courtroom to make his final presentation. Yet, his performances are acknowledged to be models of preparation and delivery. Athletes, too, champions among them, are known to suffer unmitigated torment before a tournament. In short, the day of performance is for all performers, as it is for the musician, a moment of final reckoning—a confrontation with one's art and with oneself to which others will soon bear witness. Not only does the musician assume responsibility for interpreting works that have influenced the very course of civilization, but he must also deliver his best within a designated time span—that frozen segment of time wherein not a phrase nor even a single note can be redone. It would serve no purpose, therefore, to pretend that a performance is anything other than an extraordinary feat of concentration, imagination, endurance, and dexterity. The performing musician, be he amateur or professional, deserves admiration for his ability to cope effectively with the day of his performance, whatever the state of his nerves. If some people claim that the day of performance is for them no different from any other day of their lives, that they suffer no nerves at all, the underlying reason may in fact be that they have cajoled themselves into complacency out of irresponsibility, delusions of grandeur, arrogance, or a sheer lack of musical sensibility. In any case, shame and guilt about nervousness waste our energy as much as does self-pity. Our best course of action is to face anxiety for what it really is—a normal response to and even a necessary concomitant of the function of performing. No more idle speculation then; no further need to defend yourself to those who would accuse you of histrionics; simply face the problem squarely and say, "I have a *right* to be anxious on the day of my performance."

That being the case, we must find ways to harness anxiety and direct it into positive channels. One barrier to accomplishing this can be found in the insensitivity of those close to you. The husband of one of my pupils shouted impatiently at her moments before she was to begin her recital: "What are you so nervous about? You played those pieces perfectly an hour ago!" Nonperformers—musicians and teachers among them—are perhaps the worst offenders in this regard. Safe in the audience, like the Romans viewing the gladiators, they can easily dismiss your anxiety as a symptom of emotional instability or self-indulgence. "If you are prepared," they will remind you, "you have no reason for being nervous." Or, "If performing is what you want to do, then you'd better start being more businesslike about it." As I have already suggested, all such remonstrations are to no avail. Rather, we need instead to deal with the accepted fact of nervousness so as to turn it to our advantage—by amalgamating it with the emotional content of the music. But this requires two things: control through concentration and that intense coalition of our musical functions I have called synthesis. Only then will nervousness actually heighten your natural abilities and invest your playing with a living part of your individuality.

If we cannot eradicate the cause of nervousness, we can try at least to deal with its immediate effects. Learning from the experience of others has its value, therefore, provided that we adapt what we learn to our individual needs. Here, common sense must be the ruling principle. To be sure, the methods espoused by one world-renowned artist or another may have their merits—"I sleep until noon"; "I eat Dover sole every day"; "I practice no more than one or two hours"—but, none, we must realize, is a panacea for the anxieties suffered by all performers. This, of course, is because the effects of anxiety vary with individual constitutions. Moreover, the wondrous playing of such artists derives more from their ability to channel their nervous energy than from the measures they take to allay its effects. In short, all advice must be treated with circumspection.

Conserving energy on the day of a performance would seem to be one of the most sensible things we can do. Yet, for some people, this requires special modification. On the day of his debut, a young musician dutifully followed the advice of his teacher, an experienced performer: "Go to bed and stay there. Save your energy!" No sooner did he pull the covers over him than he began to visualize his fingers on the keyboard. Soon he was in the throws of panic: "My God, I don't even know the opening notes of the piece!" As much as he hated to counter the advice of his teacher, his longing for the reassurance of the keyboard, not to mention the growing queasiness in his stomach, propelled him to the piano. There, at last, he was comforted by the reality of the keys. Far better for him, therefore, to sit in quiet contemplation at the piano than to writhe in bed in abject misery. For others, practicing apparently replenishes rather than depletes the energy. Thus, a well-known pianist insisted in a recent interview that he could not play in public unless he practiced eight hours on the day of a performance.

If the body's energy must be attended to, certainly the mind deserves no less consideration. As we all know, the memory function calls for razor-sharp alertness which must be preserved at all costs. "Don't eat before your recital," a young violinist was therefore admonished by her mother. "All your blood will rush to your stomach and your brain won't be able to work right." The scientific basis for this advice notwithstanding, here, too, individual needs must prevail. We are not all like Sherlock Holmes, certainly, who would starve himself in the interests of mental acuity for the very reasons adduced by this well-meaning mother. In any case, the poor child had to beg her mother for food before her concert, she being able—as many of us are not—to eat heartily and contentedly despite nervousness. And if her brain on this occasion was denied an adequate supply of blood, it did not affect her playing in the slightest. The security and control she evidenced obviously benefited from the nourishment she took.

My own methods for dealing with those difficult preperformance hours have changed considerably through the years. Earlier in my career, I would try to pretend that the day of a performance was no different from any other day. Thus, I continued my daily routine: I practiced in the morning, taught in the afternoon, ate normally, and even allowed myself free rein on the telephone. I discovered, however, that in trying to ignore my anxiety, I only increased it. In time, I realized that a performance could not be viewed as just another routine activity and I came to accept nervousness as its inevitable corollary. This seemed to lessen its debilitating effects for me. Now, I choose to be alone on the day of a performance—as alone, in fact, as one finds oneself on stage. Everything I do, then, is geared toward conditioning myself for this single-minded responsibility. The first requirement, as I see it, is to sleep soundly on the night before a concert. To accomplish this, I exercise vigorously and breathe deeply before going to bed. These activities tend to allay anxiety and induce sleep. Sometimes, I purposely sleep fewer hours two nights before the concert, thereby making myself tired enough to sleep soundly on the following night. On the day of the performance, I cancel all appointments and unplug the telephone. What can be more distracting or unnerving than well-wishers who compress your lifetime of practicing into a "Good luck; are you nervous?" Or even, "Please forgive me, but I cannot go to your concert." Insulating myself from all such distractions, I concentrate solely on the emotional content of the music, always keeping that synthesis of thought and feeling in touch with its physical counterpart. My intention is not just to test the security of this or that passage, but more important, to search for new insights, new sensations that will add spontaneity to my playing. Some performers would regard any such modifications of feeling or attitude so soon before a performance as risky indeed. But I believe that if one's automatic pilot has been properly conditioned, it can withstand even this. Certainly, the pressure of performance can make us acutely receptive to new interpretive and physical insights and it is this range of experience that I, for one, choose not to ignore. To be sure, anxiety is not the most pleasant of sensations. But it, too, has its place, for by heightening our perceptions, it can actually enhance our performances.

Although I usually spend most of the critical day practicing, I do conserve my energy by playing reflectively, softly, and under tempo. I give special attention to deep breathing and stop my work intermittently to exercise moderately or rest. But sometimes my mind wants an added stimulation, even on the day of a performance, and I generally gratify it by writing. This, I have discovered, seems to quicken all my creative energies and somehow makes contact with the musical currents within me that are about to be released. It provides a point of juncture at which thought and feeling find mutual stimulation. For some performers, it comes with painting; others capture it by composing. Whatever it is and however it displays itself, one thing is certain: it cannot be forced. One veteran pianist, representing the opposite extreme, reported to me: "I like to make myself feel bored on the day of a performance. I write letters, do crossword puzzles, practice a little, and nap. In fact, I get so bored that I look forward to the concert as the first excitement I will have had all day."

What to Eat

Performing taxes the body's energy as much as the most vigorous athletic pursuits. A solo recital in a major concert hall can leave a performer as bone-tired and depleted of energy as any tennis player, any tackle in football, or any wing in hockey. If athletes are scrupulous about what they eat, musicians can scarcely afford to be less so. Certainly, pianists, being in every sense of the word athletes of the keyboard, can learn much from their counterparts on the playing fields. Athletes have discovered that carbohydrates make for a greater lasting power than protein and that of all the foods we eat, sugar provides the shortest run of energy. Potatoes, noodles, and the like are now preferred over steak and other red meats. After a recent experience—or bout—with the effects of sugar, I am now and forever more a chastened advocate of noodles. I was to perform on a wintry night in upper New York State and fueled my energy a few hours before the concert with no less than six pieces of my favorite candy. The results could not have been more catastrophic. The temporary "high" given me by the sugar was exactly that—temporary. According to nutritionists, as I learned thereafter, the body processes sugar so rapidly that a very sudden drop in the body's blood-sugar content usually follows such a large intake, and this makes one a ready prey to fatigue. Given such a condition, nervousness finds free access to do its worst. Rarely, therefore, have I ever felt so nervous both before and during a performance as I did on that occasion and seldom have I felt so depleted afterward.

Drugs

Stimulants, depressants, uppers, downers, muscle-relaxers, mind-expanders—call them what you will—have become the ingenuity of our age. They solve all problems. Devised by science to mitigate the ills of mankind, they are now applied to any and every kind of situation imaginable, however unsuitable, ill-defined, or baseless. They are, to adopt one of politics' more inglorious inventions, the grand cover-up of all time. For that is the use to which they are so routinely being put: to cover up carelessness, irresponsibility, incomplete thinking, and imperfect activity in fields too numerous to mention. Even horses take drugs to run faster, not because they want to, but because they have to, so great is the public need for extravaganzas at the expense of dumb animals. Humans administer drugs to themselves in order to feel better, whether at their own expense or that of society. Athletes, we know, have learned that drugs can add to their efficiency on the field. The question is, should musicians resort to them for the same purpose?

My first—and only—experience was with tranquilizers. I was on a tour of the Far East and Southeast Asia sponsored by the State Department, in the course of which I participated in an international festival held in Singapore. With a young Chinese pianist at the second piano, I performed the *Rhapsody in Blue* by Gershwin on two successive nights. The first night was a huge success—the *Rhapsody* brought down the house; but the second night was even more memorable for me because I was "assisted" by a tranquilizer. No one coaxed me to take it. I had spent a sleepless night in the aftermath of the first concert, which was commemorated with a banquet of unmatched lavishness. On the following day, I was understandably fatigued, enough so to become a prime candidate for extreme nervousness. Even worse, I could not marshal the energy to practice properly and the hours until stage time were rapidly dwindling. Then I remembered the tranquilizer my physician had prescribed to ease the stress of travel. As expected, the drug did quiet my nerves; in fact, it made me so calm that by the time I walked on stage, I had lost all motivation to play. And when I was in fact playing, I suffered no pangs of conscience over the wrong notes and other inaccuracies I was hearing. The tranquilizer had done its job: it blocked my emotions, my concentration, my reflexes, everything, in fact, that goes into a successful performance.

Most musicians have learned by now that tranquilizers cannot be trusted. In recent years, however, a new drug has begun to gain favor among musicians for doing what other drugs cannot: inhibiting the flow of adrenalin, the secretion responsible for producing the effects of nervousness. The name of the drug is Propanalol and its intended users are heart patients. Not long ago, a controlled experiment was conducted in which a group of musicians performed three times—first, after having taken placebos; second, with Propanalol; and finally, with a stimulating drug. Propanalol, it was established, abolished the symptoms of stage fright—at least in the majority of cases—without adversely affecting the performer's mental or physical efficiency. The dose administered was 40 mg., this being somewhat lower than that prescribed for chronic heart patients. Judging from this experiment, Propanalol would seem to be the ideal solution for performers were it not for two nagging questions: what are its long-range side-effects on people without heart conditions and how does it influence a performer's physical response to the emotional impact of the music he is playing? The first question involves, of course, our fundamental life processes; the second, those of music. As matters stand, no substantive information has yet been advanced on either issue.

Using any drug to conquer fear—especially one like Propanalol whose properties have not yet been thoroughly documented—is in effect to risk one's life and health for the immediate gratification of performing in comfort and ease. If one values this latter above life itself, all argument is superfluous. Let us consider instead, then, whether the synthesis of thought, feeling, and physical co-ordination that integrates everything we project as performers can itself be adversely affected by chemical intervention. Arthur Koestler, it will be remembered (see Chapter 1), had apparently foreseen the development of a chemical harmonizer that would promote an integration of reason and emotion. But, as I have attempted to argue throughout this book, practicing for such integration is exactly what makes such chemical intervention unnecessary. Here, I would like to suggest that it is also undesirable—for purely musical reasons. If, as one performer recently remarked, "everything you *are* is reflected in the music you perform," it stands to reason that tampering with some part of yourself will have a direct bearing upon your music. Left to the power of his own talent, a musician will respond freely to the emotional content of a musical phrase and, depending upon his skill and self-mastery, will express it movingly through his own body's coordination. Emotions—joy, passion, grief, exaltation—induce in us a natural flow of adrenalin quite apart from that triggered by nervousness. Treating the effects of nervousness by inhibiting the function of the adrenal glands could also impair emotive responses independent of fear. In other words, by disposing of fear we may also be casting off something else too precious to lose—our ability to feel and act precisely on what we feel.

In Chapter 4, p. 67, I discussed how each emotion, musically or otherwise induced, provokes a physical response, and I suggested further that it is also possible to find our way to musical feeling by arriving at a correspondingly appropriate physical gesture. Now, suppose our physical state is preconditioned by drugs to manifest calmness. Would this not affect our ability to respond physically as well as emotionally? As a matter of fact, the doctors who supervised the experiment with Propanalol described above, suggested that a calm physical condition would eventually remove all the emotional symptoms of anxiety and that in time musicians would wean themselves from a dependency on Propanalol, being able by then to induce the desired calmness in themselves. Assuming that this could be done, the question remains, how would this affect the music? Could a performance glow with movement, intensity, and spontaneity with the performer in a state of glacial calm? Would he be able to communicate his feelings to us with his body chained, as it were, in an unnatural bond? Should a performer in fact try to dispel the effects of nervousness at the possible expense of his music?

Nervousness is the price we must pay for the privilege of performing. Enduring it, making it work for us, channeling it, and converting it into healthy energy is self-mastery in its highest form, and this should be one of the goals of productive practicing. All of our efforts should be directed toward achieving that synthesis of feeling, thought, and physical coordination that makes drugs an unthinkable expedient. If drugs eradicate the agony and tension associated with performing, they may also anesthetize us to the various causes of nervousness, thus seducing us into improper or inadequate practicing. Nervousness guarantees honest practicing. It comes down to this: the means of arriving at a controlled performance are as important as the results themselves. In the final analysis, a musician has two options for controlling nervousness: to search out and dispose of anything in the score that could be hazardous or to rely on drugs. Through the first, he demonstrates that what he does is attributable to what he is; by the second, he is admitting that his achievement is owing to something he cannot be. Self-mastery—our ultimate goal—is in reality self-dependence. It demands that all external dependencies be replaced by a total reliance upon our inner resources. If we hope to build our confidence and self-esteem through our musical accomplishments, we and we alone must be the controlling factor—before, during, and after a performance. In short, we must know that each phrase, each note of our performance was fashioned by the full power of our concentration and the disciplined movements of our own two hands.

The Artists' Room

Some of us call this backstage accommodation for artists "the green room" more in deference to the human condition before a concert than to the actual color of its walls. For here, the final moments of self-contained animation are lived through in rituals of various sorts all of which reflect a single truth: everything that can be done has been done. Nothing remains but to wait. And, as we all know, waiting can tax the energy seriously. To cope with this problem, musicians resort to various measures ranging anywhere from the absurd to the religious, and, certainly, to the superstitious. All have the same end in view: to protect and conserve the vital forces that are about to converge on music making. One musician will stand on his head while another sits quietly reading or studying his scores. Some will practice until the moment they must appear on stage; others avoid the artists' room altogether, preferring to arrive at the concert hall minutes before the concert. Some simply meditate.

In the artists' room, logic and reason are not infrequently supplanted by talismans and charms—anything from coins and amulets to toy raccoons and silver bells being prized for the magical properties conferred upon them. Omens, too, are studied for their meaning. "Rain. It's a bad sign for me." Or, "I won at solitaire. That means I can't fail." Some clothes are lucky, others must be avoided. "Never wear a green dress. Never wear a blue dress." One artist I know is still performing in the white gown that brought her rave reviews—patches and all. Ignace Paderewski wore the same socks for every performance.

All of this means that there are, in fact, no heroes before a concert, but only human beings—frail and panicky, yet, nonetheless admirable.

THE DAY AFTER A PERFORMANCE

The aftermath of a performance can be as trying in some ways as the event itself. Actors recognize this. So do lecturers, athletes, musicians, and, in fact, everyone who tries to do or make something memorable or beautiful. The energy expended in so taxing an enterprise as a musical performance has to be restored and until then, a performer may be prone to depression or feelings of physical debilitation. In most cases, this cannot be avoided, but it too can and must be managed wisely. Nervousness being what drains our energy the most, it has to be stripped of its most injurious effects. In the preceding pages, I offered various suggestions for doing this. Here, in focusing on the aftermath of a concert, I would add two further points for consideration. First, the more often we perform, the less we tend to suffer from the aftereffects of nervousness. The more seasoned the performer, the shorter the post-concert period of fatigue, experience being our best teacher. This is why musicians can sustain their strength over long concert tours and frequent engagements. By the third or fourth in a series of performances, they hit their optimum stride and become less nervous with each succeeding performance (unless, of course, they are called upon to change their repertory frequently). The result: less exhaustion on each succeeding day. The problem is, how does all this apply to the less experienced performer who plays infrequently and tends therefore to approach a recital with a do-or-die attitude? If the answer is obvious—by performing more often—the means for bringing this about are an altogether different matter. Second, opportunites for frequent performances being in short supply, one has to compensate for this lack by scheduling as many try-outs as possible and appearing as often in performing classes as can be arranged. This is the only way to learn how to pace yourself in terms of anxiety. If you begin to suffer pangs of fear too far in advance of the performance, the degree of exhaustion you suffer afterward will be that much greater. There is, then, no better teacher of performing than performing itself.

Despite all that can be done in the way of try-outs and trial runs in order to learn how to cope with preconcert nervousness and post-concert blues, no experience can equal that of the formal recital in a major concert hall. It is unique. With an important concert date on the calendar, we are motivated to practice and our energy is rekindled with each passing day. There is no time for exhaustion quite simply because we have work to do. The exhilaration of the concert floods each hour until the great moment arrives. Then, suddenly, it is all over. A week or even a day later, we cannot make ourselves believe that the event actually took place. "Now what," one may well ask. "What do I look forward to now? What am I to practice for now?" No less than those final agonizing minutes before the recital, this too is a time for heroics. But this is what most musicians have to face at various points in their careers: to work when there is ostensibly nothing to work for; to work when energy is depleted from unaccustomed exertion and the mind is restless for lack of a challenge. The only thing harder to endure than this is not working at all. At this low point, we have only to let music itself take charge. For every challenge we can possibly want lies before us in the vast and inexhaustible repertory that cannot but replenish our spirit. For true musicians, depression is temporary because their music is permanent.

12 Finale

An attorney, exhausted after spending a full day in court, returns home, eats dinner, and then practices the *Italian Concerto* by J. S. Bach; he is going to perform it for a music organization of which he is a member. A scholar, prominent in her field, sets aside three hours of each busy day to practice, her annual recital being the focal point of her life. Deprived of this intense musical activity, she claims she becomes ill. A surgeon places his assistant on call so that he can take a lesson with a well-known violinist on the *Archduke Trio* by Beethoven; he plans to perform it with two of his colleagues at a fund-raising concert for the hospital. Performing and practicing obviously serve a need in the lives of all these people—a need that their professions cannot fully satisfy. Without question, therefore, they would rearrange their professional schedules to meet a musical commitment; unhesitatingly, they would spend large sums of money on music lessons or the purchasing and maintenance of instruments. Stimulated at the mere thought of turning a musical phrase with control and artistry, they approach their practicing with a religious fervor and a childlike enthusiasm born of an unconditional love. No one forces them to practice; they are drawn to it. Their lives, they admit unashamedly, would be meaningless without music. Such people, though they may be highly accomplished in their chosen fields, are in truth among the most devoted servants of music. It is they who dignify the status of amateurism.

It is hard to be an amateur—harder in some ways than being a career musician. This is primarily because amateurs are, for the most part, not taken seriously. For one thing, most artist-teachers will accept only professional students or those who aspire to that status, this despite the amateur's willingness to work toward the highest standards of musicianship. Amateurs are all too often misunderstood, even by their families and friends who may look askance on so passionate an involvement in something that promises no immediate or tangible gain. Those who view music as a hobby or an amusing pastime cannot appreciate its elemental influence on the life of a serious amateur. "I wish you would spend as much time with me as you do with your music," the wife of the surgeon thus complains. "Are you still so busy with your fun and games?" a friend of the scholar asks derisively. "Here comes Horowitz!" the attorney's partners comment. Facing the attitudes expressed in such words, many amateurs are apologetic about their musical abilities. It is hard enough that they have limited time for practicing, but having their efforts undervalued by others is perhaps one of the greatest difficulties they must surmount. Even if they do manage to achieve high standards of musicianship, the world around them is not about to reward them handsomely for it. In other words, credit is more apt to go to the professionals. Somehow, though, and despite everything, the serious amateur manages to keep his music very much alive. What is it that so compels him?

In contemplating my own connection to music, I always return to the same answer—universal order. If the heavenly constellations offer us visual proof of this order, then music must be its aural manifestation. And we, being as much a part of creation as are the stars, sense in music an extension of ourselves—a reminder of our own potential for perfection. We gravitate to that which strikes a sympathetic vibration within us and we practice to express that harmony of parts of which music is the paradigm. Through its language we become one with the stars. For music, as I see it, encapsulates in its harmonies the universal order of things and transmutes its awesome dimensions into an experience that is immediate and comprehensible. Without words, music speaks concordantly to a troubled world, dispelling loneliness and discontent, its voice discovering in us those deep recesses of thought and feeling where truth implants itself. To understand the discourse of music, to reproduce it as it was humanly conceived, to grasp it in our hands—all reveal to us, perhaps for the first time, what is noblest in our nature. How? By giving us the opportunity to separate ourselves from sham and pretense. Music offers no quarter for compromise—no excuses, no subterfuge, no shoddy workmanship. We perform the way we practice. If we would be as music is—permeated throughout with order and perfection—we must rise to its demands for however long it takes. In the end, we may be given to participate in creation itself—by conceiving our own music.

The magnetic force that draws us irresistibly to music has another inexplicable property: it binds us to each other. It reaches peak intensity when we pool our resources for a common purpose—to share knowledge or to perform together. And from it there springs a camaraderie between pupils and their teachers, musicians and their colleagues, as deep and pure as love itself. Anyone who has played chamber music knows its effects all too well. That these effects could suspend, even temporarily, a revolution was something I could scarcely contemplate—at least not until I experienced it first-hand while on a concert tour of the Far East.

It was twelve noon when the students began their march toward the center of Seoul, Korea, the very hour at which I was scheduled to give a concert at Seoul National University. Their stand against a corrupt government was no less heroic than the efforts of the American ambassador—Walter P. McConaughy. He negotiated the peace, all the while exercising the greatest diplomacy in his dealings with the host of international reporters and cameramen who swarmed about him wherever he went. At 6 P.M., when the final shots echoed through the city and the fires of a dozen or more buildings glowed like so many setting suns, I sat on the edge of my hotel bed and relived the nightmarish events of the day: how the American Military Police rescued me from the auditorium of the University; how I reached the safety of my hotel just as the first shots were ringing out; how I watched, tranfixed with horror, as the battle raged in the square below. I saw them come—wave after wave—until the sheer number of dead and wounded students forced the Korean president to resign. All travel to and from Korea was banned. Martial law had been declared: everyone was to be a victim of the revolution. With my concerts canceled and my movements restricted to the Bando Hotel, I was robbed of my freedom.

The telephone rang. The American ambassador, with whom I had played chamber music just a week before, was speaking, his voice burdened with the strain of his responsibilities: "I need your help. It has been a terrible day and only music can restore me. If I send my car for you with a military escort, would you meet me at my residence at 7:30? My driver will have a note explaining your mission in case the guards stop you along the way." Within the hour, sirens announced the arrival of the embassy car. Korean guards, seeing the official insignia, stood at attention as I stepped inside. We sped through the now deserted streets where the events of only a short time ago would provide history with yet another story of heroism. The ambassador arrived a few moments later, paused only long enough to greet his wife, and then went directly to the music room, his clarinet in hand. After welcoming me warmly, he asked if we might read through the *Sonatas for Clarinet and Piano* by Brahms, his favorite music. As we played together and discussed various questions of interpretation, something in our communication dispelled all the horrors of the day—something "more restorative than food or rest," the ambassador said. We were suspended in time, lifted beyond tragedy and drawn together in music's bond—indeed, like comrades. Later, when he thanked me, I saw in his manner what lies at the core of music—warmth and humanity.

This has remained with me: how music in its wisdom can govern the way a person lives; how its uncompromising standards can make a person discriminating in everything he does. Just as a musician upholds and reveres the principles of his art, he should steer a course in life that is free of dishonesty, selfishness, and ignorance. He can draw strength from that absolute beauty he finds in music—a beauty of which he is himself a part. And as he probes into those regions deep within himself where everything is knowable, he becomes that ideal performer—a contributor not only of artistic values, but of human values as well.

Notes

1. Maynard Solomon, *Beethoven* (New York, 1977), p. 63.
2. Longinus, *On the Sublime*, 14 (Cambridge, Mass., 1965), pp. 169–171.
3. Robert Schumann, *On Music and Musicians*, ed. Konrad Wolff, tr. Paul Rosenfeld (New York, 1946), p. 31.
4. Plato, *Apology*, 38A, thus reports Socrates' famous maxim: "For a human being, an unexamined life is not worth living."
5. Frederick Perls, Ralph E. Hefferline, Paul Goodman, *Gestalt Therapy* (New York, 1951), p. 54.
6. Madame Auguste Boissier, *Liszt Pedagogue*, in *The Liszt Studies*, ed. and tr. Elyse Mach (New York, 1973), p. xiii.
7. Konrad Wolff, *The Teaching of Artur Schnabel* (London, 1972), pp. 173–174.
8. *Landowska on Music*, coll., ed. and tr. Denise Restout, assisted by R. Hawkins (New York, 1964), Pl. 21.
9. Ibid., p. 369.
10. Ibid., p. 367.
11. Eva and Paul Badura-Skoda, *Interpreting Mozart on the Keyboard* (London, 1962), p. 158.
12. Alexander Lowen, *Pleasure: A Creative Approach to Life* (New York, 1975), p. 37.
13. Heinrich Neuhaus, *The Art of Piano Playing*, tr. K. A. Leibovitch (New York, 1973), p. 89.
14. Eugen Herrigel, *Zen in the Art of Archery* (New York, 1971), see pp. 76, 77, 40, 69, respectively.
15. Ira M. Altshuler, *A Psychiatrist's Experience with Music as a Therapeutic Agent* (New York, 1948), pp. 270–271.
16. *Letters of Composers*, ed. Gertrude Norman and Miriam Lubell Shrifte (New York, 1946), p. 89.
17. Edwin Fischer, *Beethoven's Pianoforte Sonatas: A Guide for Students and Amateurs*, tr. S. Godman (London, 1959), p. 93.
18. Ibid.
19. Emile Jaques-Dalcroze, *Rhythm, Music and Education*, tr. H. F. Rubinstein (New York, 1921), p. ix.
20. Emile Jaques-Dalcroze, *The Popular Educator Library*, vol. 3, *Eurhythmics* (New York, 1938), p. 1224.
21. F. R. Levin, *The Harmonics of Nicomachus and the Pythagorean Tradition*, American Classical Studies, I (University Park, Pa., 1975), p. 1.
22. *The Portable Jung*, ed. Joseph Campbell, tr. R. F. C. Hull (New York, 1971), p. 61.
23. Ibid., p. 62.
24. Ibid., p. 319.

25. Ibid., p. 320.
26. R. T. C. Pratt, "The Inheritance of Musicality," in *Music and the Brain: Studies in the Neurology of Music,* ed. Macdonald Critchley and R. A. Henson (London, 1977), p. 26.
27. *Landowska on Music,* p. 367.
28. "The Inheritance of Musicality," p. 29.
29. The tuning fork is important for providing a standard of constancy in pitch. It was invented in the early eighteenth century by John Shore, a trumpeter for Handel and a member of an orchestra formed for Queen Anne. It was not until 1859, however, that a French government commission recommended A = 435 as standard pitch, before which time concert pitch had ranged anywhere from 415 to 450 for A. In America, A = 440 was taken as the standard, to which an international conference in London in 1939 gave its approval for universal use. On the history of the tuning fork, see Sir James Jeans, *Science and Music* (Cambridge, 1961), pp. 23–24.
30. Not all of the long pedal indications suggested by Beethoven work on the modern piano. The two examples cited here, however, are acceptable in every respect—provided that the dynamics are carefully controlled.
31. *Liszt Pedagogue,* p. xii.
32. *The Art of Piano Playing.*
33. James Cooke, *Mastering Scales and Arpeggios* (Bryn Mawr, Pa., 1913).
34. József Gát, *The Technique of Piano Playing* (London and Wellingborough, 1974).
35. For a detailed discussion of phrases, see the *Harvard Dictionary of Music,* ed. Willi Apel, 2d ed. (Cambridge, Mass., 1973), p. 668, under *Phrase* and *Phrasing and articulation.*

Index

Index

Absolute metronome, 82
Absolute pitch, 123–124, 233
Accelerandos, 94
Adler, Alfred, 112
Albee, Edward, 106
Alberti, Domenico, 178
Alberti bass, 178
Allegri, Gregorio, *Miserere*, 221
Allegro, 81
Aloneness, 11–13, 18
Analysis, 215–217
Anticipation, 58–60, 67, 103, 237
Appassionata Sonata (Beethoven), 52–53, 69
Arm weight, 128–129
Arms, 71, 193
  movement of upper, 175–180
  stabilizing, 170–172
Arpeggios, 159–170, 187–189
Art of Piano Playing, The (Neuhaus), 164
Articulation, 90
Artists' room, 280–281
Athenaeus, 221
Audience, 121–123, 212–214
Aural memorization, 233–234
Automatic pilot, 47–49, 226–228, 231–233
Awareness, 215–217

Bach, J. S., 64
  Chorale Preludes, 143
  Fugue in B major, Bk. I of the *Well-Tempered Clavier*, 54
  Partita in B flat (Minuet I), 190

Prelude in D major, Bk. I of the *Well-Tempered Clavier*, 255–258
Prelude and Fugue in D minor, Bk. II, 230
Two-Part Invention in C minor, 177–178
Two- and Three-Part Inventions, 120
Backward memorizing, 234–235
Badura-Skoda, Eva, 90
Badura-Skoda, Paul, 90
Balzac, Honoré de, 202
Baroque music, 190
Beethoven, Ludwig van, 4, 45, 81–82, 150, 151
  Appassionata Sonata, 52–53, 69
  Concerto No. 3 in C minor, Op. 37, 147
  Concerto No. 4 in G major, Op. 58, 55
  Emperor Concerto, 148
  Klavierstück (Für Elise), 56, 148
  Menuetto, 88
  Sonata, Op. 27, No. 2, 157
  Sonata, Op. 109, (third movement), 90–91
  Sonata, Op. 110, 64
  Sonata, Op. 111 (*Arietta*), 225–226
  Sonata in A flat, Op. 110, 229
  Sonata in C major, Op. 53 (*Waldstein*), 148, 149
  Sonata in D minor, Op. 31, No. 2, 149
  Sonata quasi una Fantasia, 158
Berceuse (Chopin), 182
Bernhardt, Sarah, 260, 261

Bernstein, Seymour, *The Praying Mantis*, 42
Bio-feedback, 79
Boigon, Helen, 97
Boissier, Valérie, 48, 163
Boulanger, Nadia, 92–93, 230, 258
Brahms, Johannes
  Intermezzi, 82
  Trio in B major, Op. 8, 57, 58
Brailowsky, Alexander, 136
Breathing, 65–67, 71, 72, 130
Bülow, Hans von, 220

Capriccio for Piano and Orchestra (Stravinsky), 230
Case histories of teacher-pupil relationship, 19–38
Cathédrale engloutie, La (The Engulfed Cathedral) (Debussy), 147
Chamber music, 17
Chopin, Frédéric, 46, 151, 162–163, 167
  Berceuse, 182
  Etude, Op. 10, No. 8, 68–69
  Etude, Op. 10, No. 12, 191
  Etude in C major, Op. 10, No. 1, 158–159
  Polonaise in A flat, 179–180
  Prelude in G major, 153–154
Chorale Preludes (Bach), 143
Chords, voicing, 139–143
Choreography, 173–198
Class experience, 16–19
Clementi, Muzio, 62
Collective unconscious, 112
Commitment, 215, 217–218
Concentration, 39–61, 268–270
  anticipation, 58–60
  fingering, 54–58
  inducing, 45–47
  mistakes, 49–51
  natural and deliberate, 39–40
  reflex action, 47–49
  sight-reading, 40–45
Concerto in C minor, K. 491 (Mozart), 224–225

Concerto No. 3 in C minor, Op. 37 (Beethoven), 147
Concerto No. 4 in G major, Op. 58 (Beethoven), 55
Conditioned reflex, 47–49, 226–228
Congreve, William, 80
Conscious memory, 228–229, 237
Contemporary music, 258
Contests, 206–210
Contrapuntal music, 258
Controlled tension, 130–133
Cooke, James, 164
Crescendos, 58–59
  illusion of, 86–90
  rhythmic control in, 93–94
Curves of energy, 180–186
Curzon, Sir Clifford, 54, 58, 74–75, 119, 148, 183, 192, 203, 204

Dalcroze, Emile Jaques, 95–96
Damper pedal, 143–150
Deadlines, memorization and, 229–231
Debussy, Claude, *Cathédrale engloutie, La (The Engulfed Cathedral)*, 147
Delakova, Katya, 96, 128
Deliberate concentration, 39–40
Delusions of grandeur, 264
Diminuendos, 59; rhythmic control in, 93–94
Discipline, 75, 95
Drugs, 277–280

Economy of motion, 131
Elbow, 85
Emotional tension, 132
Emperor Concerto (Beethoven), 148
Endurance, 155–156
Erster Verlust, Op. 68 (*First Sorrow*) (Schumann), 238–255
Escapement level of key, 138–142
Etude, Op. 10, No. 8 (Chopin), 68–69
Etude, Op. 10, No. 12 (Chopin), 191
Etude in C major, Op. 10, No. 1 (Chopin), 158–159
Eurhythmics, 95–96
Extension exercises (stretching), 170

Fantasia, Op. 15 (*The Wanderer*)
(Schubert), 136–137
Fantasia in D minor (Mozart), 11
Fantasy audience, 13–14, 50, 268,
269
Feeling, 48–49, 62–76, 196–197
breathing, 65–67
notation, 63–65
physical adaptability to sound, 67–
73
Fingers, 46–47, 54–58, 71, 102, 103,
152–154, 193, 196
choreography, 173–198
curved or flat, 162–163
exercises for independence of, 153–
154
scales and arpeggios, 159–170
taut, 84, 137–138, 153, 154
Flagstad, Kirsten, 124
Foot, pedalling and, 145–146
Forearm, cramps in, 136–137
Four-hand pieces, 91–92
Freud, Sigmund, 112
Fugue in B major, Bk. I of the *Well-
Tempered Clavier* (Bach), 54

Gát József, 164
Gestalt Therapy (Perls), 39
Gide, André, 208
Goldberg, Susan, 53
Gordon, Kenneth, 5
Grandeur, delusions of, 264
Grounded, 156–159
Gould, Glenn, 174

Hallé, Sir Charles, 220
Hammers, 99, 138–139
Hand position, 162–170
Handel, Georg Friedrich, 126
Height, 174–175
Herrigel, Eugen, 75
Hess, Dame Myra, 119–120

Independence of fingers, 153–154
Inspiration, 13–14

Intermezzi (Brahms), 82
Interpreting Mozart on the Keyboard
(Eva and Paul Badura-Skoda),
90
Integration of self, 5–9
Irresponsibility, 261–262

Jaw, 173
Joints, 84–86, 164
Jung, Carl, 112

Kentner, Louis, 174
Key bed, 138–139, 141, 142
Key positions, 138–139
Keyboard memory, 222–226
Klavierstück (Für Elise) (Beethoven),
56, 148
Koestler, Arthur, 5–6, 279
"Kuh-kuhing," 90, 120

Landowska, Wanda, 54, 56, 58, 60–
61, 119
Landowska on Music (ed. Restout),
54
Left pedal, 150–152
Legato playing, 145, 148
Leschetizky, 56
Listening, 110–126
audience and, 121–123
naturally, 110–114
to others, 120–121
pitch: *see* Pitch
tuning in and out, 115–116
Liszt, Franz, 45–46, 48, 160, 163–
164, 220; *Nuages Gris (Gray
Clouds)*, 71, 72
Loneliness, 11–13, 18
Long notes
filling out values of ("kuh-kuh-kuh"),
58, 90
illusion of crescendo on, 86–
90
Longinus, 13
Loudness, 134–135
Lowen, Alexander, 65

MacLean, Paul H., 6
Mastering Scales and Arpeggios
   (Cooke), 164
Matthay, Tobias, 129–130
McConaughy, Walter P., 285–295
Melodic invention, 238, 239
Memory and memorizing, 219–259
   aural, 233–234
   backward, 234–235
   conditioned reflex (automatic pilot),
      226–228, 231–233
   conscious, 228–229, 237
   deadlines, 229–231
   historical survey, 219–220
   keyboard, 222–226
   outline for memorization, 238–258,
      262
   reasons for, 220–222
   repetition, 226–228, 238
   sight-reading, 40–45
   slips, 46, 58, 60, 235–238
Mendelssohn, Felix, 221
Meno (Plato), 113–114
Menuetto (Beethoven), 88
Mettler, Barbara, 80
Metronome, 80–84, 93–94
Middle pedal, 143
Miserere (Allegri), 221
Mistakes, 49–51
Mosel, Ignaz von, 81
Mozart, Wolfgang Amadeus, 62, 64,
      65, 151, 221
   Concerto in C minor, K. 491, 224–
      225
   Fantasia in D minor, 11
   Piano Quartet in G minor, 93
   Sonata, K. 332, 87, 90
   Sonata in B flat for Violin and
      Piano, K. 454, 219
   Sonata in F major, K. 497, 89, 91–
      92
   Sonata in G major, K. 283 (third
      movement), 156–157, 194–195
Muscles, 99–100, 130; *see also* Tension
Music therapy, 80–81

Natural concentration, 39–40
Natural tension, 102, 132, 133–134, 136

Nervousness, 83, 260–282
   day after performance, 281–282
   day of performance, 272–281
   irresponsibility, 262
   responsibility, 261–262
   self-destructiveness, 263–267
   try-outs, 268–272
Neuhaus, Heinrich, 69, 164
Neurotic behavior, 8
Notation, 63–65
Nuages Gris (Gray Clouds), (Liszt), 71,
      72

Observation, 215–216
Octaves, 179–180
On the key, 138
On the Sublime (Longinus), 13
Outline for memorization, 238–258,
      262
Overpreparation, 271–272

Paderewski, Ignace, 281
Palms, 193
Papillons, Op. 2 (Schumann), 56
Partita in B flat (Minuet I) (Bach), 190
Pedalling, 105–106, 143–152
   middle pedal, 143
   right pedal, 143–150
   soft pedal, 89, 150–152
Performing, 16–19, 201–286
   audience response, 212–214
   awareness, 215–217
   commitment, 215, 217–218
   contests, 206–210
   day after performance, 281–282
   day of performance, 272–281
   as incentive to practice, 205–206
   memory: *see* Memory
   nervousness: *see* Nervousness
   reviews, 210–212
   spontaneity, 215
   synthesis, 215, 218
   try-outs, 268–272
Phrase, 238–239
Physical adaptability to sound, 67–73
Piano Quartet in G minor (Mozart), 93
Piatigorsky, Gregor, 260, 261, 272

Pitch, 110, 233
  absolute, 123–124, 233
  relative, 125–126, 233
Plato, 113–114
Playing softly, 135–136
Polonaise in A flat (Chopin), 179–180
Practicing: *see also* Concentration;
    Feeling; Listening; Performing
  coping with difficulties, 102–107
  deterrents to, 11–13
  fantasy audience, 13–14, 50, 268,
    269
  as key to self-integration, 6–9
  loneliness and, 11–13, 18
  reasons for, 3–10
  repetition, 105, 226–228, 238
  scales and arpeggios, 160–170
  slow or fast, 98–101
  supervision of, 114–115
  taping, 270–271
  teacher-pupil relationship, case
    histories of, 19–38
  ultimate goal, 9–10
Praise, need for, 8–9
Praying Mantis, The (Bernstein), 42
Prelude in D major, Bk. I of the *Well-
    Tempered Clavier* (Bach), 255–258
Prelude and Fugue in D minor, Bk. II
    (Bach), 230
Prelude in G major (Chopin), 153–154
Priorities, 267
Propanalol, 278, 279
Pulse, 94; *see also* Rhythm; Tempo;
    defined, 80

Rachmaninoff, Sergei, 267
Recordings, 49
Reflex action, 47–49, 226–228, 231–
    233
Relative pitch, 125–126, 233
Relaxation theory, 127, 129–130
Repetition, 105, 226–228, 238
Responsibility, 203–204, 261–262
Reviews, 210–212
Rhythm: *see also* Pulse; Tempo
  balance and control, 94–95
  control in crescendos and
    diminuendos, 93–94

defined, 79–80
effect on behavior, 80–81
eurhythmics, 95–96
Ries, Ferdinand, 81–82
Right pedal, 143–150
Ritardandos, 94
Role-playing, 4–5
Romantic music, 190
Rubato, 94
Rubinstein, Anton, 143
Rubinstein, Artur, 122
Rules for Young Musicians
    (Schumann), 13

Scales, 70, 159–170, 187–189
Schnabel, Artur, 54, 58, 161, 177, 227
Schnabel, Karl Ulrich, 227
Schubert, Franz, 7, 204
  Fantasia, Op. 15 (The Wanderer),
    136–137
  Serenade, 111–112
  Sonata in B flat, Op. Posthumous,
    191, 203
Schumann, Clara, 219, 220
Schumann, Robert, 13, 125, 189
  *Erster Verlust, Op. 68 (First
    Sorrow),* 238–255
  Papillons, Op. 2, 56
Self-destructiveness, 263–267
Self-integration, 5–9
Self-loathing, 263–264
Self-sacrifice, 264–266
Serenade (Schubert), 111–112
Serial music, 258
Serkin, Rudolf, 111
Shoulders, 85
  exercising, 175–176
  tension in, 173–174
Sight-reading, 40–45, 46, 160, 241
Slow practicing, 68–69
Slurs, 90
Smith, Kate, 261
Socrates, 113–114
Soft pedal (una corda), 89, 150–152
Solfege, 125–126
Sonata, K. 332 (Mozart), 87, 90
Sonata, Op. 27, No. 2 (Beethoven),
    157

Sonata, Op. 109 (third movement) (Beethoven), 90–91

Sonata, Op. 110 (Beethoven), 64

Sonata, Op. 111 *(Arietta)* (Beethoven), 225–226

Sonata in A flat, Op. 110 (Beethoven), 229

Sonata in B flat, Op. Posthumous (Schubert), 191, 203

Sonata in B flat for Violin and Piano, K. 454 (Mozart), 219

Sonata in C major, Op. 53 *(Waldstein)* (Beethoven), 148, 149

Sonata in D minor, Op. 31, No. 2 (Beethoven), 149

Sonata in F major, K. 497 (Mozart), 89, 91–92

Sonata in G major, K. 283 (third movement) (Mozart), 156–157, 194–195

Sonata quasi una Fantasia (Beethoven), 158

Sostenuto pedal, 143

Speed-distance principle, 98–99

Spinal alignment, 71

Spontaneity, 96–97, 215, 271

Stravinsky, Igor, *Capriccio for Piano and Orchestra*, 230

Supervision of practicing, 114–115

Synthesis, 215, 218

Tape recordings, 270–271

Taut fingers, 84, 137–138, 153, 154

Tcherepnin, Alexander, 51

Teacher-pupil relationship, 13–35

Teaching of Artur Schnabel, The (Wolff), 54

Technique of Piano Playing, The (Gát), 164

Tempo: *see also* Pulse; Rhythm
defined, 80
determination of, 81–83
difficult passages, 102–107

joints and, 84–86
long notes: *see* Long notes
physical response to, 84
weak beats, 92–93

Tension, 81, 173
controlled, 130–133
degree of, 134–136
endurance, 155–156
excess, 131
forearm cramps, 136–137
natural, 102, 132, 133–134, 136
taut fingers, 137–138

Thalamic reflexes, 80

Thumb
movement of, 164–169
exercises of, 164–167
scales and arpeggios, 160

Torso, 71, 193–194

Trio in B major, Op. 8 (Brahms), 57, 58

Try-outs, 268–272

Two-Part Invention in C minor (Bach), 177–178

Two- and Three-Part Inventions (Bach), 120

Una corda, 89, 150–152

Vibrato pedalling, 147

Victimization, children and, 266–267

Voice, 120

Voicing chords, 139–143

Wagner, Richard, 125

Weak beats, 92–93

Wolff, Konrad, 54

Wrist, movement of, 85, 177–191, 193

Wrong notes, 49–51

Zen in the Art of Archery (Herrigel), 75